Afropolitan Literature as World Literature

Literatures as World Literature

Can the literature of a specific country, author, or genre be used to approach the elusive concept of "world literature"? **Literatures as World Literature** takes a novel approach to world literature by analyzing specific constellations—according to language, nation, form, or theme—of literary texts and authors in their own world-literary dimensions.

World literature is obviously so vast that any view of it cannot help but be partial; the question then becomes how to reduce the complex task of understanding and describing world literature. Most treatments of world literature so far either have been theoretical and thus abstract, or else have made broad use of exemplary texts from a variety of languages and epochs. The majority of critical work, the filling in of what has been traced, lies ahead of us. **Literatures as World Literature** fills in the devilish details by allowing scholars to move outward from their own areas of specialization, fostering scholarly writing that approaches more closely the polyphonic, multiperspectival nature of world literature.

Series Editor:
Thomas O. Beebee

Editorial Board:
Eduardo Coutinho, Federal University of Rio de Janeiro, Brazil
Hsinya Huang, National Sun-yat Sen University, Taiwan
Meg Samuelson, University of Cape Town, South Africa
Ken Seigneurie, Simon Fraser University, Canada
Mads Rosendahl Thomsen, Aarhus University, Denmark

Volumes in the Series

German Literature as World Literature
Edited by Thomas O. Beebee
Roberto Bolaño as World Literature
Edited by Nicholas Birns and Juan E. De Castro
Crime Fiction as World Literature
Edited by David Damrosch, Theo D'haen, and Louise Nilsson
Danish Literature as World Literature
Edited by Dan Ringgaard and Mads Rosendahl Thomsen
From Paris to Tlön: Surrealism as World Literature
By Delia Ungureanu
American Literature as World Literature
Edited by Jeffrey R. Di Leo
Romanian Literature as World Literature
Edited by Mircea Martin, Christian Moraru, and Andrei Terian
Brazilian Literature as World Literature
Edited by Eduardo F. Coutinho
Dutch and Flemish Literature as World Literature
Edited by Theo D'haen
Afropolitan Literature as World Literature
Edited by James Hodapp
Modern Indian Literature as World Literature (forthcoming)
Edited by Bhavya Tiwari
Francophone Literature as World Literature (forthcoming)
Edited by Christian Moraru, Nicole Simek, and Bertrand Westphal

Afropolitan Literature as World Literature

Edited by James Hodapp

BLOOMSBURY ACADEMIC
NEW YORK • LONDON • OXFORD • NEW DELHI • SYDNEY

BLOOMSBURY ACADEMIC
Bloomsbury Publishing Inc
1385 Broadway, New York, NY 10018, USA
50 Bedford Square, London, WC1B 3DP, UK
29 Earlsfort Terrace, Dublin 2, Ireland

BLOOMSBURY, BLOOMSBURY ACADEMIC and the Diana logo are trademarks of
Bloomsbury Publishing Plc

First published in the United States of America 2020
This paperback edition published in 2021

Volume Editor's Part of the Work © James Hodapp

Each chapter © Contributors

Cover design by Simon Levy/Levy associates

All rights reserved. No part of this publication may be reproduced or transmitted in any form or by any means, electronic or mechanical, including photocopying, recording, or any information storage or retrieval system, without prior permission in writing from the publishers.

Bloomsbury Publishing Inc does not have any control over, or responsibility for, any third-party websites referred to or in this book. All internet addresses given in this book were correct at the time of going to press. The author and publisher regret any inconvenience caused if addresses have changed or sites have ceased to exist, but can accept no responsibility for any such changes.

Library of Congress Cataloging-in-Publication Data
Names: Hodapp, James, editor.
Title: Afropolitan literature as world literature / edited by James Hodapp
Other titles: Literatures as world literature.
Description: New York : Bloomsbury Academic, 2020.
Series: Literatures as world literature | Includes bibliographical references and index.
Summary: "Explores the disparate creative works that are characterized as "Afropolitan literature," contextualizing them within the fundamental questions of world literature, such as translation, circulation, and cultural specificity while also examining Afropolitan ideology itself as a new African way of seeing and being."-- Provided by publisher.
Identifiers: LCCN 2019026037 (print) | LCCN 2019026038 (ebook) |
ISBN 9781501342585 (hardback) | ISBN 9781501342592 (epub) | ISBN 9781501342608 (pdf)
Subjects: LCSH: African literature (English–History and criticism. | Comparative literature.
Classification: LCC PR9340 .A686 2020 (print) | LCC PR9340 (ebook) | DDC 820.996—dc23
LC record available at https://lccn.loc.gov/2019026037
LC ebook record available at https://lccn.loc.gov/2019026038

ISBN: HB: 978-1-5013-4258-5
PB: 978-1-5013-7245-2
ePDF: 978-1-5013-4260-8
eBook: 978-1-5013-4259-2

Typeset by RefineCatch Limited, Bungay, Suffolk
Series: Literatures as World Literature

To find out more about our authors and books visit www.bloomsbury.com and sign up for our newsletters.

CONTENTS

1 Introduction: Africa and the Rest   1
  James Hodapp

2 The Worlds of Afropolitan World Literature: Modeling Intra-African Afropolitanism in Yvonne Adhiambo Owuor's *Dust*   13
  Birgit Neumann

3 Strategic Label: Afropolitan Literature in Germany   37
  Anna von Rath

4 Afropolitanism and the Afro-Asian Diaspora in M. G. Vassanji's *And Home Was Kariakoo*   57
  Shilpa Daithota Bhat

5 "White Man's Magic": A. Igoni Barrett's *Blackass*, Afropolitanism, and (Post)Racial Anxieties   71
  Julie Iromuanya

6 Toward an Environmental Theory of Afropolitan Literature   85
  Juan Meneses

7 How Afropolitanism Unworlds the African World   103
  Amatoritsero Ede

8 Afropolitan Aesthetics as an Ethics of Openness   131
  Chielozona Eze

9 Fingering the Jagged Grain: Rereading Afropolitanism (and Africa) in Taiye Selasi's *Ghana Must Go*   151
  Aretha Phiri

10 "Part Returnee and Part-Tourist": The Afropolitan Travelogue in Noo Saro-Wiwa's *Looking for Transwonderland: Travels in Nigeria*   167
  M. Rocío Cobo-Piñero

11 "Something Covered But Not Hidden": Obscurity in Teju Cole's Oeuvre as an Afropolitan Way of Worlding   185
  Julian Wacker

12 The Hesitant Local: The Global Citizens of *Open City* and *Americanah*   203
  Lara El Mekkawi

Notes on Contributors   219
Index   223

1

Introduction

Africa and the Rest

James Hodapp

> 'It seems that Nigerian writers who make it are from the diaspora. I want to write a book, but I'm scared. Will I be able to publish it? People don't seem to want to read books by Nigerians living in Nigeria. Do I have to travel abroad for people to like my work?' ... She cited Kaine Agary's *Yellow-Yellow* as a book similar to [Chimamanda] Adichie's but didn't enjoy the same publicity. 'If Agary had published the book in the US, Nigerians would have taken an interest in it.'
> NOOR SARO-WIWA, *Looking for Transwonderland* (90)

> *Afropolitanism then, seems to reference a particular kind of affluent mobility in the global north, as opposed to all global mobility.*
> GRACE MUSILA Part-Time Africans, Europolitans and Africa-Lite (111)

In Noor Saro-Wiwa's travelogue, *Looking for Transwonderland*, she interviews a fledgling Nigerian writer at the University of Ibadan named Faith who wants to write stories "for the people," i.e. Africans, but is convinced that the global publishing industry is structured in opposition to her. While she would like to write about Nigerians for Nigerian readers with a domestic publisher, she believes that the experiences of authors such as Kaine Agary, published in Nigeria by Dtalkshop with limited circulation, demonstrate that an African writer's work must paradoxically originate outside of Africa to gain traction inside it. She acknowledges that publishing internationally with US or UK publishers would increase global circulations, but is frustrated that to become renowned in Africa a writer must produce for the outside world—a burden Euro-American writers do not face. Beyond the cruel irony of needing to publish outside of Africa to be legitimized inside of it, a pernicious classism imbues this publishing model because authors who choose the foreign publishing route must also have access to elite global networks to participate, or risk being characterized as a "local author" like Agary. Faith realizes that she might be able to publish in Africa, to limited effect, and that she does not have the inroads to the elite circles needed to "make it." To Faith, the system is rigged: pre-determined to favor those already operating in international circles of influence at the expense of average Africans like her. Like many of us, she yearns for an African literary meritocracy in which the quality of one's work determines success. For authors like Faith on the continent it can seem at times that the worldliness of contemporary African literature does not offer the expansiveness that we imagine it should. Worldliness appears to confine rather than liberate for the Faiths of Africa.

Faith's localized anxiety in Nigeria is confirmed on a broader scale by Grace Musila, a prominent African critical theorist. Musila provides an unflattering overview of the machinations of the most prominent kind of worldly African writing: Afropolitan literature. The elitism inherent in this system concerns Musila. For her, the "affluent mobility" of well-educated elites who vacillate between various locales around the world, being "multi-local" as the proto-Afropolitan Taiye Selasi puts it, narrowly dictates who gains global recognition as African writers (Selasi, 2015). Such authors and their works, she argues, focus on "embracing enough of Africa to retain a certain flavour that sets it apart—presumably from Euro-American—but not so much as to be *too* 'African'" (Musila, 2015: 110). Afropolitan literature in this guise is an African-flavored literature that offers Western readers a taste of Africa without alienating them too much by being "too African." She terms this literature "Africa-Lite," insinuating that Western readers would rather not get weighed down with African particularities when reading their African literature. This "lite-ness" means that a text can travel more easily because it "does not fully recognize difference," meaning Afropolitan literature does not risk alienating Western readers. Offering an even sharper critique Brian Bwesigye, a Ugandan author and critic, has argued that Afropolitan literature is most interested in "proving the Africanness of London-minded elites," confining it to a boutique status in which people who are insecure about proving their African *bona fides* successfully market African authenticity in easily accessible literature to validate themselves and their elite globetrotting lifestyles (Bwesigye, 2013).

Given the biting critiques of Afropolitan literature above, readers may wonder what value it has, and perhaps why one would begin a collection of essays on it with attempts to essentially delegitimize it. I begin with these critiques because they are salient. Afropolitanism *is* a controversial ideology and Afropolitan literature is polarizing. They are contested, they are resisted, and they are even dismissed. They are not safe, settled, or stable. One is just as likely to be on the end of intense interest as to receive eye rolls and sighs when speaking about Afropolitanism to academics, even those same critics who have contributed to the popularity of Afropolitan literature. This is to say that we are trying to figure out what exactly it is and what are the limits of its usefulness. I will touch on this later in this introduction, but the contributors' articles are what actually put Afropolitanism to the test. And it needs to be tested because if indeed it is "lite" or "elite" or narrow then we don't need it. If, on the other hand, we understand that it has been narrowly deployed but is not inherently so then we have a whole other charge: reimagine Afropolitanism as truly worldly. In other words, when Musila laments that Afropolitan literature does not reference "all global mobility" by Africans, I take that to mean that we should get to work on establishing different networks of mobility. If such global mobility is worth considering, and everyone seems to think it is, then critiquing Afropolitanism without thinking about how to amend it, supplement it, and make it better is in a nutshell a twenty-first century Afro-pessimism. *Afropolitan Literature as World Literature* acknowledges these critiques but pushes back against abandoning Afropolitanism, advocating for the notion that we can actually think about African literature that takes the globe as a unit without falling into the traps Afropolitan critiques lay out as its defining characteristics.

Saro-Wiwa and Musila highlight in their own ways the questions that many writers and scholars have about how Afropolitan literature engages the larger world. How representative of Africa is Afropolitan literature? Who are the power brokers? Who and what gets published? What is the role of African readerships? How much power do the tastes of Euro-American readers have? The timing of these questions is not arbitrary as we are experiencing an unprecedented wave of African writing that moves beyond the "writing back" of previous generations who sought to redress colonialism and its aftermath. We no longer live in a moment where we must rationalize the existence of African nations to prove to former colonial masters that Africa has culture. Instead, we have been vaulted into a time where we question the ability of largely inherited national boundaries to contain African subjectivity. Whether we think about subjectivities smaller than the nations that contain them, those that slip between national boundaries on the continent, or those that retain Africa but move beyond the continent, what it means to be African has outstripped the nation. To be African is to be global, and Afropolitanism represents that. Literature has been the realm *par excellance* that has represented this shift and the literature that embodies the elasticity of African subjectivity today—with all of the advantages and problems inherent in such a maneuver—is Afropolitan.

There are many ways to track and define Afropolitanism and Afropolitan literature, but perhaps the best way to begin to contextualize its relevance today is to acknowledge what scholars commonly contend preceded it, namely Afro-pessimism. For Simon Gikandi, Afropolitanism and Afropolitan literature "overcome the malady of Afro-pessimism—the belief that the continent and its populace is hopelessly imprisoned in its past, trapped in a vicious cycle of underdevelopment and held hostage to corrupt institutions" (Gikandi, 2011: 9). Afropolitanism and its literature has not focused on struggles against racism or fitting in abroad, but rather on normalizing the worldliness of Africans to demonstrate that being African and being worldly is entirely natural. Noted Cameroonian political theorist Achille Mbembe also finds value in Afropolitanism as "a way of being in the world, refusing on principle any form of victim identity" (29), stressing that moving beyond a particular place in Africa opens up new ways of being, new opportunities, and new worlds. In other words, being an African of the world is liberating as has been pointed out by Afropolitanism's other primary architect Ghanaian-American novelist Taiye Selasi. Selasi's literary output has also been commonly associated with Afropolitanism as has that of Chimamanda Adichie and Teju Cole, through a whole host of other authors such as NoViolet Bulawayo, Imbolo Mbue, and Dinaw Mengestu associated with the term. The literature of these authors represents Africans as worldly and no more at odds with the world than anyone else. It has quickly become the most widely read literature from the continent, and has increasingly constituted what we mean when we say African literature.

However, as noted above, the rise of Afropolitanism as an African world literature, has been derided in some African critical circles as being a fad, elitist, too commercial, not political enough, and (perhaps most damningly) too Western oriented. The major works of Afropolitanism such as Adichie's *Americanah*, Cole's *Open City*, and Selasi's *Ghana Must Go* are novels set mainly in the US about well-educated Africans and their ability to move in and out of Africa and the US as they please. The characters are not without their struggles, but being African outside of Africa is not an existential conundrum for them. For many critics of Afropolitanism (and world literature), this too easy global Africanness elides the struggles Africans continue to experience in the West as well as overlooks the lived realities of the majority of Africans living in Africa who cannot simply move freely around the world. Despite gestures to the emancipatory nature of Afropolitanism, many critics, such as Emma Dabiri, Binyavanga Wainaina, and Marta Tveit, to name just a few of many, contend that Afropolitan literature only represents a narrow subset of Africans for Western audiences with the resources, i.e., Western publishers, to popularize certain works.

Critics also point to the absence of a clear political agenda as largely missing in the ideology and literature of Afropolitanism. Unlike previous generations who focused on anti-colonialism, independence, post-independence disillusionment, poor state governance, civil unrest, neo-colonialism, and a host of other issues facing Africa, Afropolitanism seems to lack a political angle. The fact that Afropolitanism does not adhere to a strict ideological line concerning what ails Africa should not be understood though as non-political. Helon Habila points this out when he writes that those who "accuse this generation of writers of not being 'ideological' enough, fail to see that this lack of ideology could be intentional and useful, an ideology in itself" (Habila, 2011). Rather than backing a certain political bent, or what Wole Soyinka has disparagingly called "ideological prisms and tidy formations of social development" Afropolitanism's refusal to play into the hands of those who would have them take sides with regimes, movements, leaders, and other explicitly political entities that have largely failed the continent, is actually political (Soyinka, 2014: x). It is the politics of refusal, in that what is refused are the limitations of nations (and nationalisms), regimes, and promises of liberation that never materialize. It refuses victimhood by rejecting political saviors who never arrive while also refusing a new brand of Afropessimism. This is not to say that Afropolitans do not have sympathy with decolonial movements such as #mustfall, but that they understand the way movements rise, fall, and are coopted in the *longue durée*. Ironically, Afropolitanism is criticized for being a short-lived fad while its literature refuses attachments to contemporary trends, searching instead for Soyinka-esque universalism for African literature.

To these ends, Afropolitanism moves beyond the nation and the continent in terms of geography and ideology for liberation. Afropolitanism as a politics of refusal defines itself as what it is not as much as what it is. It is worldly; it is not centered on national, ethnic, or religious questions. Afropolitanism's ideology-eschewing ideology is pivotal in understanding the term's usefulness because its positivism, which can appear as naïve in light of the monumental challenges for Africa and Africans, is in fact a strategy of representation bent on escaping a defensive position for the continent. That is, rather than positioned to refute or account for the manner in which Africa is maligned, Afropolitanism seeks to assert the influence, power and worldliness of African subjectivity because it is precisely these elements that it has been deprived of in the discourses of colonialism and globalization. Its positivist, expansive, and seemingly boundless enthusiasm for celebrating all that is African while seemingly abjuring grounded political topics such as elections, corruption, neocolonialism, mineral extraction, and the like are in fact targeted political maneuvers. They do not deny the existence of Africa's well-known ills, but stress the elements of African subjectivity that have been underrepresented.

In thinking about Afropolitan literature in this worldly and expansive sense though we are not met with only negation but rather with the semi-parallel field of World Literature writ large which seeks to address how particular literatures function on a global scale. Although we cannot engage in depth all of the established and nascent theories and methodologies here, we can begin to see how Afropolitan literature presents unique challenges to World Literature systems. The most prominent of these systems is David Damrosch's by now commonplace archetype of world literature that articulates a process in which works that originally become important in their home geographies, are translated and circulate beyond their geographic origins. In this model, an internal program brings great works of a country, region, or people to the foreground almost demanding wider circulation once prominent domestic status has been achieved. For example, the best Chinese poetry of the early modern period that may have been central to Chinese literature for centuries would eventually be translated as some of the country's best literature. Then, the rest of the world would take notice and get a glimpse, mediated by translation, of Chinese poetry. Clearly though such a model of circulation does not characterize the dilemma of authors like Faith. Her work must be foreign born, enter modes of circulation in place, be already in a European language (mainly English or French), and appeal to a global audience before it can appeal to an African one. Like Afropolitanism, Damrosch's system of World Literature is also not without its elite tendencies, such as who becomes prominent in a particular culture and how decisions on translation are made in accordance with foreign markets. The system cannot simply be trusted to be organic and what emerges as World Literature may or may not represent a whole. These elite mechanisms aside, Afropolitan literature operates within an entirely different model, meaning that it is often born already global, via Western publishers and prize cultures, and gains traction as literature *of* the continent by achieving *outside* the continent.

In many ways, Afropolitan literature and World Literature as disciplines run parallel to one another. Both are accused of eschewing specificity: one in service to the idea of the global as knowable to Western audiences and one to avoid topics about Africa that might be too grounded in unfamiliar contexts. Both are accused of treating too lightly the complications, drawbacks, and inherent limitations of European languages and translation as both essentially are Anglophone phenomena with claims towards totality despite the fact that only a small fraction of the globe or Africa are English speakers and readers. Both are also working at unenviable projects that open them up to criticism despite the noble ideals of examining the world's literatures on a level field and understanding the role of Africa in the world at large. These are no minor or trivial pursuits. They are big ideas and it is their largess in addressing time and space in new ways that attracts both admirers and detractors.

Largely absent from the above is an extended genealogy of Afropolitanism. I have made rough sketches elsewhere, but I leave it to the contributors to craft their own genealogies for their own purposes, because part of the contention of this collection is not only that we must expand the geographic and temporal boundaries of Afropolitanism but also that we must think about African worldliness differently, including with different antecedents. This introduction then is less interested in providing a definition, and more interested in thinking through the ways that we can expand the usefulness of the concept.

Given the contentious discourse on Afropolitanism, *Afropolitan Literature as World Literature* intervenes in the Afropolitan debate by expanding what Afropolitanism means, reclaiming it from its current trajectory of characterizing a niche elite literature for Western readers. By thinking with and against current notions of Afropolitanism in a serious manner, this book looks beyond the usual handful of authors popularized in the West by expanding the temporal and geographic limits of Afropolitanism while re-examining those seminal to it. Temporally, this book opens up earlier and varied temporalities in African literature. Geographically, it seeks to decenter the problematic focus of Afropolitanism on the West. Africa has exchanged ideas, goods, and people with the entire world for centuries and this is reflected in its literature, but these movements, as Musila points out, are too often elided in favor of a focus on movement to and from the West. A Western focus has also been a serious detraction from World Literature, and just as World Literature is slowly becoming more worldly by moving beyond the West as a focal point, so too this book imagines a similar move by Afropolitanism. By examining intra-African, Indian Ocean, and other circulations, this book challenges a Western oriented Afropolitanism as well as redefines movement within Afropolitanism so that, for example, a late nineteenth century South Asian crossing the Indian Ocean on a *dhow* to British East Africa is as Afropolitan as a twenty-first century socialite who jets in from Lagos to attend an Afropunk concert in London.

This collection participates in two larger projects concerning Afropolitanism. Firstly, it contributes to a debate about what constitutes Afropolitanism because even though important work has been done by the likes of Selasi, Mbembe, Gikandi, and Habila, the concept has been hardly fleshed out. Secondly, and more importantly, it develops the future direction of Afropolitanism. We aim to think about the ways that Africans and their texts circulate within Africa, the Global South, and many other networks not limited to well-worn oscillations between Africa and the West—including some interactions with the West that have been understudied. This collection challenges this narrowness. There is nothing inherent in a formulation of African worldliness that means that it must apply to a few well-heeled global socialites. In fact, just the opposite is true. A global African subject paradigm should be expansive and difficult to contain. It should be multifarious and difficultly tracked. The contributors and I believe that we can make what we will of the global aspirations of Afropolitanism. We refuse to buy into strict diasporic or tourist themed notions in order to open up this idea because to us it seems that if we acquiesce to a definition of African worldliness that settles for narrowness then we are buying into notions that Africa's worldliness is limited and that the continent is outside most networks of consideration. Indeed, to take the notion of multiple networks to its logical conclusion, there are many Afropolitanisms and in principal, if not always in practice, we are interested in them all.

In some ways it is tempting to call this collection "Beyond Afropolitanism" or "Afropolitanism 2.0" because it seeks to expand what the term means beyond the initial catalyst and backlash. This collection though proposes that the limited purview defined early on for Afropolitanism has been exhausted but that its potential has not been nearly entropized. In this way, this collection of articles on Afropolitanism is late on the scene, but in a good way. Afropolitanism was a phenomenon for a moment a few years ago, peaking around 2015 and 2016. Predictably, an immediate anti-Afropolitan push back arrived resulting in several collections and special issues of academic journals weighing the pros and cons of this critical lens and type of writing. Among the noteworthy collections that captured this lightening in a bottle were *Negotiating Afropolitanism* (2011), *Afropolitanism: Reboot* (2016), and *In Search of the Afropolitan* (2017), along countless popular and scholarly articles and blog posts. These collections gathered the disparate views on Afropolitanism as a way of being in the world, a critical lens, and a type of literature, serving as a useful snapshot of the initial critical reactions to Afropolitanism, but this collection aims to update, overtake, and expand on these approaches.

In his 1964 Egyptian Anglophone novel *Beer in the Snooker Club*, Waguih Ghali characterizes the relationship of Egyptian elites through the eyes of the main character Ram. Ram, an Egyptian, defines himself in ways that embody the worst elements of Afropolitanism:

> It was Edna who introduced me to Egyptian people. It is rare, in the milieu in which I was born, to know Egyptians. She explained to me that the Sporting Club and the race meetings and the villa-owners and the European-dressed and -traveled people I met were not Egyptians. Cairo and Alexandria were cosmopolitan not so much because they contained foreigners, but because the Egyptian born in them is himself a stranger to his land.
>
> (53)

Clearly Ram's Afropolitanism, or proto-Afropolitanism, lives on today, though usually expressed in less straightforward and unsympathetic ways.

Ram is an Afropolitan that predates Afropolitanism, one of many ignored figures who can stretch the fairly arbitrary temporal and geographical limitations placed on it. He goes so far as to argue that even though he was born in Egypt and often lives there, he is actually not Egyptian at all. His elite class status presents a barrier between him and the majority of people in the country. As the quote indicates though he is self-aware. Unlike many of his ilk, he knows that he is a stranger in his own land and he tries for much of the novel, through intellectual struggles with Arab nationalism and communism and creating new social circles to overcome the narrow perspective his status has imposed. As Anglophone readers, writers, and scholars of global Anglophone African literature, we too can choose the narrow horizons that easily come our way in considering Afropolitanism and its literature, or like Ram we can challenge those boundaries and think about Afropolitanism outside our troubled inheritance. This collection chooses to challenge both the norms of thinking on Afropolitanism and the narrow scope of literature deemed Afropolitan to prove that Afropolitanism can accommodate the Rams and Faiths as well as many other types of global Africans.

The articles in this collection approach these issues in a number of innovative and intriguing ways, and it is in them that this collection ultimately demonstrates its value. Opening the collection with a striking take on an almost universally praised novel, *Dust*, is Birgit Neumann's essay on Intra-African Afropolitanism. This article addresses the almost entirely overlooked circulations of Africans inside of Africa in African literary and Afropolitan studies. The scale of Africa with its scores of nations and thousands of languages and ethnicities is a world in and of itself. To wit, Neumann challenges many of the most deeply imbedded assumptions about who is and is not worldly and Afropolitan. Similarly, expanding the geography of Afropolitanism, Anna von Rath focuses on a queer German language novel by SchwarzRund, the child of African immigrants who grew up in the Caribbean and then migrated to Europe. In tracking an author and her work that is part of what SchwarzRund terms an African "double diaspora" (displaced from Africa to the Caribbean and then to Germany), von Rath's essay brings in multiple elided Afropolitan geographies.

Shilpa Bhat's article also explicitly confronts underrepresented groups and geographies by turning to South Asians in East African literature. Her essay challenges the notions of Afropolitan movement to include migration to Africa and to consider how and why Africans of Asian descent, often historically inhabiting a precarious space between colonizer and colonized, are dismissed as African. By examining the work of M.G. Vassanji, arguably the most prominent Asian-African writer of East Africa, she argues for an expansion of Afropolitanism to include this overlooked, and even at times maligned, group of Africans. Similarly, Julie Iromuanya's take on A. Igoni Barrett's *Blackass* both rescues the novel from a simplistic "writing back" paradigm in which the novel's only intertext is Kafka's *Metamorphosis*, and invokes global south affinities between African and African-American literature. Iromuanya borrows the notion of "passing" in African-American literature to Afropolitanism as an essential interlocutor, creating a dialog between African and African-American literary studies often missing.

In addition to these important expansions of Afropolitan geographies and mobilities, several authors take Afropolitanism in new theoretical and methodological territory. Because Afropolitanism is at times critiqued as under-theorized, these interventions resonate and speak to its long-term viability. Juan Meneses innovatively puts Afropolitanism in conversation with Environmental Theory, which is not only timely given the current exigence of the subjects, but also stresses a different kind of worldliness: an ecology-based African world sensibility. If Africa is worldly as all the authors in this collection argue, then the hitherto unprecedented impact of humanity in and from Africa on the environment on the continent cannot be overlooked. In general, more work on the environment and African literature needs to be done, especially within Afropolitan literature, and Meneses' essay represents an important first in this regard for Afropolitanism.

Continuing the theoretical expansion, both Amatoritsero Ede's "How Afropolitanism Unworlds the African World" and Chielozona Eze's "Afropolitan Aesthetics as an Ethics of Openness" bring Afropolitanism into conversation with several large-scale theoretical concerns. Ede's article embodies the notion that this collection is not meant to cheerlead for Afropolitanism, by being critical of it, yet importantly also bringing in the almost totally ignored Francophone Afropolitanism, e.g., "Afropean," into the conversation. In most African literary scholarship the Anglophone and Francophone are siloed off from each other, one rarely engaging the other, and Afropolitanism is no exception. Ede's positioning then is most welcome and necessary, creating another type of expansion of Afropolitanism by transgressing linguistic disciplinary boundaries. Eze's article builds on his influential previous work on Afropolitanism as openness to consider the role of aesthetics and its ability to expand ethical horizons. By examining two poets (in itself unorthodox as scholarship on Afropolitan literature is almost exclusively on novels), Eze establishes Afropolitan ethics and aesthetics to provide not only needed formalism to Afropolitanism, but also to speak to its emancipatory capabilities.

In considering this collection as a reassessment of Afropolitanism, it is fitting that Aretha Phiri is "Re-reading Afropolitanism (and Africa) in Taiye Selasi's Ghana Must Go" in her subtitle to her article both because Selasi and her novel are pivotal to Afropolitanism, but also because clearly we need a reassessment of Afropolitanism beyond the original articulation and reaction. Phiri's original approach synthesizes Afrodiasporic blues music with Selasi's novel to open up new possibilities in realizing a more tenuous Afropolitanism than the novel is generally credited with, injecting critiques of the novel with new life. Rocío Cobo-Piñero's article on Noor Saro-Wiwa's *Transwonderland* also brings Afropolitanism into a realm in which it is rarely considered: travel writing. Cobo-Piñero demonstrates that rather than the typical Westerner "discovering" the wonders of Africa, Noor Saro-Wiwa, daughter of Ken Saro-Wiwa, acts as an Afropolitan both attached to and alienated from her Nigerian Igbo heritage. Considerations of genre typically elude scholarship on Afropolitanism literary criticism, but here they are central.

Although many authors compete for the title of ultimate Afropolitan, Teju Cole repeatedly emerges both because he does not shirk the Afropolitan tag, as he expressed in an interview with me, but he also writes and publishes in global circuits on Africa. The variety of his work is highlighted in Julian Wacker's article on Cole's unique style of worlding. Wacker investigates Cole's novels, but also examines Cole's work on photography as both a photographer, writer of captions, and as a critic to give a rounded sense of both Cole's Afropolitan output and as an Afropolitan himself. Lara El Mekkawi stresses the need to recover cosmopolitanism as an operative lens for Afropolitanism by re-examining the work of Cole as well as of Chimamanda Adichie. Both a theoretical and novelistic reassessment, Mekkawi's article speaks both to the need to fully flesh out the elements of Afropolitanism's natural theoretical interlocutors and the need to re-examine seminal Afropolitan novels in relation to that theory.

Ultimately, this truly global collection crafted by scholars in Africa, the Middle East, Asia, Europe, the Caribbean, and North America harnesseses the high level of interest in Afropolitanism. Their contributions provide Afropolitanism and its literature with the historical and geographical depth they deserve so that we do not lose important elements of this Afro-centric critical apparatus. Africa is and always has been complexly worldly; this book, in part, tells the story of how we arrived at our present notions of African literary worldliness and expands and diversifies those notions to align with Africa's complex history and literature.

Works cited

Bwesigye, Brian. "Is Afropolitanism Africa's New Single Story?" Aster(ix) Journal. 22 Nov. 2013. Web. 1 Nov. 2018.
Coetzee, Carli. *Afropolitanism: Reboot*. Routledge, 2019.
Ghali, Waguih. *Beer in the Snooker Club*. New York: Vintage International/Vintage Books, a division of Random House LLC, 1964.
Gikandi, Simon. Foreword. *Negotiating Afropolitanism Essays on Borders and Spaces in Contemporary African Literature and Folklore*. Rodopi, 2011. 9–11.
Habila, Helon. Introduction. *The Granta Book of the African Short Story*. Ed. Helon Habila. London: Granta, 2011.
Knudsen, Eva Rask, and Ulla Rahbek. *In Search of the Afropolitan: Encounters, Conversations, and Contemporary Diasporic African Literature*. Rowman & Littlefield International, 2016.

Mbembe, Achille. "Afropolitanism." *Africa Remix: Contemporary Art of a Continent*. Ed. Simon Njami. Ostfildern-Ruit: Hatje Cantz, 2005. 26–29.

Musila, Grace. "Part-Time Africans, Europolitans and 'Africa lite.'" *Journal of African Cultural Studies*, 2015: 28(1), 109–113.

Saro-Wiwa, Noor. *Looking for Transwonderland: Travels in Nigeria*. London: Granta, 2013.

Selasi, Taiye. "Don't Ask Me Where I'm From, Ask Me Where I'm Local." Ted Talks. 20 Oct. 2015. YouTube. Web. 1 Feb. 2019.

Soyinka, Wole. Introduction. *Africa 39: New Writing from Africa South of the Sahara*. Ed. Ellah Wakatama Allfrey. New York: Bloomsbury, 2014.

Wawrzinek, Jennifer, and Justus Makokha. *Negotiating Afropolitanism Essays on Borders and Spaces in Contemporary African Literature and Folklore*. Rodopi, 2011.

2

The Worlds of Afropolitan World Literature

Modeling Intra-African Afropolitanism in Yvonne Adhiambo Owuor's *Dust*

Birgit Neumann

Introduction

In the last decade or so a remarkable number of African literatures have entered the world literary canon, reminding us once again of the complex and shifting dynamics underlying the making of world literature.[1] Surprisingly—or maybe unsurprisingly—the majority of these literary texts have been written by diasporic authors and explore the trajectories between Africa and the Western metropolis, the predicaments of migration, and possibilities of a cosmopolitan ethos. Works by Teju Cole, Taiye Selasi (born Taiye Tuakli-Wosornu), Chimamanda Ngozi Adichie, NoViolet Bulawayo, and Dinaw Mengestu are the most obvious cases in point. Taking their cue from Selasi's viral essay "Bye Bye Barbar," published in *LIP* magazine in 2005, critics were quick to subsume these authors under the label 'Afropolitan.' According to Selasi, the term designates the stylish "ethnic mixes," the seemingly effortless multilingualism, "academic successes" and rather hip lifestyle of the "newest generation of African emigrants."[2] This new generation of twenty-first century African emigrants is no longer defined by the legacies of transatlantic slavery or other forms of colonial violence; the Afropolitans do not leave Africa behind to escape poverty or oppression in the postcolonial nation-state. Rather, they embrace the opportunities offered by a globalized world, readily mobilizing their cultural hybridity to secure individual success. Selasi thus offers the term as a core element of contemporary "African identity politics,"[3] which, steeped in neoliberal individualism, is designed to counter so-called Afro-pessimism and to celebrate a genuinely "African ethos"[4] in the world.

Ever since its popularization by Selasi, the term Afropolitanism has sparked a number of critical debates. While some celebrated the term as liberating and as a "significant attempt to rethink African knowledge outside the trope of crisis,"[5] others dismissed it for its apparently elitist, Western-oriented, and "product-driven" thrust.[6] From the latter perspective, the concept not only fails to address economic inequalities but also propels the commodification of mobility and African identity.[7] While such criticism can certainly claim some validity,[8] my critical engagement with the term follows a different track. In line with those critics who draw attention to the multi-directional relations between Africa and the world,[9] I seek to move beyond the identification of Afropolitanism with global networks and transatlantic entanglements. This association, I argue, has inevitably led to a neglect of those African works that focus on the African continent and that explore different forms of movement, traveling, and exchange across Africa.[10] The fact that Afropolitanism is "a resource mainly for those of African descent in the Diaspora"[11] causes significant problems for the understanding of various forms of African cosmopolitanism and notions of Afropolitan world literature.[12] While, in a phase of mass migration to the West, it is of course important to pay attention to diasporic African literature and to examine how it models a distinctively African cosmopolitanism, it is equally necessary to focus on those African literatures that tell a different story, a story about traveling within Africa and crossing the continent. These literatures confirm the centrality of the continent in histories of global exchange, a centrality that, according to Achilles Mbembe (2005), is the essence of Afropolitanism. A recognition of literatures that put a spotlight on the African continent is vital to account for the pluralities of African modernities and the complexities of Afropolitanism.[13]

This essay outlines some contours that make such a recognition possible, first by discussing concepts of Afropolitanism (Part 2) and second by exploring the complex relations between Afropolitan literature and world literature (Part 3). To do justice to the plurality of Afropolitan world literature, it is necessary to decouple the standard association of world literature with circulation on a global market and to develop critical attention to literary acts of world-making. In Part 4, I examine configurations of intra-Afropolitanism in Yvonne Adhiambo Owuor's novel *Dust*, focusing on the trajectories, entanglements, and migratory patterns to and across the African continent. How capable is postcolonial African literature of imagining new, possibly Afropolitan forms of community that transgress national, ethnic, or Pan-African categories? Owuor's *Dust*, I maintain, is Afropolitan not only because it shows that both the African continent and African ways of being in the world are deeply steeped in movement and that even the so-called local is always formed by exchange and translocation.[14] Just as importantly, *Dust* figures Afropolitanism "into an idea of epistemological narration,"[15] i.e., it creates an aesthetically complex, polycentric, and multilayered narrative that is modeled on and emerges from processes of mixing, movement, and circulation. As such, the postcolonial novel invites us to rethink the world and community from a distinctively African perspective, gesturing toward an Afropolitanism yet to come.

Roots vs. Routes? Reading Africa into Afropolitanism

My suggestion to put greater emphasis on the African continent does not intend to pit routes against roots, traveling against situatedness, the global against the local, etc. Rather, I take my cue from Achille Mbembe who proposed the term Afropolitanism in his 2005 article "Afropolitanisme" to recall the histories of mobility, exchange, and collision on the African continent.[16] Undoing the equivalence between Afropolitanism and transnational diaspora, Mbembe claims that the "cultural history of the continent can hardly be understood outside the paradigm of itinerary, mobility, and displacement."[17] Though Mbembe[18] acknowledges that "part of African history lies somewhere else, outside Africa", he puts a spotlight on exchange *within* Africa, highlighting the cultural entanglements between different African locales. According to this logic, Afropolitanism designates a polycentric network that binds continental Africa as well as the various diasporic spaces in the Americas, Europe, and elsewhere into mutually transformative patterns of exchange. It is an ever-becoming space, in the sense described by Doreen Massey,[19] a space that only emerges from movement and relations and that is never closed, uniform, and stable.

Mbembe's formidable intervention invites us to move beyond the Atlantic-studies frame, which has dominated scholarship in the field of Afropolitanism and which presupposes that texts that portray transnational movement and diasporic life in the Western metropolis spur the most topical debates. The black Atlantic paradigm, influentially spelled out in Paul Gilroy's 1993 study *The Black Atlantic: Modernity and Double Consciousness*, has explicitly been designed as a critique of the Pan-African model and a concomitant fetishizing of autochthonous roots and origins, presumably untouched by the ruptures of modernity.[20] And yet, while

Gilroy's approach effectively redresses nativist and nationalist notions of ancestral Africa as a stable origin for African identity, it "fails to provide any alternative way of thinking about Africa."[21] Broadly speaking, the black Atlantic model, as noted by Yogita Goyal,[22] excludes "Africa from discussions of modernity," pitting the presumably homogeneous time of Africa against the disjunctive temporalities characteristic of diasporic spaces.[23]

The political urgency of Mbembe's notion of Afropolitanism resides in the fact that it allows him to consider Africa as an active participant in the dynamics of modernity rather than as the static, homogenous, and premodern other of the West. Mbembe[24] insists that a genuinely African tradition never existed because African cultures have always been shaped by "processes of mixing, blending and superimposing": The "[a]wareness," Mbembe[25] continues, "of the interweaving of the here and there, the presence of the elsewhere in the here and vice versa, the relativisation of primary roots and memberships and the way of embracing, with full knowledge of the facts, strangeness, foreignness and remoteness .... It is this cultural, historical, and aesthetic sensitivity that underlies the term 'afropolitanism.'" That is to say that Afropolitanism, for Mbembe, first and foremost describes a "way of belonging to the world" and "of being in the world." This way of being is marked by "the interweaving of worlds,"[26] while also being committed to an Afrocentric worldliness. Opening up the term to new transcultural bonds, Mbembe stresses that Afropolitanism recognizes "the multiple origins of those who designate themselves as 'African' or as 'of African descent'"[27] and is therefore a powerful means to combat–racial, ethnocentric or national–narratives of homogeneity. To the extent that Afropolitanism designates a post-racial "way of belonging to the world,"[28] it also provides the conceptual means by which non-black Africans can claim an African identity.

Mbembe's understanding of Afropolitanism is radically different from Selasi's take on the term. Rather than promoting an ideology of unconstrained mobility and neoliberal individualism, which ultimately invests "in cultural difference at the expense of concern for class difference,"[29] Mbembe emphasizes the cultural sensitivity and awareness of processes of mixing. He energetically reconsiders African identity from the perspective of the community, instead of the mobile individual. For Mbembe, Afropolitanism not only circumscribes a certain position, a location, in the world. Rather, it also indexes a specific orientation and "disposition towards the world."[30] In a recent conversation with Sarah Balakrishnan, Mbembe specifies that "Afropolitanism is a name for undertaking a critical reflection on the many ways in which, in fact, there is no world without Africa and there is no Africa that is not part of it."[31] That is to say that Afropolitanism is also an epistemic principle, an articulation of African self-knowledge that recognizes the reciprocal relations between Africa and the world. Following Mbembe, I understand Afropolitanism as an ongoing and open-ended process of thinking about African cultures, histories, and subjectivities in terms of an inherent relationality and a dialogical relationship to multiple places, debates, traditions, and practices. As a "poetic" principle[32] it gives rise to multifaceted narratives that stress Africa's centrality—however fragile and contested that centrality might be. Moreover, the formal characteristics of these narratives foster an awareness of Africa's complex historical connections to localities within and beyond the continent.

Afropolitan Literature as World Literature? Rethinking the Worlds of Literature

While the association of Afropolitanism with oceanic crossings is one factor that led to the relative neglect of literatures dedicated to African localities, this neglect has also been facilitated by "the cultural sphere now generally identified as world literature."[33] According to Aamir Mufti,[34] world literature, has, from its inception, "functioned ... as a border regime, a system for the regulation of movement," which has been and continues to be dominated by literary institutions located in the Global North. While Emily Apter's[35] claim that world literature ultimately propels an aesthetically flattening and politically impotent "oneworldedness" seems unnecessarily pessimistic, the extent to which the making of world literature is steeped in geopolitical power relations and the dynamics of a global book market can hardly be denied.[36] A number of largely sociologically inspired studies have illustrated that the world literary canon is closely tied to the economic dominance of the West and largely caters to Western expectations, tastes, and reading practices. Drawing attention to the dominance of Western publishers and the ways in which this dominance influences the stories that African authors tell, Nigerian writer Adaobi Tricia Nwaubani remarks: "Some of the greatest African writers of my generation may never be discovered, either because they will not reach across the Atlantic Ocean to attract the attention of an agent or publisher, or because they have not yet mastered the art of deciphering Western tastes."[37] As indicated by the make-up of the world literary canon, "Western tastes" seem partial to migrant literatures, which negotiate belongingness in the diaspora and which allude to the experiences of their respective authors.[38] The reasons for this penchant are manifold and complex. It is not unlikely that the celebration of Afropolitan authors such as Cole, Selasi, and Adichie, all of whom embody privileged and successful forms of diasporic African identity, is linked to a neo-colonial guilt and the West's compensatory longing for positive images of the African immigrant.[39]

To overcome the Western-oriented thrust of world literature and to allow for a more fine-grained, pluralized understanding of Afropolitanism, I want to put forward a different understanding of world literature, one that pays greater attention to the singularity, agency, and experientiality of literature. As suggested by Pheng Cheah, the world of world literature should not primarily be tied to circulation in a global book market but to literary acts of creation, invention, and imagination.[40] Literature, after all, not only travels through the world but also has, as Cheah[41] puts it, a capacity "'to world'", i.e., a capacity to open other, imaginative worlds. The aesthetic, affective and ethical worlds of literature cannot be contained by the frequently market-driven world and the technologies of globalization, though literature is inevitably shaped by them.[42] While world-making is, of course, characteristic of all literature, world literature, I argue, engages with the world in more explicit and specific ways: it translates between transcultural connectivity and topographical singularity, between the translocal and the local, between knowledge of a shared world and the irreducibility of situated embodiment and affective experience.[43] This double gesture frequently finds its expression in a poetics that is marked by uneven histories of exchange, translation, and hybridization. In this understanding of world literature circulation and translation are not secondary activities. Rather, as noted by Susan Stanford Friedman,[44] translation and "[c]irculation impact . . . art *before* and *during* the creative process as well as *after*." But though foregrounding transfer, mixing and traveling, the poetics of world literature remains sensitive to the transformative and unassimilable force of locality.

The proposed conceptualization of world literature is particularly apt for analyses of Afropolitan world literatures. Mbembe, after all, understands Afropolitanism as "an aesthetic and a particular poetic of the world."[45] This poetic is based on the mingling and the interweaving of worlds and is therefore opposed to nativist politics and concepts of *négritude*, which posit autochthonous articulations of Africanness. Afropolitan world literature, I want to suggest, thrives on a narrative that resides in processes of exchange. It binds distinct creative practices into mutually transformative relationships, while exploring these entanglements from a specifically African perspective. Such a narrative has transformative potential because it can raise the awareness of the cultural mixing and travelling at the heart of an African worldliness and, simultaneously, illustrates that these processes always take shape in distinct local contexts. Owuor's novel *Dust* displays such an Afropolitan 'sensibility,' which means not so much that it celebrates mobility but that it fosters, by means of a complex narrative poetics, consciousness of the entanglements between the local and the translocal and that it gestures toward new modes of community building. Political concerns related to Afropolitanism are thus inserted into the heart of narrative forms, compelling readers to think of African spaces, histories, and ways of being in terms of their inherent relationality and trajectories.

Yvonne Adhiambo Owuor's *Dust*— Afropolitanism to Come

Yvonne Adhiambo Owuor's first novel *Dust* presents a sustained engagement with Africa in ways that exemplify, but also considerably complicate Mbembe's understanding of Afropolitanism, not least because it highlights how precarious African subjectivities and communities can be.[46] *Dust*, which has been shortlisted for the Folio prize, traces, in discontinuous and fragmentary ways, the story of the Ogandas, a Kenyan family. It is a story of suffering and grief that is closely entwined with the country's colonial and post-colonial pasts. The narrative begins with a loss, yielding a constitutive absence that propels the plot: In a poetically dense scene, we witness the death of the son, Odidi Oganda, who is fatally shot by the police in the 'post-election violence' of 2007 on the streets of Nairobi. The novel links the weeks of violence following the contested inauguration of Mwai Kibaki to earlier historical atrocities in response to the anti-colonial Mau Mau movement in the 1950s, in which Odidi's father, Aggrey Nyipir Oganda, supported the loyalists. Learning about Odidi's death, his sister Ajany, a painter, returns from Brazil, where she had escaped to, following the sound of "Far Away"[47] that weighed on her since childhood. As the family re-unites in their unloved home Wuoth Ogik, located in the northern drylands around Lake Turkana, an unexpected British visitor, Isaiah Bolton, arrives. Isaiah seeks to reconstruct the circumstances that led to the death of Hugh Bolton, a colonial settler, whom he believes to be his father. In frequently painful memory-work, the narrative gradually uncovers that it was Nyipir, then working as Bolton's assistant, who killed the latter in an attempt to protect his future wife, Akai Lokorijom. What unites all major characters—and what separates them—is the fact that they are implicated in histories of violence, which frequently blur facile distinctions between victim and perpetrator. All of the characters are haunted by their memories, ghosts, as they are repeatedly called, which conjure up the many unspeakable conflicts of their past: "*Memories are ghosts. . . Places are ghosts, too.*"[48] The uncanny sense of a persistent spectrality, the presence of "unseen things,"[49] questions what Jacques Derrida calls the "reassuring order of presents and, especially, the border between the present, the actual or present reality of the present, and everything that can be opposed to it: absence, non-presence, non-effectivity, inactuality, virtuality."[50] For Derrida, this "being-with specters" implies a "politics of memory, of inheritance, and of generations"[51] that acknowledges the marginalized and forgotten.

Largely made up of the protagonist's memories, which persistently seep into the present to engender a multilayered temporality, the novel attests to the bourgeoning of historical fiction in Kenya and Eastern Africa.[52] These revisionist historical novels re-member the colonial and post-independence pasts to envision new modes of identification in contemporary Africa; they are as much shaped by the past as they are oriented towards the future. Experimenting with innovative ways of storytelling, they test the capacity of African literature to provide new symbolic forms with which to approach the socio-political fragmentations caused by the violence of colonialism and the failures of the postcolonial nation-state.

From its beginning, *Dust* makes it clear that the vision of a multi-ethnic and liberal Kenya, in which people from different cultural backgrounds freely mingle, has been irretrievably lost: "A mosaic people ... Wanderers, cattlemen, camel herders, fishermen and hunters, dreamers, strangers, gatherers and farmers, trading nations, empire builders, and the forgetful. Such were the people for whom Nyipir had carried the new Kenya flag ... Blended cultures, intoxicating fusion—the new, revised Kenya."[53] Narration emerges in *Dust* from the loss of such a multi-ethnic community and the struggle to think of alternative possibilities of community today, after African decolonization and beyond the crippling national homogenization. Memory-work, i.e. the working through the past, becomes a crucial force in imagining pluralized modes of sociality that open a different, more peaceful and just future. Although Owuor's elaboratively self-reflexive novel does not yet fully articulate this Afropolitan vision on the diegetic level, it consistently hints at the power of literature to make available the necessary symbolic forms underlying such an open community.

The Kenya that is portrayed in Owuor's epic novel is a country that is marked as much by cultural exchange, movement and transfer as by social fragmentation, violence, and conflict; it is a fluid, dynamic site of mixing and a site of violent repression of this very mixing. Echoing Mbembe's understanding of Afropolitanism, Kenya is a world in movement, intricately entangled with an array of other places across and beyond the continent, with Ethiopia, Somalia, Sudan, Eritrea, Egypt, Burma, Great Britain, France, Portugal, Brazil, and many more. The influx of different ethnicities and peoples has produced all sorts of intersections and translocations, which cut across clearly delimited nations or countries. Nyipir's name, alluding to the eponymous Luo king, is an evocative reminder of the patterns of migration and collision that have been formative of Kenya and the continent since pre-colonial times. Plurilingualism is the enabling condition for navigating the country's inherent plurality: "Pulse of language—Kiswahili for trade, English spots, and fifteen murmured dialects—this was how they crossed worlds."[54] Even rural, seemingly remote places such as Wuoth Ogik, are caught up in complex patterns of exchange and circulation. The secluded Wuoth Ogik is not a pastoral idyll, untouched by global histories and the ruptures of modernity. Rather, it is a site in which multiple histories, private and public wars, converge in frequently violent ways, illustrating that the local "is not purely indigenous, but a 'cradling' of the global within one particular site":[55]

"This place. Wuoth Ogik. Forces converged here. People left stories at springs."[56] The smallest objects in the house, traveling objects par excellence, bear the traces of other cultures and index the extent to which the seemingly local and indigenous is entrenched in global networks: books by Charles Baudelaire, George Sand, Charles Dickens, the Brontës, Carle Vernet, and Gustave Flaubert are placed next to Ethiopian Orthodox art and a painting "of a green robed Saint George conversing with a resigned gold-sashed, golden-fire-sworded Archangel Uriel."[57] Built by the English settler Hugh Bolton during the British colonization of East Africa and later becoming the residence of the Ogandas, Wuoth Ogik, literally meaning "journey's end,"[58] deeply enmeshes the characters into the place's repressed history of violence. It is in the crumbling farming homestead where Nyipir kills Bolton and this unspeakable atrocity binds him and Akai, almost against their will, to Wuoth Ogik and entangles their children in a network of secrets, lies and silences.[59] As the characters struggle with their "[c]easeless unbelonging"[60] and "efficient out-of-place-ness,"[61] the novel works against facile oppositions between home vs. diaspora, roots vs. routes. *Dust* locates the ruptures and discontinuities that Paul Gilroy in *The Black Atlantic* (1993) identifies as constitutive of transatlantic diaspora within the continent and in so doing radically undoes the conventional opposition between the 'modern' instabilities of displacement and the 'premodern' stasis of African places. As Ajany comes to realize that 'her' home might in fact be Isaiah's home,[62] Owuor's novel suggests that conventional notions of 'home' as a stable point of origin have lost their epistemological plausibility in a world shaped by movement and exchange. 'Home', Rushton argues in her reading of the novel, is always shot through by otherness, translocation, and displacement.[63]

Kenya, in *Dust*, is modeled as a meshwork of open and dynamic relationships—between people, places, and histories—which underlie the generativity of an emergent world. In contrast to a network, a meshwork, according to Tim Ingold,[64] consists "not of interconnected points but of interwoven lines," i.e., trails "*along* which life is lived." These trails disclose a relation that creatively transforms the nodal participants in unpredictable ways.[65] And indeed, Owuor's Kenya is populated by people of many provenances, by Turkana, Luos, Kikuyu, Somali herdsmen and traders, by turbaned Bohra men, Eritreans, Indian shopkeepers, British colonials, and Irish missionaries, by a German ecologist, an Estonian filmmaker, a Scottish explorer, and a Japanese businessman. It is the common people and not the economically privileged jet-setters, who, in *Dust*, epitomize Afropolitan ideas of cultural plurality and movement: The desert peddler, *duddaani-nyaatte*, whose "father might be the old Kenyan Punjabi trader who once lived in Ethiopia"[66] and who "spoke all the tongues of the desert, mimicked accents and postures, dialogued in the gist of some European languages, including Croatian";[67] the police officer Ali Dida Hada, who "had walked away mid-battle from Eritrea through Ethiopia and into Kenya"[68] and the shopkeeper Babu Paratpara Chaudhari, whose father's father "had gone to Ethiopia"[69] and whose "family ... left East Africa for Rushey Mead, Leicester, England."[70] The central characters of the novel are constantly on the move and are predominantly defined by their travels, movements, and trajectories, suggesting that their identities will always be in the making. Conversely, their travels bring forth new cartographies, which entangle African spaces in a dense meshwork. Nyipir frequently disappears for weeks from Wuoth Ogik, pursuing illegal trade and then "coming home from secret journeys, bearing gifts of livestock and assorted weapons like a fourth magus."[71] The enigmatic Akai Lokorijom relentlessly roams the land, trying to escape the "ghosts," "devils," and "secret nightmares"[72] that haunt her. Ajany dreams of leaving home behind, almost obsessively painting rivers and ships that take her "Far Away."[73] To overcome the spatial confines of their home and its stifling atmosphere, Odidi creates "story-words" that, just as "vessels," "always carried" Ajany "into safe border."[74] He seeks to make up for their solitude by imagining relatives, "a web of doting dream relations into which he and Ajany inserted their longing to leave."[75] The fact that these dream relatives never materialize only strengthens Ajany's wish to escape Wuoth Ogik. Ajany beseeches her brother to accompany her, but he insists on his sense of belonging, which, for him also entails a moral obligation for Africa's future: "'Here, we belong ... We stay here,' 'Jany. . . *This* is home.'"[76] She finally decides to turn her back to Kenya, relocating to Brazil, where she hopes to pursue her career as a painter and sculptor. Odidi, in turn, moves to Nairobi, determined to build a water system across the country. The fact that he eventually becomes the leader of a criminal gang and is killed in the streets of Nairobi conveys a strong sense of pessimism concerning the possibility of change, i.e., of establishing a free, democratic, and just Kenya that overcomes the tyrannies of colonial violence, economic exploitation, and political corruption. Increasingly, in modern Kenya authoritarian rule and corruption weaken the meaning of the political, replacing it with "an implicit, tenuous moral contract of material benefits in return for political quiescence."[77] It is in this sense that Odidi's death metonymically stands in for the fate of the nation: "*This is how we lose the country, one child at a time,*"[78] one character bitterly notes.

From its beginning, a beginning that is at the same time an end, *Dust* illustrates that the cultural mixing and heterogeneity that have gone into the making of Kenya do not automatically translate into Afropolitan attitudes. While movement and circulation might indeed be the essence of Afropolitanism, they are hardly sufficient for bringing forth Afropolitan sensibilities. If, as Mbembe argues, Afropolitanism entails an awareness of the ways in which acts of blending shape one's positionality in the world, then *Dust* first and foremost exposes the limits of Afropolitanism. The multi-ethnic Kenya that Mboya envisioned and that Nyipir once fought for, is buried by the nation's unifying forces: "After Mboya," the heterodiegetic narrator states, "Kenya's official languages [were]: English, Kiswahili, and Silence."[79] Rather than experiencing cultural plurality as an enrichment, most characters see it as a threat and are willing to remodel their identities to comply with the nationalist 'pedagogy' of unity.[80] Contemporary Kenya is a burning and crumbling country in which "most citizens understated ethnic roots, overemphasizing Kenyan-ness in brash Kiswahili and even louder English. Renegotiating belonging, desperate faith in One Kenya."[81] Throughout, the novel accentuates that the political formation of the nation is inadequate to harbor the kind of plurality and worldliness that is constitutive of Kenya's society. In line with much postcolonial criticism,[82] the nation in *Dust* turns out to be a totalizing, ethnically absolutist force that is antithetical to the Afropolitan embracement of plurality. Political unity is exposed as an ideologically powerful chimera, a longing for togetherness and not a foundational characteristic of the nation. Rather than enabling political action, it ignites a spiral of violence, fear and repression; "the nation, slow horror."[83] As Ajany anxiously seeks to grasp the reasons that led to Odidi's death and to unlock the secrets of her family's past, her stutter becomes an evocative reminder of the discrepancies within the national community; it registers, as Rebecca Walkowitz writes in a different context, "antagonisms within a civic rhetoric that claims to be uniform and consistent."[84]

The suppression of cultural heterogeneity that *Dust* problematizes on the diegetic level, i.e., the level of the story, is powerfully counteracted by a reverse impulse at work, an impulse that highlights the creative intervention made possible by literary forms. In an important sense, Owuor's novel can be read as an Afropolitan narrative that disturbs the "ideological manoeuvres"[85] through which the nation and nativist nationalism claim their unity. Afropolitanism, in *Dust*, is a generative poetological principle that gives rise to a complexly patterned narrative, which thrives on processes of entanglement, while stressing a locally inflected worldliness. The narrative of *Dust* does not follow a coherent plot or display a full-blown, chronologically ordered and teleological structure. It consists of a multiplicity of small accounts, focalized by different characters and only loosely held together by a heterodiegetic narrator. Each of the accounts registers different, subjective and highly affective ways of experiencing life in Kenya. The bits and pieces refuse to congeal into a closed and coherent narrative structure; they produce an open, polyphonic, and discontinuous narrative that aptly reflects the diversity of Kenyan society. It is only toward the end of the novel, after the characters have worked through their sinister past and hesitantly broken their silences, that affinities between the characters' impressions become more pronounced and that the single vignettes begin to resonate with one another. Revealing frictions and differences, *Dust* strategically undoes the close links between the novel and the nation, prominent in particular to eighteenth-century European literature. In his essay "The national longing of form," Timothy Brennan has characterized the eighteenth-century novel as "a composite but clearly bordered work of art,"[86] which provides the symbolic means for the imagination of community and unity of the nation. If Owuor's novel does imagine a community, this community is certainly one "without unity";[87] it is a community that is built on difference, pluralism, and traumatic exchange, but not on 'natural' genealogical relations. The frequent use of Kiswahili words, phrases, and songs, which are only sometimes translated, powerfully asserts difference as a cornerstone of the community. Creating a "metonymic gap"[88] between local and colonial culture, Kiswahili, in *Dust*, contests the authority of hegemonic, totalizing orders to bolster alternative knowledges and plural identities. Mboya's Afropolitan vision of Kenya as one of "blended cultures, intoxicating fusion"[89] is therefore not only a ghostlike memory. It is also and more importantly a future possibility made available by the performative force of *Dust*'s narrative.

In *Dust*, the rapid shifts between the characters' thoughts, memories, and impressions give rise to a genuinely achronological, non-linear narrative, in which the conventional tripartite division between past, present, and future is dissolved. What emerges is a multidirectional temporality, in which past, present, and future are bound into many loops of relation: "The past's beckon is persistent,"[90] the narrator remarks. Time is not only moving forward, but also "backward-turning" and "sideways-sliding";[91] according to the narrator, "[t]ime shifts, a chain of moments leading … across thresholds."[92] The narrative's continual oscillation between the Mau Mau uprisings of the early 1950s, the political assassination of Tom Mboya in 1969 and the post-election violence of 2007 shows that the past expands, as a latent and haunting force, into the present. Such latent living on, a *survivre* in the Derridean sense, indexes an intractable presence of the past—a "shadowed historical persistence"[93]—that conjures up alternative, largely forgotten histories, which are, nevertheless, immanent in the present. The bones that Nyipir eventually excavates symbolize such latent histories, which must be affirmed to enable regeneration and to promote justice. The temporalities modeled in *Dust* provide opportunities to connect actuality, latency, and potentiality, death to life, gesturing towards a "new set of historical possibilities",[94] which also affect Afro-futures. The many "staccato phrase[s]"[95] and the constant changes in narrative tempo displace any sense of linear progress and produce a disjunctive rhythm that lays bare the incommensurability of Kenya's global contemporary. While some passages offer detailed, poetic, and slowly unfolding descriptions of, e.g., the landscape, others quickly jump from one episode, memory or impression to the next. Time and again, the narrative circles back through different variations of a specific memory, producing a multilayered narrative that spans the distance between different times and people and that introduces "a potentially infinite series of submovements punctuated by jerks."[96]

According to Cheah,[97] the modeling of alternative temporalities that disrupt "the teleological time of Western's modernity's universal narrative progress" lies at the heart of postcolonial world literatures. For Cheah, world literature consists first and foremost of a process of worlding through which suppressed or disqualified non-Western temporalities are revitalized. These temporalities are major resources for displacing Western teleological time, which underpinned colonial conquest and which persist in the present as the basis of capitalist globalization and exploitation. Broadly speaking, the unifying potential of Western teleological time incorporates the non-synchronicity of heterogeneous spaces into the same, seemingly natural and abstract order, thus producing an ideologically charged opposition between the modern vs. the premodern, the civilized vs. the uncivilized, and so on.[98] By performatively creating a new, fluid, and rhythmic sense of temporality, which is derived from local experiences, *Dust* resists the totalizing thrust of capitalist globalization[99] and opens up worlds that confirm the epistemic centrality of Africa in a transculturally entangled, though clearly uneven word.

Importantly, in *Dust*, time and temporality are not pitted against the presumed stability of space and spatial matter.[100] Rather, they are wrested from landscape; they are inscribed into and evolve from the dynamics of a mythical, active, and changing landscape: "As so often across the Global South," Russell West-Pavlov remarks, "political alternatives are not merely human inventions, but devolve from the environment, frequently a sacred space in which creation histories (or more accurately, history as creation) are coeval with the landscape itself."[101] Conversely, landscape and space are not conceived as inert, passive, and static, but as agents in history, which produce their own kind of language and knowledge: "Mount Kulal" is "the storykeeper of this land";[102] "winds carry songs,"[103] and "every crevice contains a story."[104] The time of landscape troubles the dualism of time and space that structures Western epistemes, inviting readers to consider space and history as interlocking forces. Spaces and places are open sites in the *becoming*, even sites of an excessive vitality, which resist mastery, possession, and instrumentalized quantification: There is "[t]oo much life; everything breathes here, even the damn stones. Too much space,"[105] Isaiah claims about the arid landscape surrounding Wuoth Ogik. In highlighting the agency of space, *Dust* radically challenges the notion of a blank space that, after all, was central to colonizing Africa and that today appears to legitimize the ongoing exploitation of the environment. The decoupling of nature from history, as Mary Louise Pratt[106] has convincingly argued, helped obscure colonialism's histories of conquest, exploitation, and violence and ultimately naturalized Europeans' "global presence" by construing a seemingly natural, undifferentiated, and abstract space. The novel's understanding of both space and time are fittingly encapsulated by the eponymous dust: Dust is a dynamic particle; it is animated matter, which is imbued with a distinct agency and as such references unpredictable metamorphosis and vibrant vitality.[107] As dust is turned into agential force, underlying a complex and spiralling narrative, the novel invites us to think "ourselves as embedded in geologic temporalities,"[108] highlighting that narratives that limit themselves to human agency are too narrow to capture our being-with-the-world.

The poetics of time and space in *Dust* can claim socio-political importance precisely because it is posited as an element of Afropolitanism that allows us to think differently, disjunctively, about the world and community. *Dust* reworks many epistemic premises that underlie traditional, Western concepts of cosmopolitanism, including its presumed universalism. Step by step, the novel creates a conceptual basis for a more modest and worldly, i.e., a distinctively African, vernacular, or rooted, but unavoidable cosmopolitanism.[109] This kind of cosmopolitanism acknowledges the historical and geographical particularity of ideas, norms, characters, and historical trajectories, without forfeiting "an ethos of macro-interdependencies," as Paul Rabinow[110] puts it. More specifically, *Dust* questions Western, anthropocentric conceptions of cosmopolitanism that understand the world and community as an exclusively human property. In contradistinction, Owuor's novel makes it clear that the world is shared by human and non-human actors and encourages us to imagine biocentric and possibly more sustainable conceptions of community, kinship and solidarity.

Throughout, *Dust* inscribes into—what was once—the Western genre of the novel the transformative force of African knowledge and confronts the novel's seemingly modern world with its repressed and discredited alternatives. The fictional world of *Dust* is inhabited by ghosts, devils, spirits, and necromancers and thrives on African myths, rituals, traditions, and folk practices. In this world, spirits, animals, and landscapes co-exist with humans in a web of ethically meaningful relationships. The result is an open, emergent, and relationally constituted world that cannot be claimed by anyone. Animist cosmology, *Dust* suggests, constitutes an alternative form of worlding that offers ethically nuanced and politically valuable interpretations of the many forces that make up the world.[111] It functions as a regenerative memory, which becomes a precondition of the characters' psychological healing. Importantly, animism also extends beyond human history and compels characters to grasp human life within the non-human temporalities of natural history;[112] "people", according to the narrator, "listen to four winds"[113] and recognize nature as a source of wisdom. Thriving on alternative knowledge produced by the material world's "elastic time"[114], the novel brings to the fore the non-synchronicity of our broad present and gradually develops a non-Eurocentric understanding of modernity. *Dust* illustrates that modernity is far from singular and that the meta-narrative that imagines the West as the origin of modernity and a unique site of epistemic creativity has lost its plausibility. Underneath the presumed modernity of the Western, bourgeois nation-state and capitalist globalization are alternative modernities, other epistemologies and other, horizontally structured, forms of political communities that are not and possibly cannot be represented by Western discourses, genres and institutions.[115]

Conclusion

The Afropolitanism of Yvonne Adhiambo Owuor's novel *Dust*, I have argued, does not primarily reside in the celebration of mobility or an allegiance to a worldwide African community. Rather it emerges from the novel's powerful imagination of alternative symbolic forms and epistemes, which both articulate an African worldliness and express an acute consciousness of the exchange processes that have gone into the making of Kenya. As such, they actively rework the orders, structures, and shapes of Western knowledge and produce new models by which a community beyond the nation, race, and ethnicity can be imagined. It is by means of its genuinely pluralized and open poetics that the novel points toward new allegiances and solidarities within Kenya and across Africa–a community that, in the sense of Giorgio Agamben (1993),[116] is yet to come.

According to Mbembe,[117] Afropolitanism has the potential to bring "something new and meaningful to the world in general." In a similar vein, *Dust* highlights that "[t]o name something is to bring it to life"[118] and in so doing self-consciously confirms its power to make a worldly intervention. As an instance of Afropolitan world literature, Owuor's novel tells a story that inscribes distinctively African perspectives and experiences into cosmopolitanism, thus participating in the concept's "scaling down, its pluralizing and particularizing."[119] By creating new categories, epistemes and forms, which are derived from African historical and geographic contexts, *Dust* insistently confirms the centrality of Africa as a site of epistemic intervention and cultural reinvention. As it decenters the hegemony of the West in the fabrication of knowledge and offers new conceptions of the world, *Dust* takes a step towards achieving greater epistemic justice.

Notes

1 In Part I and II of this essay I draw on ideas I have developed in Birgit Neumann and Gabriele Rippl, "Celebrating Afropolitan Worlds? Contemporary African World Literatures in English," *Anglophone World Literatures*—Special Issue of *Anglia*, 135.1 (2017): 159–85.

2 Taiye Selasi, "Bye-Bye Babar," *The LIP #5 AFRICA*, March 3, 2005, n.p. Available online: http://thelip.robertsharp.co.uk/?p=76 (accessed January 11, 2018).

3 Betiel Wasihun, "Afropolitan Writing," in *Handbook of Transatlantic Studies*, ed. Julia Straub (Berlin/Boston: De Gruyter, 2016), 393.

4 Selasi, "Bye-Bye Babar," 528.
5 Simon Gikandi, "Foreword: On Afropolitanism," in *Negotiating Afropolitanism: Essays on Borders and Spaces in Contemporary African Literature and Folklore*, ed. Jennifer Wawrzinek and J.K.S. Makokha (Amsterdam: Rodopi, 2011), 9.
6 Cf. Emma Dabiri, "The Pitfalls and Promises of Afropolitanism," in *Cosmopolitanisms*, ed. Bruce Robbins and Paulo Lemos Horta (New York: New York UP, 2017).
7 Cf. Binyavanga Wainaina, qtd. in Stephanie Bosch Santana, "Exorcizing Afropolitanism: Binyavanga Wainaina" explains why "I am a Pan-Africanist, not an Afropolitan" at ASAUK 2012', *Africa in Words*, February 8, 2013, n.p. Available online: https://africainwords.com/2013/02/08/exorcizing-afropolitanism-binyavanga-wainaina-explains-why-i-am-a-pan-africanist-not-an-afropolitan-at-asauk-2012 (acessed January 11, 2018); Brian Bwesigye, 'Is Afropolitanism Africa's New Single Story?', *Aster(ix) Journal* November 22, 2013, n.p. Available online: <http://asterixjournal.com/afropolitanism-africas-new-single-story-reading-helon-habilas-review-need-new-names-brian-bwesigye/> (accessed May 6, 2019).
8 Cf. Neumann and Rippl, "Celebrating Afropolitan Worlds?"
9 Cf. Dabiri, "The Pitfalls and Promises of Afropolitanism"; Achille Mbembe, "Afropolitanism," in *Africa Remix: Contemporary Art of a Continent*, ed. Simon Njami (Johannesburg: Jacana Media, 2007); S. Okwunodu Ogbechi, "Afropolitanism: Africa without Africans (II)," *Aachronym*, April 4, 2008, n.p. Available online: <http://aachronym.blogspot.com/2008/04/afropolitanism-more-africa-without.html> (accessed September 5, 2018).
10 The distinction between texts which focus on movement across the African continent and those which explore transatlantic routes is not always straightforward since many texts portray moments of transition, arrival, and return. The same holds true for writers, many of which divide their time between different places.
11 Dabiri, "The Pitfalls and Promises of Afropolitanism," 210.
12 Maureen Moynagh is right to note that "[t]here is an uneasy tension between those who understand Afropolitan to mean primarily those with connections to Africa who have grown up in the West or who reside primarily in Europe or the US, and Mbembe, who is clearly more interested in Afropolitans resident on the continent" (2015: 283).
13 Gikandi warns us not to ignore the "negative consequences of transnationalism, the displacement of Africans abroad, the difficulties they face as they try to overcome their alterity in alien landscapes, the deep cultural anxieties that often make diasporas sites of cultural fundamentalism and ethnic chauvinism" (2011: 11).
14 See in this context also Gikandi's understanding of Afropolitanisms as a "new phenomenology of Africanness—a way of being African in the world" (2011: 9).
15 Achille Mbembe and Sarah Balakrishnan, "Pan-African Legacies. Afropolitan Futures. A Conversation with Achille Mbembe," *Transition* 120 (2016): 28–37, 31.
16 Mbembe's article "Afropolitanisme" was originally published on December 20, 2005 in *Le Messager*; its English translation appeared in 2007.

17 Achille Mbembe, "Afropolitanism," in *Africa Remix: Contemporary Art of a Continent*, ed. Simon Njami (Johannesburg: Jacana Media, 2007), 27.

18 Ibid., 28.

19 Doreen Massey, *For Space* (London: Sage, 2005), 9.

20 Yogita Goyal, "Africa and the Black Atlantic," *Research in African Literatures* 45, no.3 (2014): v–xxv

21 Ibid., v.

22 Ibid., iv.

23 Paul Gilroy, *The Black Atlantic: Modernity and Double Consciousness* (London: Verso, 1999), 197.

24 Mbembe, "Afropolitanism," 27.

25 Ibid., 28.

26 Mbembe, "Afropolitanism," 28.

27 Mbembe and Balakrishnan, "Pan-African Legacies," 30.

28 Mbembe, "Afropolitanism," 28.

29 Bruce Robbins and Paulo Lemos Horta, "Introduction," in *Cosmopolitanisms*, ed. Bruce Robbins and Paulo Lemos Horta (New York: New York UP, 2017), 11.

30 Miriam Pahl, "Afropolitanism as Critical Consciousness: Chimamanda Ngozi Adichie's and Teju Cole's Internet Presence," *Journal of African Cultural Studies* 1 (2016): 73–87, 74.

31 Mbembe and Balakrishnan, "Pan-African Legacies," 29.

32 Mbembe, "Afropolitanism," 29.

33 Aamir R. Mufti, *Forget English! Orientalisms and World Literatures* (Cambridge, MA: Harvard UP, 2016), 9.

34 Ibid.

35 Emily Apter, *Against World Literature; On the Politics of Untranslatability* (London/New York: Verso, 2013), 70.

36 Graham Huggan, *The Postcolonial Exotic. Marketing the Margins* (London/New York, NY: Routledge, 2001); Sarah Brouillette, *Postcolonial Writers in the Global Literary Market Place* (Houndmills/Basingstoke: Palgrave Macmillan, 2007).

37 Adaobi Tricia Nwaubani, "African Books for Western Eyes," *New York Times*, November 28, 2014, n.p. Available online: <https://www.nytimes.com/2014/11/30/opinion/sunday/african-books-for-western-eyes.html> (accessed January 11, 2018). In a similar vein, Helon Habila and Ben Okri have complained about the narrow range of topics that African writers are expected to engage with.

38 Cf. Mads Rosendahl Thomsen, "Changing Spaces: Canonization of Anglophone World Literature," *Anglia*. Special Issue: *Anglophone World Literatures* 135, no. 1 (2017): 51–66.

39 Cf. Neumann and Rippl, "Celebrating Afropolitan Worlds?"

40 Pheng Cheah, *What Is a World? On Postcolonial Literature as World Literature*. (Durham, NC: Duke UP, 2016); Neumann, Birgit and Gabriele Rippl, "Celebrating Afropolitan Worlds"; Birgit Neumann, "Vernacular Cosmopolitanism in Anglophone World Literatures—Comparative Histories of Literary Worlding," in *Global Perspectives on European Literary Histories.* Special Issue, *Arcadia* (2018).

41 Cheah, *What is a World?*, 8.

42 This is not to deny the role of economic and socio-political factors shaping the field and practice of world literature. The literary text, however, is imbued with a distinct force, an agency that cannot be understood in the terms established by a global market. See in this context also Debjani Ganguly, *This Thing Called the World: The Contemporary Novel as Global Form* (Durham, NC: Duke UP, 2016), 24.

43 Cf. Vittoria Borsò, „Markt Macht Vergessen: Wie der Medialitätsraum der Literaturen der Welt zur kommunikativen Formel der Weltliteratur wird," in *Verlag Macht Weltliteratur. Lateinamerikanisch-deutsche Kulturtransfers zwischen internationalem Literaturbetrieb und Übersetzungspolitik*, ed. Gesine Müller (Berlin: Tranvía, 2014), 41.

44 Susan Stanford Friedman, "World Modernisms, World Literature, and Comparativity," in *The Oxford Handbook of Global Modernism*, ed. Mark Wolleager and Matt Eatough. (Oxford: Oxford UP, 2012), 503.

45 Mbembe, "Afropolitanism," 28.

46 The novel was first published in 2013 by the Nairobi-based publisher Kwani; in 2014 Knopf published a slightly modified version.

47 Yvonne Adhiambo Owuor, *Dust* (New York: Knopf, 2014), 50.

48 Ibid., 123; 121.

49 Ibid., 78.

50 Jacques Derrida, *Specters of Marx: The State of the Debt, the Work of Mourning and the New* International (London: Routledge, 2006), 48.

51 Ibid., xviii.

52 Cf. Russell West-Pavlov, "Temporality and Quantum Theory in the Contemporary Global South Novel," in *New Approaches to the 21st-Century Anglophone Novel*, ed. Sibylle Baumbach and Birgit Neumann (Basingstoke: Palgrave Macmillan) (in print).

53 Owuor, *Dust*, 25.

54 Owuor, *Dust*, 120.

55 Wai Chee Dimock, "African, Caribbean, American: Black English as Creole Tongue," in *Transforming Diaspora: Communities beyond National Boundaries,* ed. E. Field and Parmita Kapadia (Madison, NJ: Farleigh Dickinson UP, 2011), 41.

56 Owuor, *Dust*, 240.

57 Ibid., 54.

58 Ibid., 170.

59 Cf. Amy Rushton, "No Place Like Home: The Anxiety of Return," in Taiye Selasi's *Ghana Must Go* and Yvonne Adhiambo Owuor's *Dust, Études Anglaises. New Diasporas, New Directions* 70, no. 1 (2017): 45–62, 57.

60 Owuor, *Dust*, 219.

61 Ibid., 19.

62 Ibid., 335.

63 Cf. Amy Rushton, "No Place Like Home," 52.

64 Tim Ingold, *Being Alive: Essays on Knowledge, Movement and Description* (Oxon/New York, NY: Routledge, 2011), 69–70.

65 Ibid., 67–75.

66 Owuor, *Dust*, 82.

67 Ibid.

68 Ibid., 219.

69 Ibid., 27.

70 Ibid., 27.

71 Ibid., 68.

72 Ibid., 51.

73 Ibid., 52.

74 Ibid., 19.

75 Ibid., 117.

76 Ibid., 119.

77 Bruce J. Berman, "Nationalism in Post-Colonial Africa," in *The Oxford Handbook of the History of Nationalism*, ed. John Breuilly (Oxford: Oxford UP, 2013), 361.

78 Owuor, *Dust*, 187.

79 Ibid., 274.

80 Cf. Homi K. Bhabha, "DissemiNation: Time, Narrative, and the Margins of the Modern Nation," in *Nation and Narration*, ed. Homi K. Bhabha (Oxon/New York, NY: Routledge, 1990).

81 Owuor, *Dust*, 192.

82 Cf. Homi K. Bhabha (ed.), *Nation and Narration*; Paul Gilroy, *The Black Atlantic*.

83 Owuor, *Dust*, 25.

84 Rebecca L. Walkowitz, *Cosmopolitan Style: Modernism beyond the Nation* (New York: Columbia UP, 2006), 136.

85 Bhabha, "DissemiNation," 300.

86 Timothy Brennan, "The National Longing of Form," in *Nation and Narration*, ed. Homi K. Bhabha (Oxon/New York, NY: Routledge, 1990), 48.

87 Jonathan Culler, "Anderson and the Novel," *Diacritics* 29, no. 4 (1999): 19–39, 32.

88 Bill Ashcroft, "Bridging the Silence: Inner Translation and the Metonymic Gap," in *Language and Translation in Postcolonial Literatures. Multilingual Contexts, Translational Texts*, ed. Simona Bertacco (New York: Routledge, 2014), 24.
89 Ibid., 25.
90 Ibid., 24.
91 West-Pavlov, "Temporality and Quantum Theory in the Contemporary Global South Novel."
92 Owuor, *Dust*, 64.
93 Peter Boxall, *Twenty-First-Century Fiction: A Critical Introduction* (Cambridge/New York: Cambridge UP, 2013), 62.
94 Ibid., 81.
95 Owuor, *Dust*, 117.
96 Brian Massumi, *Parables for the Virtual: Movement, Affect, Sensation* (Durham, NC: Duke UP, 2002), 40.
97 Cheah, *What Is a World?*, 12.
98 See Dipesh Chakrabarty, *Provincializing Europe: Postcolonial Thought and Historical Difference* (Princeton: Princeton UP, 2008. Chakrabarty notes: "Historicism is what made modernity or capitalism . . . global *over time*, by originating in one place (Europe) and then spreading outside it . . . Historicism thus posited historical time as a measure of cultural distance . . . that was assumed to exist between the West and the non-West." (7).
99 Cf. Cheah, *What Is a World?*, 11.
100 West-Pavlov, "Temporality and Quantum Theory in the Contemporary Global South Novel."
101 Ibid.
102 Owuor, *Dust*, 117.
103 Ibid., 110.
104 Ibid., 43.
105 Ibid., 78.
106 Mary Louise Pratt, *Imperial Eyes: Travel Writing and Transculturation* (London: Routledge, 1992), 28.
107 West-Pavlov, "Temporality and Quantum Theory in the Contemporary Global South Novel."
108 Kathryn Yusoff, "Geologic Life: Prehistory, Climate, Futures in the Anthropocene," *Environment and Planning D: Society and Space* 31.5 (2013): 779–795, 785.
109 Cf. Homi K. Bhabha, "Unsatisfied Notes on Vernacular Cosmopolitanism," in *Text and Narration*, ed. Peter C. Pfeiffer and Laura García-Moreno (Columbia, S.C. Camden House, 1996); Mitchell Cohen, "Rooted Cosmopolitanism," *Dissent*, 39, no. 4 (1992): 478–83.

110 Paul Rabinow, "Representations are Social Facts," in *Writing Culture: The Poetics and Politics of Ethnography*, ed. James Clifford and George E. Marcus (Berkeley: U of California P, 1986), 258.

111 West-Pavlov, "Temporality and Quantum Theory in the Contemporary Global South Novel."

112 See, in this context, Dipesh Chakrabarty, "The Climate of History: Four Theses," *Critical Inquiry*, 35, no. 2 (2009): 197–222, who suggests giving up the "the age-old humanist distinction between natural history and human history" (201) to account for the fact that human and natural forces intermingle.

113 Owuor, *Dust*, 41.

114 Owuor, *Dust*, 47.

115 Cf. G.K. Bhambra, *Rethinking Modernity.Postcolonialism and the Sociological Imagination* (Basingstoke: Palgrave Macmillan, 2007), 1.

116 Giorgio Agamben, *The Coming Community* (Minneapolis: U of Minnesota P, 1993).

117 Mbembe and Balakrishnan, "Pan-African Legacies," *Transition*, 120 (2016): 28–37, 29.

118 Owuor, *Dust*, 35.

119 Bruce Robbins. "Introduction Part I: Actually Existing Cosmopolitanism," in *Cosmopolitics: Thinking and Feeling Beyond the Nation*, ed. Bruce Robbins and Pheng Cheah (Minneapolis: U of Minnesota P, 1998), 3.

Works Cited

Agamben, Giorgio. *The Coming Community*. Minneapolis: U of Minnesota P, 1993.

Apter, Emily. *Against World Literature; On the Politics of Untranslatability*. London/New York: Verso, 2013.

Ashcroft, Bill. "Bridging the Silence: Inner Translation and the Metonymic Gap." In *Language and Translation in Postcolonial Literatures. Multilingual Contexts, Translational Texts*, edited by Simona Bertacco, 17–31. New York: Routledge, 2014.

Berman, Bruce J. "Nationalism in Post-Colonial Africa." In *The Oxford Handbook of the History of Nationalism*, edited by John Breuilly, 359–76. Oxford: Oxford UP, 2013.

Bhabha, Homi K. "DissemiNation: Time, Narrative, and the Margins of the Modern Nation." In *Nation and Narration*, edited by Homi K. Bhabha, 291–322. Oxon/New York, NY: Routledge, 1990.

Bhabha, Homi K. "Unsatisfied Notes on Vernacular Cosmopolitanism." In *Text and Narration*, edited by Peter C. Pfeiffer and Laura García-Moreno, 191–207. Columbia, S.C. Camden House, 1996.

Bhambra, G.K. *Rethinking Modernity. Postcolonialism and the Sociological Imagination*. Basingstoke/New York, NY: Palgrave Macmillan, 2007.

Borsò, Vittoria. „Markt Macht Vergessen: Wie der Medialitätsraum der Literaturen der Welt zur kommunikativen Formel der Weltliteratur wird." In *Verlag Macht Weltliteratur. Lateinamerikanisch-deutsche Kulturtransfers zwischen internationalem Literaturbetrieb und Übersetzungspolitik*, edited by Gesine Müller, 21–46. Berlin: Tranvía, 2014.

Bosch Santana, Stephanie. "Exorcizing Afropolitanism: Binyavanga Wainaina explains why 'I am a Pan-Africanist, not an Afropolitan" at ASAUK 2012'. *Africa in Words*, February 8, 2013, n.p. Available online: https://africainwords.com/2013/02/08/exorcizing-afropolitanism-binyavanga-wainaina-explains-why-i-am-a-pan-africanist-not-an-afropolitan-at-asauk-2012 (accessed January 11, 2018).

Boxall, Peter. *Twenty-First-Century Fiction: A Critical Introduction*. Cambridge/New York: Cambridge UP, 2013.

Brennan, Timothy. "The National Longing of Form." In *Nation and Narration*, edited by Homi Bhabha, 44–70. Oxon/New York, NY: Routledge, 1990.

Brouillette, Sarah. *Postcolonial Writers in the Global Literary Market Place*. Houndmills/Basingstoke: Palgrave Macmillan, 2007.

Bwesigye, Brian. "Is Afropolitanism Africa's New Single Story?" *Aster(ix) Journal* November 22, 2013, n.p. Available online: http://asterixjournal.com/afropolitanism-africas-new-single-story-reading-helon-habilas-review-need-new-names-brian-bwesigye/ (accessed January 11, 2018).

Casanova, Pascale. *The World Republic of Letters*. Cambridge, MA: Harvard UP, 2004.

Chakrabarty, Dipesh. "The Climate of History: Four Theses." *Critical Inquiry*, 35, no. 2 (2009): 197–222.

———. *Provincializing Europe: Postcolonial Thought and Historical Difference*. Princeton, NJ/Oxford: Princeton UP, 2008.

Cheah, Pheng. *What Is a World? On Postcolonial Literature as World Literature*. Durham, NC: Duke UP, 2016.

Cohen, Mitchell. "Rooted Cosmopolitanism." *Dissent* 39, no. 4 (1992): 478–83.

Culler, Jonathan. "Anderson and the Novel." *Diacritics* 29, no. 4 (1999): 19–39.

Dabiri, Emma. "The Pitfalls and Promises of Afropolitanism." In *Cosmopolitanisms*, edited by Bruce Robbins and Paulo Lemos Horta, 201–11. New York: New York UP, 2017.

Derrida, Jacques. *Specters of Marx: The State of the Debt, the Work of Mourning and the New International*. London: Routledge, 2006.

Dimock, Wai Chee. "African, Caribbean, American: Black English as Creole Tongue." In *Transforming Diaspora: Communities beyond National Boundaries*, edited by Robin E. Field and Parmita Kapadia, 37–64. Madison, NJ: Farleigh Dickinson UP, 2011.

Friedman, Susan Stanford. "World Modernisms, World Literature, and Comparativity." In *The Oxford Handbook of Global Modernism*, edited by Mark Wolleager and Matt Eatough, 499–525. Oxford: Oxford UP, 2012.

Ganguly, Debjani. *This Thing Called the World: The Contemporary Novel as Global Form*. Durham, NC: Duke UP, 2016.

Gikandi, Simon. "Foreword: On Afropolitanism." In *Negotiating Afropolitanism: Essays on Borders and Spaces in Contemporary African Literature and Folklore*, edited by Jennifer Wawrzinek and J.K.S. Makokha, 9–12. Amsterdam: Rodopi, 2011.

Gilroy, Paul. *The Black Atlantic: Modernity and Double Consciousness*. London: Verso, 1999.
Glissant, Édouard. *Caribbean Discourse. Selected Essays*. Trans. J. Michael Dash. Charlottesville, VA: UP of Virginia, 1989.
Goyal, Yogita. "Africa and the Black Atlantic." *Research in African Literatures* 45, no. 3 (2014): v–xxv.
Habila, Helon. "We Need New Names by NoViolet Bulawayo—Review." *The Guardian*, June 20, 2013, n.p. Available online: https://www.theguardian.com/books/2013/jun/20/need-new-names-bulawayo-review (accessed January 11, 2018).
Huggan, Graham. *The Postcolonial Exotic. Marketing the Margins*. London/New York, NY: Routledge, 2001.
Ingold, Tim. *Being Alive: Essays on Knowledge, Movement and Description*. Oxon/New York, NY: Routledge, 2011.
Massey, Doreen. *For Space*. London: Sage, 2005.
Massumi, Brian. *Parables for the Virtual: Movement, Affect, Sensation*. Durham, NC: Duke UP, 2002.
Mbembe, Achille. "Afropolitanisme." *Le Messager*, December 20, 2005, n.p. Available online: http://africultures.com/afropolitanisme-4248/ (accessed January 10, 2018).
Mbembe, Achille. "Afropolitanism." In *Africa Remix: Contemporary Art of a Continent*, edited by Simon Njami, 26–29. Johannesburg: Jacana Media, 2007.
Mbembe, Achille, and Sarah Balakrishnan. "Pan-African Legacies. Afropolitan Futures. A Conversation with Achille Mbembe." *Transition* 120 (2016): 28–37.
Mignolo, Walter D. "Second Thoughts on *The Darker Side of the Renaissance*. Afterword to the Second Edition." In *The Darker Side of the Renaissance: Literacy, Territoriality, and Colonization*, by Walter D. Mignolo, 427–57. Ann Arbor: U of Michigan P, 2003.
Moynagh, Maureen. "Afropolitan Travels: 'Discovering Home' and the World in Africa." In *New Directions in Travel Writing Studies*, edited by Paul Smethurst and Julia Kuehn, 281–96. Basingstoke/New York: Palgrave Macmillan, 2015.
Mufti, Aamir R. *Forget English! Orientalisms and World Literatures*. Cambridge, MA: Harvard UP, 2016.
Neumann, Birgit, and Gabriele Rippl. "Celebrating Afropolitan Worlds? Contemporary African World Literatures in English." *Anglophone World Literatures*—Special Issue of *Anglia*, 135, no. 1 (2017): 159–85.
Neumann, Birgit. "Vernacular Cosmopolitanism in Anglophone World Literatures—Comparative Histories of Literary Worlding." In: *Global Perspectives on European Literary Histories*. Special Issue, *Arcadia* (2018). [in print].
Nwaubani, Adaobi Tricia. "African Books for Western Eyes." *New York Times*, November 28, 2014, n.p. Available online: https://www.nytimes.com/2014/11/30/opinion/sunday/african-books-for-western-eyes.html (accessed January 11, 2018).
Ogbechi, S. Okwunodu. "Afropolitanism: Africa without Africans (II)." *Aachronym*, April 4, 2008, n.p. Available online: http://aachronym.blogspot.com/2008/04/afropolitanism-more-africa-without.html (accessed September 5, 2018).
Okri, Ben. "A Mental Tyranny is Keeping Black Writers from Greatness." *The Guardian*, December 27, 2014, n.p. Available online: https://www.theguardian.

com/commentisfree/2014/dec/27/mental-tyranny-black-writers (accessed January 11, 2018).

Owuor, Yvonne Adhiambo. *Dust*. New York: Knopf, 2014.

Pahl, Miriam "Afropolitanism as Critical Consciousness: Chimamanda Ngozi Adichie's and Teju Cole's Internet Presence." *Journal of African Cultural Studies* 1 (2016): 73–87.

Pratt, Mary Louise. *Imperial Eyes: Travel Writing and Transculturation*. London: Routledge, 1992.

Rabinow, Paul. "Representations are Social Facts." In *Writing Culture: The Poetics and Politics of Ethnography*, edited by James Clifford and George E. Marcus, 234–61. Marcus Berkley: U of California P, 1986.

Robbins, Bruce, and Paulo Lemos Horta. "Introduction." In *Cosmopolitanisms*, edited by Bruce Robbins and Paulo Lemos Horta, 1–20. New York: New York UP, 2017.

Robbins, Bruce. "Introduction Part I: Actually Existing Cosmopolitanism." In *Cosmopolitics: Thinking and Feeling Beyond the Nation*, edited by Bruce Robbins and Pheng Cheah, 1–19. Minneapolis: U of Minnesota P, 1998.

Rosendahl Thomsen, Mads. "Changing Spaces: Canonization of Anglophone World Literature." *Anglia. Special Issue: Anglophone World Literatures* 135, no. 1 (2017): 51–66.

Rushton, Amy. "No Place like Home: the Anxiety of Return in Taiye Selasi's *Ghana Must Go* and Yvonne Adhiambo Owuor's *Dust*." *Études Anglaises. New Diasporas, New Directions* 70, no. 1 (2017): 45–62.

Selasi, Taiye. "Bye-Bye Babar." *The LIP #5 AFRICA*, March 3, 2005, n.p. Available online: http://thelip.robertsharp.co.uk/?p=76 (accessed January 11, 2018).

Walkowitz, Rebecca L. *Cosmopolitan Style: Modernism beyond the Nation*. New York: Columbia UP, 2006.

Wasihun, Betiel. "Afropolitan Writing." In *Handbook of Transatlantic Studies*, edited by Julia Straub, 391–419. Berlin/Boston: De Gruyter, 2016.

West-Pavlov, Russell. "Temporality and Quantum Theory in the Contemporary Global South Novel." In *New Approaches to the 21st-Century Anglophone Novel*, edited by Sibylle Baumbach and Birgit Neumann, n.p. Basingstoke: Palgrave Macmillan [in print].

Yusoff, Kathryn. "Geologic Life: Prehistory, Climate, Futures in the Anthropocene." *Environment and Planning D: Society and Space* 31, no. 5 (2013): 779–795.

3

Strategic Label

Afropolitan Literature in Germany

Anna von Rath

> *It could just as well be called queer, neuro-diverse, crazy, diasporic or Black. These are all main themes of the novel. In the end, I decided to call it Afropolitan, because my own Afropolitan perspective includes all of this. Thus, it is my Afropolitanism.*
> SCHWARZRUND 2017

In the statement of the author SchwarzRund, which I quoted above, she addresses the process of categorizing her own novel, *Biskaya*. She makes clear that she chose one particular label from a selection of already existing ones. Something will have caused her preference for Afropolitan, especially because, in her opinion, neuro-diverse, crazy, diasporic and Black would have fit her novel just as well. By using one label in particular, Afropolitan in this case, she claims allegiance, but she also makes Afropolitanism her own and shapes what it contains.

Generally speaking, the term Afropolitan has not been around for very long. The two cultural critics who are still the first association with the concept are Taiye Selasi and Achille Mbembe. They introduced Afropolitanism to describe a specific identity (Sealsi 2005) and an aesthetic and ethics of being African in the world (Mbembe 2007). Since its emergence, the concept has been picked up by other individuals to describe themselves. Moreover, it appears often with reference to contemporary art, fashion, and literature. In this essay, I will focus on literature, specifically on SchwarzRund's *Biskaya*. Reading her novel, I can recognize influences of Selasi and Mbembe's theories, but in the end, SchwarzRund creates her own notion of Afropolitanism adapted to her own creative context, Germany.

To my knowledge, *Biskaya* is the first novel written in German which wears the label Afropolitan.[1] SchwarzRund demonstratively claims association with the concept and other Afropolitan authors by putting the declaration "*Afropolitaner Berlin Roman*" (Afropolitan Berlin novel) on the front cover of her book, underneath the title. While Afropolitanism is highly controversial, Susanne Gehrmann rightly praises the novels, which are marketed as Afropolitan, for opening up "a fruitful literary landscape for the uncovering of contemporary Afro-diasporic identity politics traversing America, Africa and Europe" (Gehrmann 2016: 69). When making this statement, Susanne Gehrmann probably had the celebrity authors Taiye Selasi, Chimamanda Ngozi Adichie and Teju Cole in mind, and not SchwarzRund. But *Biskaya* similarly interrogates the processes constituted in and through power relations that structure the everyday experiences of mobile Black people in a predominantly *white* society.[2] In this essay, I argue that SchwarzRund's Afropolitanism is the creative process of dealing with the anxiety of non-belonging and not fully retraceable diaspora histories by creating new networks and ways of expression. The book illustrates the local malleability of a globally marketed concept. Considering the linguistic and geographical context of *Biskaya*, I have a whole set of questions: With regard to content, characters, and setting, what kind of an Afropolitanism does the novel express? What is the appeal of the label Afropolitan or why is it strategically useful for SchwarzRund to write herself into the controversial realm of African inflected cosmopolitanism? What is the relationship of this German Afropolitan novel and Afropolitanism as a wider (literary) phenomenon which has, so far, been predominantly shaped by Anglophone, and to some extent Francophone, writers? This essay will explore the Afropolitanism depicted in *Biskaya* and elaborate on the strategic choice of label to negotiate the local and the global, worldliness and cultural specificity.

Biskaya—An Afropolitan Berlin Novel

In *Biskaya*, SchwarzRund creates a world that adds an otherwise often invisible perspective to the literary landscape of Germany. The narrative focuses on the transformation of a Black musician from a person who tries to fit into societal norms—in which she never feels comfortable—to a person who tries to work against those oppressive norms. *Biskaya* is the story of the 35-year-old Tue Millow and it is set in Berlin a few years ahead of our time. Tue was born and raised on the imaginary island Biskaya. But her parents die early and she moves to Germany to live with her grandmother. After finishing school, she spends a few years roaming on the streets. Later, she moves into a queer flat share in Berlin and manages a breakthrough with her band. Tue's life, however, does not remain calm and successful for long. One of her housemates commits suicide, leading Tue into a crisis. She receives stationary psychiatric treatment for a couple of months. This experience as well as a few more details on her family's diaspora history make her change her goals in life. Tue realizes that she can barely endure the racism anymore that has been her constant company since she moved to Germany. She does not want to continue to boil her music down for her mainly *white* audience's taste. Instead, she wishes to write meaningful, political texts. Slowly she begins to find new terms for her art. Her *white* male band colleagues react disgruntled to the changes and their ways part. I argue that SchwarzRund's depiction of Tue represents her notion of Afropolitanism, particularly Tue's process of dealing creatively with her anxiety of non-belonging and her life circumstances (a consequence of her migration). The novel challenges the relative ease with which characters of the more visible and famous Afropolitan novels move around the world. In Tue's life fitting in is never easy, because of racism and homophobia.

SchwarzRund thus adds to a debate which has been started by Taiye Selasi and Achille Mbembe who introduced Afropolitanism as a novel term at the core of which are questions of African and Afro-diasporic identities and their positioning(s) in an interconnected world. The Afropolitan subject that Mbembe describes is very similar to Selasi's in the sense that he refers to people who come and go, who live or have lived in several places (on the African continent and/or elsewhere), people who are likely to speak several languages and who "developed a wealth of perception and sensitivity in the course of movement" (Mbembe 2007: 29). Unlike Selasi, Mbembe's vision of the contemporary Afropolitan subject is not restricted to the well-educated middle class, even though he specifically refers to African artists, musicians, composers, writers, poets, and businesspeople (Mbembe 2007: 29). SchwarzRund presents similar, yet again slightly different ideas of Afropolitanism, she gives the concept a German touch, visible in a political urgency brought about by the isolation of the Black German community and the sheer inexistence of colonialism in Germany's memory culture.

Throughout the novel SchwarzRund describes her protagonist Tue as a mobile, successful Black artist who spends her nights with her Black friends in Europe's hip (fictitious) nightclubs.

Es war eine dieser Nächte, in der Club, der sonst nur von weißen Queers besiedelt war, ihnen zu gehören schien. Die Biskayani und sie [Tue] tauschten kontinuierlich Blicke aus, webten ein Band durch die staubige, verrauchte Luft. Dies erlaubte ihrem Körper, sich der Musik endlich ungezwungen hinzugeben. All die Projektionen, die ansonsten einhergingen mit ihren Schwarzen queeren Körpern und Musik, schienen in diesen wenigen Nächten an Relevanz zu verlieren.

SCHWARZRUND 2016: 143

It was one of those nights, in which the club, which was usually filled with white queers, seemed to belong to them. The Biskayani and she [Tue] continually exchanged glances, weaving a connecting thread through the dusty, smoky air. It allowed her body to move unconstrained to the music. All of the projections, which are otherwise provoked by her Black queer body and music, seemed to lose relevance in these few nights.[3]

This description—except for the emphasis on queerness—immediately brings to mind Taiye Selasi's essay "Bye-bye Babar (Or: Who is an Afropolitan?)" in which she characterizes the contemporary Afropolitan generation as follows:

It's moments to midnight on Thursday night at Medicine Bar in London. Zak, boy-genius DJ, is spinning a Fela Kuti remix. The little downstairs dancefloor swells with smiling, sweating men and women fusing hip-hop dance moves with a funky sort of djembe. The women show off enormous afros, tiny t-shirts, gaps in teeth; the men those incredible torsos unique to and common on African coastlines. The whole scene speaks of the Cultural Hybrid: kente cloth worn over low-waisted jeans; African Lady over Ludacris bass lines; London meets Lagos meets Durban meets Dakar.

SELASI 2005

Quite clearly, SchwarzRund and Selasi agree that people express their Afropolitanism in outer appearance, favored activities and their knowledge of major cities around the world. Wherever they dance, they acknowledge each other. SchwarzRund as well as Selasi propose that music, dancing, and creative self-expression create connections and relief. While Afropolitans may appear to be rather privileged Black hipsters on the surface, it does not mean that there is no depth to the Afropolitan. SchwarzRund further presents *her* Afropolitanism as cherished moments of undermining exclusive dominant structures and as a process of developing less discriminatory ways of interaction.

In *Biskaya*, one of SchwarzRund's main concerns is the socially constructed idea, yet lived experience, of race. The Afro- in her Afropolitanism quite clearly denotes a group which Taiye Selasi tends to call "beautiful brown people" (Selasi 2005) who try to articulate their perspectives on the day-to-day life in a European city. SchwarzRund asserts that in a country in which the majority of the population is *white*, her Black protagonist Tue experiences episodes of everyday racism whenever she moves in the public sphere, at parties, at work, at the doctor's. When I speak of everyday racism, I refer to a concept first introduced by Philomena Essed. She uses it to describe the interaction between individuals, routine practices that reinforce racism's ideological and structural dimension (Essed 1991: 2). It helps to think of it as walking through a minefield. Tue never knows where and how hard the next racist incident will hit her. She cannot avoid it, but she can develop possible ways of acting against it within her spheres of influence.

Already the first couple of pages of *Biskaya* set the tone in depicting one of the many episodes of everyday racism which Tue experiences throughout the novel. In the first chapter, Tue attends a party in the art studio of the Black artist—later her best friend—Matthew. Two *white* people, who were not invited, offend the host. Matthew tells them to leave which results in a brief verbal fight. Then, one of the *white* intruders uses the N-word to defend her *white* friend:

> [*white* uninvited guest calls out:] Das ist Rufmord! Du kannst doch ihn hier nicht einfach als Rassisten bezeichnen! Keiner hat was Rassistisches gesagt, ey, is' ja nicht so, dass er dich N-
> Nur das Klirren von Tues Schüssel, die an der Wand zersplitterte, verhinderte die letzten Buchstaben, die durch viele vorherige Verletzungen bereits in ihren Kopf gebrannt grell aufleuchteten, in Erwartung der erneuten Erniedrigung.
>
> SCHWARZRUND 2016: 13

> [*white* uninvited guest calls out:] This is slander! You cannot just call him a racist! Nobody said anything racist, hey, it's not like he called you n-
> Only the clattering of Tue's bowl, which shattered on the wall, prevented the last letters of the word, which, already burned into her mind because of earlier hurtful moments, appeared as bright flashes, in expectation of repeated humiliation.

While the *white* uninvited guest apparently knows that the N-word is offensive, she still does not mind saying it right into Matthew's face. She expresses a feeling of entitlement by believing that she has the right to be there and by behaving disrespectfully and ignorantly towards the host, while at the same time crying out that nobody is allowed to insult her *white* friend. She is not willing to read the space she has just entered, but simply believes that her own worldview—*white* as the norm—applies everywhere. While she is wrong, she wrongs the Black man. To show this, SchwarzRund lets Tue interrupt the situation. Tue's spontaneous throwing of the bowl, symbolically, interrupts *white* power to define. The broken porcelain stands in for what words can break in people, especially when repeated over and over again. In this situation, Tue's intervention into the structures of *white* supremacy is still an unconscious reflex. But the Afropolitanism in *Biskaya* is the process of finding ways to deal in creative and challenging ways with the painful fact that a Black person in Germany is always defined by *white* others. Tue stops allowing the *white* person to call her and other Black people what she wants. This first chapter of the novel is the beginning of Tue's often painful journey to find her own terms of definition, of who she wants to be and of how she wants to express herself within hostile structures of *white* supremacy and heterosexism.

At times, Tue's journey is challenging and not every move entirely motivated by her own will. In the early chapters of the novel, she still straightens her hair to provide her mainly *white* surroundings with a pleasing image of herself. Even though hair-straightening is a painful and smelly procedure, *white* beauty standards almost force her to do it, just to get a little closer to an unspoken norm and to crush the imposed feeling of deviation, of "otherness." Tue is not an individual case. Hair is also an important theme in more famous Afropolitan novels, especially in Chimamanda Ngozi Adichie's *Americanah* (2013). Furthermore, Grada Kilomba stresses in her book *Plantation Memories. Episodes of Everyday Racism* that "[Black] women see themselves forced to deracialize their hair" (Kilomba 2008: 73). SchwarzRund describes how this nasty affair, in the end, only destroys the hair structure. Deracialization is a painful myth. Tue has to finally cut her hair off, because it is damaged beyond repair.

> Später würde Tue behaupten, es [das Haareschneiden] wäre ganz klar gewesen, später wäre es ein revolutionärer Akt aus Überzeugung. Aber heute erlebte sie leider das Jetzt, in seiner ganzen profanen Unsicherheit. . . . Wie ihre Band reagieren würde, wie die Reaktion der Medien wäre? Wäre dies das Ende der Zeit in der sie das good black girl der sonst so weißen typenlastigen Hamburger Schule gewesen war?
>
> SCHWARZRUND 2016: 17

> Tue would later claim that it [to cut her hair] had been very clear, later it would be a revolutionary act of conviction. But today she experienced the Now, with its completely profane insecurity. . . . How would her band react, what would the reaction of the media be? Would this be the end of the time in which she had been the good black girl of the otherwise so *white* male Hamburg School?

After cutting off what has been left of the damaged hair strands, Tue suffers. Her first feelings are anxiety and loss of a protective shield. However, her thoughts do not stay with herself, they lead her right away to wonder about the *white* gaze—represented here by her band colleagues and the German media. How would they judge her? Tue anticipates that her change of hairstyle will cause her problems. Subsequently, her band members touch her hair without asking and make derogatory references about its supposed resemblance to pubic hair (SchwarzRund 2016: 35). Clearly, hair straightening used to be a preventive measure for Tue to minimize comments and actions of others which cross her boundaries. It was not Tue's choice to wear natural hair. But she knows that it is a political statement that she admires and eventually grows into. Her natural hair will force her to talk back more often.

Afropolitanism is found in this constant negotiation. SchwarzRund asserts that a Black person has to negotiate between openly displaying her own politics and complying with *white* standards in order to earn money. Adichie sends a similar message in *Americanah*, when the protagonist Ifemelu receives the following advice before going to an important job interview. "Lose the braids and straighten your hair. Nobody says this kind of stuff but it matters. We want you to get that job" (Adichie 2013: 202). Just like Ifemelu, Tue's job forces her to play a particular role which comes hand in hand with conforming to *white* beauty standards. SchwarzRund's protagonist is part of the *Hamburger Schule*, a traditionally *white* Indie music school which originated in the city of Hamburg. Well-known *Hamburger Schule* bands are, for example, the all male, all *white Die Sterne* and *Tocotronic*. The *Hamburger Schule* stands out because of its often intellectual lyrics and use of the German language. As a Black lesbian, Tue is not readily accepted into that music school.

> Es war schon zu oft zur Sprache gebracht worden, dass sie [Tue] als Schwarze Femme nicht die erste Assoziation zur Hamburger Schule war. In nahezu jedem Interview wurde gefragt, wie es zu dieser *spannenden* Kombination gekommen war. Musikmagazine suchten in jedem Lied nach besonderer Impulsivität und sie reagierte, indem sie alles was als Schwarz kodiert wurde, auf der Bühne versuchte zu unterlassen.
>
> SCHWARZRUND 2016: 93

It had been brought up too often that she [Tue] as a Black femme was not the first association of the Hamburg School. In almost every interview she was asked, how this *exciting* combination came about. Music magazines looked for notable impulsivity in every song and she reacted by trying to refrain from everything that was coded as Black when she was on stage.

SchwarzRund alleges that the persistent, but rarely spoken of understanding of race in Germany makes the *white* public believe that a Black person has a different nature, is innately different from *white* people. While innate impulsivity or musicality can still be interpreted as positive attributions, the assumption of a causality between a person's character or talents and that person's skin color remains erroneous. (Furthermore, the assigned characteristics are not always positive.) It seems as if Tue can either choose to deracialize her looks and behavior or to stir up unwanted attention and commenting. But, this time drawing on Mbembe's notion of Afropolitanism as "a way of being in the world, refusing on principle any form of victim identity" (Mbembe 2007: 28), SchwarzRund refuses to make her protagonist the victim of German society or that music school. Tue splits with her band and starts to become truer to herself, creating art that works much better for her. Tue's financial stability allows her to follow her own ideas of right and wrong. SchwarzRund is not uncritical of her own protagonist, she repeatedly points to Tue's privileges. I read this as an implicit critique of the Afropolitan idea which, so far, mostly attracts the well-educated elite.

While the *white* colleagues and media react teasingly or critically to Tue's change of hairstyle without knowing about the deeper meaning of it, her Afropolitan community has a more profound understanding of the extent of the pain such changes can potentially cause. Her friend Matthew, who is also Black, does not anticipate or judge immediately, but first asks why she did it.

[Matthew:] Bevor ich reagiere—wie geht es dir damit und wie kam es dazu? Verblüfft hielt sie [Tue] ein, starrte ihn an. Sie hatte mit allem gerechnet, dass sie lügen, eine Heldengeschichte über sich erdichten oder aber ihn zusammenstauchen würde wegen seiner Rechthaberei. Mit allem hatte sie gerechnet, nur nicht, dass er sich vorstellen konnte, dass es ihr damit nicht gut ginge.

SCHWARZRUND 2016: 23

[Matthew:] Before I react—how do you feel about it and why did this happen? She [Tue] paused perplexed, stared at him. She had expected everything, that she would have to lie, that she would have to come up with a heroic story about herself or that she would have to slate him because of his bossiness. She had expected everything except for one thing, that he could imagine that she didn't feel well with it.

Matthew's reaction surprises Tue positively. He expresses empathy for her and real interest which is uncommon, but exactly the kind of support she needs in this situation. Matthew and Tue know that sometimes, even if one understands the political importance of a certain action and theoretically supports it, it is actually difficult to act accordingly. Matthew often functions as Tue's safety net. The Afropolitan space SchwarzRund creates shows possible ways of respectful interaction. Furthermore, this episode exemplifies the essential role of community in SchwarzRund's Afropolitanism, which connects well with Taiye Selasi's notion of Afropolitanism. Selasi emphasizes that the Afropolitan is not only an identity but also a means to generate networks and exchange. Afropolitanism opens up a space for a self-defined group of people to celebrate and discuss similar experiences of (non-)

belonging, restrictions and enrichment, which mobility brings about (Selasi 2005).

Afropolitanism in SchwarzRund's novel focuses on a person's learning process and her openness to change, rather than on prescribed or prescribing ways of being, which I relate to Achille Mbembe's understanding that Afropolitanism is a new ethics of being (2007). The lesson for the protagonist as well as the reader is that one should respect everybody's private sphere at all times. Even antipathy should not lead to disrespect. While Tue often finds herself in situations in which people overstep her boundaries, it does not keep her from sometimes dropping a brick herself. She outs her band mate as gay, a man who tried his best to provide the world with an image of heterosexual masculinity of himself.

> 'ne Femme als Chefin, eine Femme im Bett, tjoa, so ist der Gute. Aber nach vorne hin straightest boy alive Sie [Tue] lächelte immer breiter, der Alkohol und die Wut stiegen ihr zu Kopf.
>
> SCHWARZRUND 2016: 104

> A femme as boss, a femme in bed, well, that's our good guy. But publicly the straightest boy alive. Her [Tue's] smile grew wider, the alcohol and her anger were making her heady.

Tue dislikes this particular band colleague, and drunk, after a concert, she makes a point of humiliating him in front of the band. It is again Matthew with whom she has an honest conversation about her behavior. He strongly criticizes her for what she did and cuts their contact until she rethinks her hurtful remarks.

Respect for individual expressions of identities is at the core of SchwarzRund's Afropolitanism. Apart from addressing race and sexuality, she also refers to the constructedness of gender, the heteronormative idea of a nuclear family that consists of mother, father and child, and adultism. One day, a young person shows up at Tue's doorstep. "Sie [Tue] bot der jungen Person ihren Sessel an, erfuhr, dass ihr Name Sarah, Pronomen: sie, war" (SchwarzRund 2016: 211). "She [Tue] offered her an armchair, learned that her name was Sarah, pronoun: she." The message is that one should not assume too much about the people one meets, but learn about them in conversation and treat them the way they want to be treated. It is challenging, even for Tue, who often demands that others should respect her sociopolitical positions. Societal norms are often so internalized that it becomes a default reaction to reproduce them. Tue, for example, corrects Sarah when she refers to her Mama as *mein Mama*:

> Du meinst: meine Mama, es heißt meine Mama und nicht mein. Ihrem oberlehrerinnenhaften Moment folgte ein angemessenes Augenrollen

seitens des Kindes. Es heißt mein Mama, wenn es um mein Mama geht, weil sie das schöner findet. Oder halt meine Papa. Halt irgendwie nicht so: Mann, Frau, fertig.

SCHWARZRUND 2016: 209⁴

You mean: my [female pronoun] mom, it is my [female pronoun] mom and not my [male pronoun]. Her head-teacher-moment was followed by an appropriate rolling-of-eyes by the child. It is my [male pronoun] mom, if we're talking about my [male pronoun] mom, because she prefers it that way. Or my [female pronoun] dad. Just not so: man, woman, done.

As an adult, Tue automatically assumes the role of the educator; Sarah, as a youth, has to be educated. That is how it always is. But Sarah teaches her that it can also be the other way around. Adults can learn from children. And in Sarah's family there is "mein Mama" and "Mutter," not *Mama, Papa, Kind*.

For SchwarzRund, the Afropolitan space is a queer space. The café which Tue often visits is called *der*die Ecke* (the corner), and whenever possible, SchwarzRund refers to people in a gender inclusive way, e.g. *Köch*innen* (cook). In written German, the asterisk indicates that all genders are included (and not only cis genders). The asterisk, a star, points in many different directions and symbolizes a vast number of possibilities (AG Feministisch Sprachhandeln der Humboldt-Universität zu Berlin 2014). It is, however, a writing practice associated with queer activism and it is rare to see it used in a literary work. The queer aspect of her novel is not only notable because of the unusual writing practice but also because Afropolitanism comes across mostly as rather heteronormative. In *Ghana Must Go* (2013), Selasi hints at Sadie's preference for women, but only very few other characters who are part of sexual or gender minorities, who are not cisgender or heterosexual, appear in better-known Afropolitan novels—at least so far.

SchwarzRund does not only challenge Afropolitan conventions by making it an explicitly and unmistakeably queer space, she further departs from Selasi and Mbembe's focus on the African continent. SchwarzRund's inquiries into global Blackness or being Black in the contemporary world, do not need Africa as a key factor in the argument. Selasi and Mbembe emphasize either a strong connection with African (Selasi 2005) or concentrate entirely on the population of the continent (Mbembe 2007). SchwarzRund does none of that. Her protagonist Tue was born on the imaginary island Biskaya which is part of Europe and that is where her emotional ties still lie. There is an actual bay of Biscay in Europe, along the Western coast of France and the Eastern coast of Spain. But the island and its history in the novel are pure fiction. SchwarzRund criticizes Europe for not accepting that parts of it are Black, so she suggests that parts of Europe are Black, but those parts are not accepted as equal. In the novel, Germany and France have distributed

Biskaya's landmass and people among themselves. The island has the status of a dependent supplier for the European powers. The predominantly *white* nations on the mainland exploit the mostly Black and of Color island population as workers. The island population is divided into conformists and anti-colonial resistance fighters. Because of this ongoing turmoil, many Biskayani decide to live on the mainland.

SchwarzRund further explains that diaspora histories are often unreconstructable. Close to the end of the novel, Tue learns that one of her forefathers was a man called Achmed, a servant at the Prussian court. In the eighteenth century, the European aristocracy found it fashionable to have "exotic" Black servants at court to demonstrate their far-reaching influence and high status. SchwarzRund thus asserts that Tue probably has African roots, but those roots are rather unknown to her, due to European colonialists renaming of the Black servants and the lack of documentation about their lives before and after arriving in Germany. These Black people often only appear in the background of portraits still found in the Prussian castles. Achmed is a real figure, who SchwarzRund integrates in her story. His portrait can still be seen in the Glienicke Palace in Berlin-Wannsee. It is not certain where exactly he came from, but he served under Prince Carl of Prussia (SchwarzRund 2016: 174).

Afropolitanism is the consequence of histories of movement. Initiated by forced migration represented by Achmed and continued by contemporary political unrest, which naturally follows colonization represented by the island state Biskaya. To focus on forced movement as a starting point for Afropolitanism comes across as unconventional—Taiye Selasi only refers to voluntary movement and Achille Mbembe mentions displacement (the transatlantic slave trade) as a mere side note—however, movement remains the key concern. Afropolitanism in *Biskaya*, then, is a wish to deal creatively with the gaps in a person's family history—to relieve the feeling of anxiety those gaps have caused—and a dedication to work for social justice. By creating an imaginary island as the home of most of Germany's Black population, SchwarzRund counters what according to Tina Campt has thus far marked the Black German community, the "[. . .] absence of the shared narratives of home, belonging and community which sustain so many other Black communities and on which they draw (i.e., make use as 'resources,' diasporic or otherwise) in numerous ways" (Campt 2003: 290). SchwarzRund spatially defines a shared home base, though the real location does not matter. The shared narrative for Black Europeans is found in the effects of colonialism and stories of migration. It is found in having to live with ambivalences, with the knowledge that every home is imaginary, caught between a sense of familiarity and a gap of knowledge (cf. SchwarzRund 2016: 151).

SchwarzRund, Selasi and Mbembe formulate slightly differing versions of Afropolitanism, but they agree on one thing. Essential to the concep—as an identity, an art form or literary category—is a broad-mindedness and an evaluation of the position of the self as an actor in a complicated, globalized world. Afropolitanism, thus, shows itself as a space for negotiation, a constant process of becoming. The novel *Biskaya* depicts an Afropolitanism for a specific context, while staying dedicated to a broader project. Afropolitanism in *Biskaya* is an opening and not an end, it is an ongoing process in order to survive sanely in a world full of barriers.

The Appeal of Afropolitanism

After exploring Afropolitanism in *Biskaya*, the question remains, why did SchwarzRund choose this label? Her Afropolitanism appears as a fuzzy, not easy to grasp concept that overlaps with various other theories. I am directly reminded of identity politics, intersectionality, and social justice. Furthermore, SchwarzRund's approach seems contradictory at first: Even though she could have called her novel queer, neuro-diverse, diasporic or Black, she chose Afropolitan. While she wrote an outspokenly political novel, she labeled it with a term often critically denounced as apolitical. Using Afropolitanism, she seems to aim at a rather mainstream audience, but at the same time, she published with a small, activist publishing house. While attempting to tap into the transnational cultural and literary capital of Afropolitanism, the language of the book is German and restricts it to the German-speaking parts of the world. In the following, I will briefly contextualize Germany as a site of Afropolitanism and the hopes expressed by the choice of label. Afterwards, I will discuss *Biskaya*'s relationship with other Afropolitan literatures and the context-dependent malleability of Afropolitan political aims and claims within literature/ the literary market.

Biskaya is written in German and set in Berlin. Matching Afropolitanism and German(y) causes attention, because Afropolitanism is, so far, a rather unheard-of topic in this region. So far, the concept predominantly floats around in the English-speaking parts of the world, followed by French. The Black German academic activist Natasha A. Kelly sees the cause for the peripheral appearance of the term in the German(-speaking) context in the fact that *Afropolitanismus* does not easily roll off the tongue. But another reason for the lesser visibility of Afropolitanism in Germany may be, according to Kelly, that Germany's Black community is smaller than the British or US-American and afro-urban structures are still much more under construction (Kelly 2016: 23). Sheila Mysorekar, a Black German activist, poet, and journalist addresses the lack of diaspora visibility in much more drastic terms than Kelly. "As Black Germans, we are painfully aware that in times of danger we have no community to turn to. . . . The prominent feature of Black German life is its complete isolation" (Mysorekar in Faymonville 2003: 367). Even though Black presences in Germany go back a couple of centuries (to Achmed and all the other displaced Black people), the existence of Black people in the streets still often surprises the *white* majority society which SchwarzRund also reflects in her novel. Black experiences, which intersect with many other aspects of a person's identity, still often remain silenced in German public discourse.

The isolation of Black Germans makes Afropolitanism attractive. Afropolitanism offers a different route for establishing networks and creating greater visibility of Black Germans in Germany and beyond. Tina Campt argues that Black Germans always had to articulate their situation via borrowing from or comparing themselves to African US-Americans (Campt 2002: 110). Afropolitanism, however, allows to speak from a position that loosely forms part of a larger diasporic group, a group that finds itself in a continuing formation process. SchwarzRund sets up a relation of similarity between her Germany-specific Afropolitanism and other Afropolitans by drawing on the potential commonality of Afropolitan experiences—experiences of young, urban, mobile Blacks working in the field of arts and culture. Kelly commends the appearance of Afropolitanism in general, but also in the German context as a form of self-designation. Kelly is convinced that only if you clearly name your own position, it becomes possible to make social realities and experiences perceptible. Specific terms for lived realities help to strengthen peoples' understanding of social hierarchies (Kelly 2016: 23).

In *Biskaya*, the Black characters make no claim to Germanness. They may have the passport—or not—but to be German is not presented as a defining aspect. Neither do these characters make a claim to any other nationality to show their refusal to give too much importance to this complicated and restricting category of identity. Tue and most of her Black friends and contacts are Biskayani which could refer to any formerly colonized nation state that still depends on Europe. Afropolitanism is critical of the concept of the nation because Afropolitans can never tie their sentiments to one single nation. Tue has a history of migration that starts with Achmed on the African continent, leads to Germany, to Biskaya and back to Germany—and those are only the known of places. Afropolitans are almost forced to find home and valuable aspects in many places and to cherish whatever they experience as good. Furthermore, most Afropolitans are well acquainted with the exclusivity of the concept of the nation and therefore, know of its limits. Pheng Cheah points out that "contemporary critics of nationalism regard it as a particularistic mode of consciousness or even a privative ethnic identity that disguises itself as a universalism" (Cheah 1998: 21). As a consequence, he asserts, "cosmopolitanism is the obvious choice as an intellectual ethic or political project that can better express or embody genuine universalism" (Cheah 1998: 21). SchwarzRund's vision of Afropolitanism, as a form of cosmopolitanism, similarly functions as a transnational political project for exchanging ideas of less discriminatory ways of interaction and then establishing them. To SchwarzRund the prefix

Afro- is essential as—in her opinion—it emphasizes a sensitivity for the diverse, intersecting and context-dependent positions of (non-)privilege in human interaction.

Even if Afropolitanism is a global concept that propagates a universal set of ethics, one of the strengths of the Afropolitan generation is its awareness of differences between its individual members. A Black businessman who is the board member of a big company in London, has different problems than a Black female musician in Berlin, who, alongside to playing music, has to work in a café to survive. But they can both claim to be Afropolitans, if they are dedicated to Afropolitanism's essentials (broad-mindedness, self-reflexivity concerning their context dependent socio-political positions). In conversation with Ulla Rahbek and Eva Rask Knudsen, for example, Kwame Anthony Appiah commends the ability of Afropolitans to acknowledge the context dependency of articulations and dealings with race.

> How you will be racially understood in different places and that means that if you listen to conversations among the people who talk about Afropolitanism, they actually have a subtle sense of distinction between London, New York, and Paris. Of course, they know that when they are in one of their homes in Africa then 'race' is a completely different subject.
>
> RAHBEK AND RASK KNUDSEN 2016: 146

The discourse on race and racism or "racial literacy" as Alana Lentin calls it (Lentin 2017), needs to improve for the challenges ahead. Clearly, the Afropolitans' worldliness, their cultural capital enables them to push certain agendas in their particular spheres of influence. Afropolitan literature is a fruitful source for taking certain discourses ahead. Especially, because SchwarzRund—like other Afropolitan authors—emphasizes in her novel that one cannot deal with race and racism in isolation as they intersect with many other factors such as gender, sexuality, class, age, etc.[5] Afropolitanism, in turn, is not a project that focuses only on one aspect of a person's identity, but on many. With her choice of Afropolitanism, SchwarzRund avoids hierarchizing between other possible labels—as either Black or queer or neurodiverse would have done—because her Afropolitanism accommodates them all.

Clearly, labels are always complicated. No label will ever be uncontroversial or satisfy everybody.[6] Its function is to send a short and poignant message which can still be relatively general. As SchwarzRund says, she makes it her own Afropolitanism, she takes it, shapes it, and does not waste time coming up with a new term (which, surely, would also be controversial). At the center of all of this is self-determination and a call to radically respect self-determination. SchwarzRund sees the potential of Afropolitanism in creating spaces for self-expression and establishing connections between people. Not taking solidarities for granted, but actively creating them. Even a loose transnational network is a network.

Afropolitan Literature in Germany and Elsewhere

Biskaya might be an entry point for Afropolitanism to spark more in-depth attention beyond the English and French speaking contexts. Vice-versa, Afropolitanism may be an entry point for SchwarzRund to awaken broader interest for her work. The combination of both asks for a discussion of some of the controversies surrounding Afropolitan literature.

So far, "the literatures of the African continent as well as literature of the African diaspora based in Germany occupy a rather marginal space on the German book market," Susanne Gehrmann observes (2016: 66). But Adichie, Selasi and Cole's works—to name only a few of the more famous Afropolitan writers—have all been translated into German, they did readings in Germany and stirred quite some attention. The more people in Germany who have taken note of the hip Afropolitans, the more likely it is that they might stumble over the lesser-known Afropolitan authors like SchwarzRund. Gehrmann, however, critically notes that "[t]he marketability of Afropolitan authors—largely sustained by their American publishing houses' systematic publicity campaigns—points again to its commodification. Yet, books that sell well are not necessarily bad books" (Gehrmann 2016: 66). The marketization of Afropolitanism can clearly lead into reductive and bothersome directions. But then again, Afropolitan literature is insightful and nuanced in showing different people's experiences, the daily ups and downs always influenced by power relations. In the German context, SchwarzRund's book can function as a unique starting point for gaining racial literacy, for questioning patriarchy and for insights into queer lifestyles.

Adding to Gehrmann's critique of the commodification of Afropolitan literature in the Global North, Amatoritsero Ede fears that "the Afropolitan's first audience is the powerful metropolitan public" (Ede 2016: 93). Ede criticizes the successful authors for their lifestyle and symbolic character that seems to cater to the West rather than the African continent.

> [T]he Afropolitan writer merely globetrots between Africa and the West, his or her primary base, where he or she is viewed by the metropolitan gaze (and acts) as a voice for the minority public within the Metropolis. The same metropolitan gaze also sees the Afropolitan as the 'face' of Africa (that is of the primordial and civic publics) in the metropolitan public.
>
> EDE 2016: 97

According to Ede, the celebrated Afropolitan authors become the new faces of Africa, even if their experiences are far removed from many ordinary Africans. However, Ede's partly valid critique does not include lesser-known Afropolitan authors who diversify Afropolitanism.

SchwarzRund's case is different. She lives in Germany and that is also her site of action (even more so because she writes in German) and she does not represent Africa or Africans at all (though Biskaya could be interpreted to symbolize Africa or, for that matter, the Caribbean). She clearly targets the Black German and queer communities as her audience. On the cover of her book, her readers find three short reviews by a transgender author, a feminist magazine, and a Black Namibian German. They recommend the book as "afrofuturist intervention," for its "radically feminist approach to storytelling" and for its "bringing literature and politics together." Furthermore, SchwarzRund's readings of *Biskaya* usually take place in activist spaces, e.g., at the *Werkstatt der Kulturen* in Berlin, one of the few cultural institutions that reserves its stage for Black people and People of Color, or at the queer book fair *Queeres Verlegen*.

SchwarzRund's goal is to criticize existing structures of inequality. But she does not stop there, she also wants to create new visions. She says about her work that

> In the past, my focus was on deficiencies (which I still find important and great), but by now I try to look at the beauty and uniqueness which develops as a consequence of the pain of oppression. To find, search for and create resistance in art is what interests me at university, in my journalistic work, in my blog and in my novel.
>
> SCHWARZRUND 2017

The novel expresses SchwarzRund's wishes for a more just society. Elsewhere, she formulated concrete steps that should be taken:

> I wish for the reflection of Black history in school and university books. I wish for policies that acknowledge colonial liabilities and appropriate reparations. I wish for curricula at universities which hold lecturers accountable to keep pace with the times and to question every scientific presupposition.
>
> SCHWARZRUND 2017

Apart from being a critique of the status quo, Afropolitanism appears to invite imaginative play with visions of ways of being and expressing the self.

Finally, the appeal of Afropolitanism lies in its ability to open worlds to readers and its strength is that it remains in a process of development. *Biskaya* does exactly what Pheng Cheah observes to be a primary quality of postcolonial literary works, they aid in worlding the world in ways that do not follow Eurocentric traditions. "Put another way, they generate alternative cartographies that enable a postcolonial people or a collective group to foster relations of solidarity and build a shared world in which self-determination is achieved" (Cheah 2016: 17). According to Cheah postcolonial world literature "points to the opening of other worlds, such a literature is a real and ongoing process of the world, a principle of change immanent to the world" (Cheah 2016: 210). Cheah emphasizes that worlding and reworlding remain a continuous project (Cheah 2016: 194). The aim is to make a diversity of perspectives visible, instead of homogenizing or reinterpreting the dominant examples.

No matter how Afropolitanism is defined or positioned, it is a concept with the ability to nurture discourses on a possible reconciliation between worldliness and locality, desirable forms of internationalism and identity politics beyond the margins of the nation state.

Conclusion

Biskaya shows exemplary that Afropolitanism is not a unitary or clearly defined project. What binds all the Afropolitan (literary) projects together is an interest in representing a variety of (success) stories of mobile Black people/ people of African descent. Afropolitanism explores a still continuing history of movement which, in many cases, involves dealing with race in different contexts and unreconstructable gaps in family histories, interrogating notions of borders and nations, creating community and connections, etc. Apart from these shared concerns, Afropolitanism develops local specifics, here referring to geographic places and particular spaces (e.g., mainstream or activist). The German context with its small Black community and its prevailing lack of interest in dealing with colonialism and racism, led SchwarzRund to make use of Afropolitanism. Her Afropolitanism is an exploration into possible survival strategies within an oppressive *white* supremacist and heterosexist society. She convincingly conveys that Afropolitanism has political potential in spite of its alleged apoliticalness.

In the end, I read the label Afropolitan on SchwarzRund's book as an expression of several hopes: the hope to build a loose transnational community and to work against Black German isolation; the hope to find a more elaborate and less hurtful terminology to address people's life conditions in relation to other groups; the hope to change the discourses on structural inequalities, to make inequalities addressable. Afropolitanism as a rather new label rings the promising sound of energizing discourses on home and belonging, on mobility and identity, on colonialism and social justice.

Notes

1 It is unusual that an author labels her or his own novel on the front cover and it would not necessarily have to mean that this is the first Afropolitan novel written in German. There could be other novels by Afro-German writers who

just did not officially label their works as SchwarzRund did. But, that is not the case. As the Afro-German community is comparably small, the number of fiction writers among them is equally small. Additionally, Black Germans favor political essays, poetry, and autobiographies (e.g., Abini Zöllner's *Schokoladenkind. Meine Familie und andere Wunder* (2003), Senait Mehari's *Feuerherz* (2005), or Theodor Wonja Michael's *Deutsch sein und Schwarz dazu: Erinnerungen eines Afro-Deutschen* (2013)). The somewhat more famous Afro-German fiction writers often write in English (like Sharon Dodua Otoo or Olumide Popoola).

2 Throughout the essay I write *white* in italics to indicate that this term is a social construction and is freed of its biologistic connotations. It serves to emphasize that *white* refers to a political position of power. Similarly, I capitalize the term Black, referring to a collective experience of oppression. Here, I follow Eggers et al. (2005) who suggest that both of these distinct forms of notation serve to counter the historical position of *white* domination and Black subjugation.

3 All English translations of quotes from the novel are my own.

4 In German there are three articles: die—female, der—masculine, das—neutral. Pronouns like "my" are also gendered in German: meine—female, mein—male, meins—neutral. Mom or mother would in a grammatically correct way be paired with the female article or pronoun. In certain political circles, a grammatically incorrect way of using articles and pronouns wants to draw attention to the limiting nature of socially constructed ideas of gender and normative notions of family.

5 So far, within the Afropolitan discourse most attention has been given to the intersections between race and gender or race and class. Even if the connection between Afropolitanism and queerness has incited less discussion and comes across as somewhat unconventional, SchwarzRund is not the first or only one to address queerness. Other notable literary works are, for example, Chris Abani's novel *The Virgin of Flames* (2007) and Mark Gevisser's memoir *Lost and Found in Johannesburg* (2014). Furthermore, Minna Salami, the founder of the blog Ms Afropolitan, has repeatedly emphasized that the Afropolitan space is a queer space (Salami).

6 Think of the funny episode in Chimamanda Ngozi Adichie's *We Should All be Feminists* (2014). She starts out by calling herself a feminist. But people comment on her choice of label and she adapts it a couple of times to counter people's criticism until she becomes "a Happy African Feminist Who Does Not Hate Men And Who Likes To Wear Lip Gloss And High Heels For Herself And Not For Men" (Adichie 2014: 10–11). The word feminist is heavy with baggage and so is Afropolitan, although the term is a lot younger. Some criticize it, others love it, but more than anything, it is complicated.

Works cited

Abani, Chris (2007), *The Virgin of Flames*. London: Penguin Books.
Adichie, Chimamanda Ngozi (2014), *We should all be feminists*. London: Fourth Estate.

Adichie, Chimamanda Ngozi (2013), *Americanah*. London: Fourth Estate.
AG Feministisch Sprachhandeln der Humboldt-Universität zu Berlin (2014), „Anregungen zum antidiskriminierenden Sprachhandeln„. Available online: http://feministisch-sprachhandeln.org/ (accessed November 12, 2017).
Campt, Tina (2002), "The crowded space of diaspora: Intercultural address and the tensions of diasporic relations," *Radical History Review*, (83), 94–113.
Campt, Tina (2003), "Reading the Black German Experience: An Introduction," *Callaloo, Vol. 26, No. 2*, 288–294.
Cheah, Pheng (1998), "Introduction Part II: The Cosmopolitical—Today." In: Pheng Cheah and Bruce Robbins (eds). *Cosmopolitics: Thinking and Feeling beyond the Nation*, 20–44, Minneapolis: University of Minnesota Press.
Cheah, Pheng (2016), *What is a world? On postcolonial literature as world literature*, Durham: Duke University Press.
Ede, Amatoritsero (2016), "The politics of Afropolitanism," *Journal of African Cultural Studies*, 28, (1), 88–100.
Eggers, Maureen Maisha and Grada Kilomba, Peggy Piesche, Susan Arndt (2005), „Konzeptionelle Überlegungen", in: ibid. (eds): *Mythen, Masken und Subjekte*, 11–13, Münster: Unrast.
Essed, Philomena (1991), *Understanding Everyday Racism. An interdisciplinary study*, London: Sage Publications.
Faymonville, Carmen (2003), "Black Germans and transnational identification," *Callaloo, Vol. 26, No. 2*, 364–382.
Gehrmann, Susanne (2016), "Cosmopolitanism with African roots. Afropolitanism's ambivalent mobilities," *Journal of African Cultural Studies*, 28, (1), 61–72.
Gevisser, Mark (2014), *Lost and Found in Johannesburg*. New York: Farrar Straus Giroux.
Kelly, Natasha A. (2016), "Afropolitan Studies„—Interview mit Natasha A. Kelly über Afrokultur in Deutschland," *Iz3w, No. 375*, 23.
Kilomba, Grada (2008), *Plantation Memories. Episodes of Everyday Racism*, Münster: Unrast Verlag.
Lentin, Alana (2017), "With our narrow interpretations of racism it's too easy to deny that we are racist too," *The Guardian*. October 27. Available online: https://www.theguardian.com/commentisfree/2017/oct/27/with-our-narrow-interpretation-of-racism-its-too-easy-to-deny-that-we-are-racist (accessed November 1, 2017).
Mbembe, Achille (2007), "Afropolitanism," in: Simon Njami (ed.). *Africa Remix. Contemporary Art of a Continent*, 26–30, Johannesburg: Johannesburg Art Gallery.
Mehari, Senait (2005), *Feuerherz*. München: Knaur.
Michael, Theodor Wonja (2013), *Deutsch sein und schwarz dazu: Erinnerungen eines Afrodeutschen*. München: dtv.
Rask Knudsen, Eva and Ulla Rahbek (2016), *In Search of the Afropolitan. Encounters, Conversations, and Contemporary Diasporic African Literature*, Lanham: Rowman & Littlefield.
Salami, Minna, "My views on Afropolitanism." *Ms Afropolitan*. Available online: https://www.msafropolitan.com/my-views-on-afropolitanism (accessed August 21, 2018).

SchwarzRund (2016), *Biskaya*, Wien: Zaglossus Verlag.
SchwarzRund (2017), Interview by Anna von Rath: "I wish for an Achmed Street in Potsdam." January 25. Available online: https://postcolonialpotsdam.wordpress.com/2017/01/25/i-wish-for-an-achmed-street-in-potsdam/ (accessed October 20, 2017).
Selasi, Taiye (2005), "Bye-by Babar (Or: Who is an Afropolitan?)." *The Lip*. March 3. Available online: http://thelip.robertsharp.co.uk/?p=76 (accessed October 5, 2016).
Selasi, Taiye (2013), *Ghana Must Go*. London: Penguin.
Zöllner, Abini (2003), *Schokoladenkind: Meine Familie und andere Wunder*. Berlin: Rohwolt.

4

Afropolitanism and the Afro-Asian Diaspora in M. G. Vassanji's *And Home Was Kariakoo*

Shilpa Daithota Bhat

Introduction

The interplay of colonizing forces and international migrants in the African continent has resulted in an African discourse that happens to exclude adequate representation of Asians in the Afropolitan discussions in contemporary debates. Intriguingly, the Asians who migrated to Africa in the early nineteenth century and continued to reside there with the subsequent generations born and brought up in the place, engendered African identities in their psyche, rather than Asian. Their ancestral Indian connections persisted merely as fragmentary memories and therefore meant little to them making them see themselves as Africans rather than Asians. This perception is predominant in the creative expressions of writers like M. G. Vassanji who has been explicitly asserting that he is an African—not an Indian or Canadian. While all his works straddle Africa, India, and Canada, Vassanji has been underlining that Africa is an inseparable part of his identity and therefore figures predominantly in his narratives creating diasporic subjectivities and constructing selfhood. Africa becomes a major ground for the enactment of history and politics of the world. African history, necessarily intertwined with international and colonial politics, inhabits his oeuvre and this problematic and layered colonial history necessitates a revisiting and reconceptualization of the notion of Afropolitan—an already contentious term, that cannot be exclusivist in its allusions of members of the African race or in the Western portrayal of Africa. Such an interpretation is myopic and distorted and aggravates Afropolitan's connotations to complete negativity and precariousness.

Asian presence in Africa has been elaborately expatiated by writers like Gunvantrai Acharya who in his *Dariyalal* (1936) shows how Gujarati Indians migrated to Africa for trade and business during the seventeenth century. The omission of Asians in Afropolitan conversations or in its significations highlights that the term is exceedingly restrictive and confining in its terminology. This viewpoint of Asian exclusion in African discourses has been articulated by Gaurav Desai in his work *Commerce with the Universe: Africa, India, and the Afrasian imagination* (2013) where he suggests that Asians have never been seen as important to African history, despite the fact that they made enormous contributions to African economy and culture. Consequently, there is barely any representation of Asia in African literature. Gijsbert Oonk uses the term "settled strangers" in his research study to gesture at how Gujaratis were always strangers in Africa (also because they frequently visited home and aspired to return at some point of time in their lives) and that how their history has not been included in Indian or African discourses. This essay seeks to address the gap and will attempt to examine Asian interventions in Africa through the study of *And Home Was Kariakoo* (2013) by M. G. Vassanji with reference to Afropolitanism deliberations. The non-fiction work traces the entry of Asians in East Africa[1] and underlines the intermingling and interactions of Africans and Asians. I argue that through the format of a travelogue, Vassanji's work signals at how Asian presence in Africa can manifest and problematize the notion of Afropolitan being exclusively African in its tenor.

Afropolitanism and
And Home Was Kariakoo

While critiquing the work *Yoruba Girl Dancing*, James Hodapp (2016) suggests that it is a

> proto-Afropolitan novel that anticipates the emergence of Afropolitanism, acting as a bridge between the been-to genre of the 1960's and 70's and the increasingly influential Afropolitan genre of the 21st-century. I also advocate for a revised conception of literary Afropolitanism itself ... its roots are more temporally and spatially complex.... Literary Afropolitanism has roots and and influences that reach well beyond those texts currently dubbed Afropolitan....
>
> (132)

This observation is critical and applicable by extension to a wide variety of texts by writers whose home Africa has been and who continue to write from the continent as their point of origin. I shall in this segment, discuss the arguments that articulate the concept of Afropolitanism and how this is theoretically applicable to *And Home Was Kariakoo*. The memoir by M. G. Vassanji focuses on the childhood experiences of the writer, how the world sees Africa through the prism of history and politics and how migrants transcending borders for personal advancement view Africa upon return or revisitation. With a nostalgic slant, the writer states that "That feeling about my African home would never change over the years and decades that followed, during which I would go to many places, including Canada, which gave me a home, and my Indian ancestral homeland, which partially claimed me back". (1–2). The author straddles generations and continents through the representation of his affiliations with Africa, Canada, and India. Their existence in his consciousness in the framework of nostalgia, memories, and physical revisiting[2] of the places underlines the cosmopolitan nature of the migratory process. At the same time, he clearly underscores that in terms of identity, his connection with his ancestral homeland is tenuous and not deep enough for him to consider it his home. Canada gives him "a home" (Ibid), a place he adopts making the country an adopted homeland. It is Africa that would remain unchangeable for the writer, strongly rooted in his consciousness and memories, as a home that cannot be replicated anywhere else. He might have fragile connections with the notion of home elsewhere in the world but Africa possesses his psyche, as a real home that is unrecreatable.

While representing generational movements, Vassanji recounts "Many from my generation left during those heady 1960's and 70's of the last century, soon after independence. Most went away to the United Kingdom, Canada, and the United States, and some have returned for visits. . ." (2). The association with Africa as a nation, with reference to its Independence, underscores how deeply the author, as someone with ancestral connections with Asia, feels for the continent, not only personally but also in terms of nationalist sentiments. The politics of the nation is important for the author in delineating his affiliations and identity, in what he actually feels in relation to belongingness. Therefore, wherever he goes, when he thinks about home, Africa becomes the vantage point for returning and that becomes a defining point that the author determines as his "home." This homing poetics is essential in circumscribing his identity as one that transcends international borders but one that is able to return to Africa, albeit with a different worldview, nevertheless locating the self in the cultural, political, and historical milieu of the continent. It is in this context that discussion of Afropolitanism and its relevance to Africans of Asian descent becomes critically significant. It also generates the debates of whether the term is exclusivist or possibly inclusive in theoretical implication.

In his critical research study "The Politics of Afropolitanism" (2016), Amatoritsero Ede traces the genesis of the term Afropolitanism and notes that Taiye Selasi "first deployed it as a neologism to describe globetrotting, mixed-race blacks or migrant and newly-diasporized Africans—including herself—whose self-perception transcends geographies, nationalities, languages or time zones". (88). The emphasis on international migration as a liberatory dynamic with reference to African past is palpable and reminiscent of Simon Gikandi's acute observation when he stated that "all current debates about the future of Africa ... are attempts to overcome the malady of Afro-pessimism—the belief that the continent and its populace is hopelessly imprisoned in its past, trapped in a vicious cycle of underdevelopment, and held hostage to corrupt institutions". (2011, 9). Gikandi identifies Afro-pessimism as "hard to dislodge because it seems to be the only logical response to political failure and economic stagnation in Africa". (Ibid). Afropolitanism in contemporary discourses, appears to be an oppositional energy, in that it seems to detach the notion of an excruciatingly painful past from the present and articulates experiences that connect Africa to the rest of the world through demographic movements. Taiye Selasi in her essay "Bye-Bye Babar (What is Afropolitanism?)" (2005) states that "Afropolitans—the newest generations of African emigrants, coming soon or collected already at a law firm/chem lab/jazz lounge near you. You'll know us by our funny blend of London fashion, New York jargon, African ethics, and academic successes. . . . We are Afropolitans: not citizens, but Africans of the world" (Selasi, "Bye-Bye"). These statements have multiple significations—the most significant being, an optimistic strand that stands out as distinctive in comparison to Afro-pessimism. Definitively, demographic movements and the effects of such migration on individual's culture, life, education, employment, income, and future, are advocated in Selasi's opinions. Her statements gesture at the meagerness of the term in describing contemporary migrants belonging to diaspora. Madhu Krishnan referring to Selasi's *Ghana Must Go*, states that her "insistence on Afropolitanism as a means of constructing her vision of contemporary African subjectivities in ways which are often contradictory ways" (21). Eze (2014) points out "Afropolitanism ... is plagued by flaws, the most crucial of which is its name ... suggests an application of the idea of cosmopolitanism on the African continent or on people of African ancestry. If it is an African way of being cosmopolitan, what do you call a European or Asian way of being cosmopolitan, Europolitanism or Asiapolitanism?" (239–240). The term has been severely criticized for its multifarious suggestions and critical questions are raised perpetually by scholars regarding its several confusing insinuations. Eze in an essay published subsequently in 2016 clarified:

> I am in sympathy with those who are cynical about Afropolitanism, understood as a market ploy, or associated with well to do Africans who

can afford to travel the world and be at home in African and Western cities. It seems, though, that the concept points to a fundamental shift in conceptions of African identity, especially in the twenty-first century, a shift that highlights the fluidity in African self-perception and visions of the world. It is on this basis that I interpreted the term within the context of cosmopolitanism.... What I mean is that one cannot understand Afropolitanism without understanding cosmopolitanism, whose idea it replicates in an intellectual mimetic gesture.

(214)

Eze through this highlights a drastically different idea advocating Afropolitanism as consequential in contemporary times and as essential in identifying the "selves" of Afrikaners who cross borders of their countries. These various debates concerning Afropolitanism underline that complexities that characterize the connotations of the term—meaning different things to different scholars and argued from various theoretical standpoints. The danger here within the heated debates of Afropolitanism is the exclusivising proclivities of the term and this is perhaps one of the greatest repercussions of the use of the word.

While the term diaspora has evolved in its implications, encapsulating the demeanour of present migratory processes as opposed to earlier migrations (chiefly that of the indentured system, a reinvention of the institution of slavery in India for instance that emphasized reluctance to cross borders and therefore pain-giving; or the institution of slavery with reference to Africa and so on), the suggestion of a cosmopolitan outlook in transcending geographical boundaries is critical in underscoring that contemporary diasporas emanating from Africa are contented at the prospect of international migration. Such migratory processes resulting in upward mobility, better quality of life, education, and employment, thereby cancelling or at least mitigating the connotations of trauma, nostalgia, and grief in a globalized world. Migration becomes a scenario that an individual anticipates, not something that one might wish to shun, in fear of imaginary agony. It is this spirit of optimism and hope that Afropolitanism seems to endorse, making scholars support and embrace it with reference to a painful past and in hope of a cheerful future.

However, Marta Tveit in her blog article "The Afropolitan Must Go" (November 2013) points out that "Selasi's representation of Afropolitans in general (a group to which I too apparently belong and for which Selasi has taken it upon herself to speak) is weirdly prejudiced .... what about the non-affluent African diaspora? What about insanely hideous brown-skinned people? What about white African natives? What about Africans who despise jazz?" (Blog, http://africasacountry.com, November 28, 2013). In the context of African citizens, making a differentiation between people residing in Africa, and citizens who belong to elite classes and who are able to voluntarily travel and benefit out of that, seems discriminatory and biased as Tviet insinuates. The term dangerously marginalizes the African elite from the "others," alienating and othering the remaining people by default. Hence, there are possibilities of abuse of the term. Still, the term can be helpful to define certain strands in theoretical analyses as illustrated in this study. Referring to Johannesberg, Sarah and Mbembe (2007) remark,

> During apartheid, the right of black people to live in the city was constantly threatened. They were to work in the city but not to live in it. This explains perhaps the force and power of attempts to conquer the right to be urban in the present. To occupy the center of the city, its subjective core, to produce forms of city style at such velocity. To draw on a culture of indifference and restlessness that nourishes self-stylization. To produce an original form, if not of African cosmopolitanism, then of worldliness. The Afropolitan? Afropolis? At least, the entanglement of the modern and the African.
>
> (282)

The comparison of apartheid policy that was alive and devastating in African history and the association of Afropolitanism with modernity suggests the complicated evolution through ages of the travails of African citizens. Moreover, it alludes to a departure from a history of pain. It also clearly highlights how the Afropolitan concept is associable with modernity, urbanity, new forms of diaspora migration, cosmopolitanism, border crossing, discrimination between migrant Africans and "sedentary" citizens, and new types of elitism.

Nevertheless in the context of this essay, I wish to clarify that the suggestion of the term is in defining the *migratory* aspect of African citizens of Asian descent, perhaps elite and advantaged but those who travel over borders, and do not as easily and generally presumed, lead rosy lives but in fact encounter challenges of racialization, acculturation, and settlement in alien spaces. An outright rejection of Afropolitanism is to obliterate an entire discussion that could be critical to the understanding of diasporic movements as also with reference to Afro-pessimism (since the two can be interestingly compared). There is no disagreement in so far as the idea of implied marginalization goes in Selasi's use of the term and Tviet's response to the essay. Yes, there is the perilous likelihood of the element of demarcation and creation of superior/inferior categories through the use of the term. The objective here is applying the term Afropolitan to examine diaspora communities through the lens of migration, the intertwining of internationalization and movement in search of better opportunities for personal advancement—a drive in life that most diasporic migrants today take up for selfhood construction.

When applying Afropolitanism to narratives, the sociological and theoretical implications of the term happen to apply to writing as well.

J. K. S. Makokha points out that "Afropolitanism ... is the spirit that emanates from those cultural narratives and fictional memories being generated by migrants and their descendants who live in racial minorities across Africa, such as the Asians of Eastern and Southern Africa ... currently located in the Diaspora. Afropolitanism ... calls for innovations in modes and genres used to transport contemporary cultural narratives and motifs". (2011, 19). This opinion of Makokha includes in the discussion of Afropolitanism, other "racial minorities" (Ibid) not only sociologically and politically but also culturally and in the cultural productions of the "migrants and their descendants" (Ibid). It is this acknowledgment that becomes a critical point in perceiving the contributions of Afro-Asians or Africans of Asian descent to their natural inclusion within the implications of the term Afropolitan. The Asians therefore cannot be segregated on account of their ancient history of migration and settlement in the continent, their feelings of allegiance and loyalty to the African society, stemming rather instinctually rather than by feelings of compulsion. At the same time, it is interesting to consider how Afropolitan literature sits within the genre of World Literature, that seems all encompassing and therefore devoid of political positioning. Afropolitanism and literature belonging to this category undoubtedly cast historical, colonial, diasporic, modern, urban signs to the cultural productions. It is a clear demarcation from African past and an optimistic dive into the future—a hopeful emotion that seems to surpass historic anguish.

Makokha's perceptions when evaluated against the poetic descriptions of Vassanji's non-fiction, highlights the emotional engagement with which the author relates himself to Africa in intensified and heightened moving descriptions of the place. His passionate excitement while returning to his African homeland is articulated thus: "Down below, out the airplane porthole, lay the vast unconquered landscape of Africa—so different from the parceled geometry of Europe which I had crossed over or the grey, highway-girded northeastern United States where I had made my home for the time being". (1). It is notable that throughout his work, Vassanji's discourse is one of spanning generations and border-crossings. This naturally imparts the proclivity to an incorrigible cosmopolitan demeanour. It confronts the author's consciousness throughout the narrative and this interestingly alludes to the notion of Afropolitanism and whether and to what extent it can be applicable to his work.

The use of the term Afropolitan in the essay is not to suggest a contest for admission of Africans of Asian descent into a group that can be called Afropolitan (and so elite, urbane by extension), rather the term is being used as an instrument to determine the theoretical ramifications when studied in the framework of diasporic migration of Asians, and Africans across borders. In the context of Asian migrants, particularly those belonging to the second generation, the definition of Afropolitan becomes intriguing and raises pertinent questions related to how the term can describe their existence in

Africa with reference to their long history of migration and settlement in the continent. The first-generation migrants would have experienced ethnic liminality due to their unique placement in terms of geographical experiences, memories of homeland and the decision to continue living in the African society. However, for those who were born and brought up in the continent, Asia would predominantly have been a narrative experience, coupled with visits to their ancestral homeland. Hence the connection was necessarily fragile. Two questions that this entire debate hinges on are the following:

(i) While the first generation Asian Gujarati migrants might have felt psychologically closely connected to Gujarat, what about those who were born and raised in Africa?
(ii) What becomes of their identity that rejects their ancestral homeland which is not their birthplace but rather an imagined space of origin, being more narrative in nature than actual lived experience?

This ambiguity can be a source of considerable mental trauma for Asians who do not call themselves Asians but are described so due to racial perceptions. To address these problematics, the examination of M. G. Vassanji's recent non-fictional writing, *And Home Was Kariakoo* is valuable. The work is critical in unearthing the notion of Afropolitanism which is not explicitly stated in terms of the use of the concept in the narrative but the viewpoints that Vassanji resorts to, clearly underline the theoretical and conceptual subtexts that Afropolitanism signifies. It is also necessary to mention that the Asian reference in the ambit of Afropolitan is not a special pleading but rather a reality that has not been acknowledged as explicitly as it should have been. One reason for this could be ascribed to the fact that historically, the amalgamation of several communities and races in the continent necessitate appellations to differentiate the various people that inhabited the region. Since Gujarati Asians traversed the Indian Ocean to reach Africa, there could be greater clarity in using the term *Indian Ocean Afropolitanism*. This evokes the entire history of the migration of Asians to Africa. Nevertheless, what problematizes this term and the terrain, when critiquing a work like *And Home Was Kariakoo*, is the fact that there is the author who emphasizes that he is an African by identity. He travels the world and it is this migratory process that calls into investigation the application and relevance of the term Afropolitan, since Vassanji fits the description advocated by those who introduced the term in current discussions on migration, the movement of Africans away from the continent, and the hybridization of their identities and cultures in the wake of such coalescing forces. However, Indian Ocean Afropolitanism most appropriately describes Asian entry, settlement and pertinence to Afropolitanism discussion.

The use of the term "Asian" in this essay is to emphasize the ancestral origins of Africans of Asian descent, and doesn't connote Asian in terms of identity crisis when describing second and subsequent generations of migrants. Asia exists only in the narratives of Africans of Asian descent and signals memories that have been handed down to second, third (and so on) generations. These are theoretically explored taking Vassanji's work as a case study. Perceptual understanding of Africa in Vassanji's *And Home Was Kariakoo* clearly gestures at how strongly rooted are the individuals in Africa and not feeling strong connections to Asian ancestry.

In this work, Vassanji traveling from Canada, revisits Africa and experiences intense nostalgia remembering his childhood experiences in East Africa. He recounts colonial occupation of the continent and how the land was ravaged brutally by the Germans and the British leading to destruction of the African psyche and mass displacement due to African slavery. The African Gujaratis preserved their culture as much as they possibly could but simultaneously hybridized in the host African society. Regular interactions with Africans and colonizers, and propensity to migrate took them to various parts of the world for education, employment ultimately leading to settlement at multiple locations.

Idi Amin's agenda of ethnic cleansing played a preponderant role in displacing Africans of Asian origin to the United Kingdom, Canada, and the rest of the world, influencing the outlook and identity of such individuals. In this context, how does the term Afropolitan apply to displaced Africans belonging to the Asian race, is a question that deserves a nuanced investigation. Many of those who were displaced from Africa returned to the continent after several years[3] since they considered Africa their home. Wherever else they traveled, ultimately it was to Africa that they wished to return. How can those individuals be identified in terms of belonging? This question will be investigated in the next section with reference to Afro Asian history.

Indian Ocean and Historical Interventions

The presentation of connections between Gujarat in India and Dar-es-Salaam in Vassanji's work under examination takes place via the ocean; and the process is shown casually, as if it was a routine (which it was). The author remarks that "For decades now by Dar Es Salaam's lovely, open seashore its Asians have arrived in numbers to stare out at the ocean, carrying out a mysterious communion with the water. . ." (4). The migration of Indian Gujaratis via the Indian Ocean to the African continent created a paradigm—a model for other Indian Gujaratis to follow the earlier travelers to explore Africa. This happened through the metaphor of journey over the ocean since that was the connecting point between the two regions in the Global South. Further, this connection and travel happened incessantly taking into its fold Gujarati migrants, their kith and kin, other traders who came to know of business possibilities across the ocean, in Africa. The pattern of using existing social capital of Indians in Africa became a path to follow, for the subsequent generations of aspiring travelers.

This historical intervention is captured by Vassanji when he describes this as his personal experience intertwined with the history of the continent: "My forefathers left the small towns of Western Gujarat—Jamnagar, Junagadh, Porbandar—with populations of 15,000 to 20,000 at the turn of the twentieth century, to settle on the East African coast". (6). Many of those who migrated from India and made it big in Africa, did not return to India but rather continued to permanently settle in the hostland and made it their home. The fact that their relatives and friends also joined them intensified the progression of stable settlement and this eventually became the point from where they dispersed to different parts of the world as part of the African diaspora with remote past Asian associations. Consequently, India became an ancestral connection that materialized through frequently visiting the place, the narrative and cultural experiences transmitted to the migrants by their parents, grandparents, other relations, and friends. India also vivified memories through myths[4] and stories and experiences of the earlier generations. Indian Ocean became a preeminent site for South Asian migrants and their stay in Africa influenced knowledge networks and cultural constructions. The knowledge networks continue to this day and these exchanges have only deepened the ties between the two regions with reference to their history. Isabel Hofmeyr refers to the

> ... new intellectual networks that have grown between India and South Africa since the latter's 1994 political transition. The chair of Gandhi-Luthuli Peace Studies at the University of Kwa-Zulu Natal, in Durban, is partly funded by India, and in 2008 the University of the Witwatersrand, in Johannesburg, established the Centre for Indian Studies in Africa, the first such center on the continent (cisa-wits.org.za). Such circuits between the two countries have prompted new scholarship on lateral connecting histories in the Indian Ocean.
>
> (2017, 726)

Gandhi's stay in Africa and the unfolding of the history of protest for Indian Independence, as also its implications on the apartheid policy, shows how infectious the movement for freedom from colonial rule was. Additionally, the interest in history relating to the Indian Ocean becomes significant when looking at the idea of Indian Ocean Afropolitanism and yet it is intriguing to note that Vassanji as a child was oblivious to his Indian connection. He suggests that "As Asians growing up in East Africa we didn't know how our forefathers had arrived, how they lived, or even what they looked like. It was later, while living abroad, that this information seemed vital for my sense of who I was". (133). Such was the detachment from the ancestral Gujarat. The fact that Africans of Asian descent related more to Africa than Asia strongly underlines the inadequacies of the term Afropolitanism. In the context of Vassanji's work, the search for identity happens in the intersections of Indian Ocean Afropolitanism and migrations that take the authors to different places for his education. Therefore, Indian Ocean Afropolitanism becomes layered, subtly implying overlapping histories when dissecting the notion of Afropolitanism.

The production of multiple Afropolitanisms therefore becomes inevitable, since Africa was occupied by Europeans and Arabs too. Does this suggest the making of new labels, perhaps inadvertently with reference to the coining and experience of the term Afropolitanism? It does and fascinatingly so, because it generates within its discourse the critical theoretical question of exploring the various dimensions that are associable with international migration of African citizens and diaspora. It also insinuates the shifting away from the connotations of a traumatic past related to the concept of Afro-pessimism. Together, these arguments have the tendency to create fresh possibilities of innovative introspections into Afropolitanisms. The primary reason for not including writers like M. G. Vassanji in Afropolitan discussions could be ascribed to the fact that the migratory routes represented by him are not usually those that are taken up by African writers. Nevertheless, from Africa onwards, Vassanji's outlining and plot development subscribe to the routes and trajectories amounting to Afropolitan theoretical reinforcements. It is problematic however, to bowdlerize the Indian Ocean discourse from Asian historical representations since that is the connecting point in all Asian African narratives. In one context in *And Home Was Kariakoo*, Vassanji states:

> Where are the Asians? This question is asked at Kenyatta University when I speak there. There is not a single brown face but mine in the packed hall. I put his question to Sarita, a brilliant young Kenyan who studied at Cambridge and London and returned. She is of the new generation. For her holidays she goes up Mount Kenya with her young family. But in answer to my question, she replied that local facilities at the universities are so inadequate that she herself would prefer to send her kids to Oxford or Cambridge if she could. As would many others, undoubtedly, of whatever race—but would these Kenyan Asians of a fourth generation return? Or will the Asians only continue to deplete and further marginalize themselves?
>
> (368)

The questions that Vassanji asks highlight the predicaments of individuals who are aspirational to make careers through education that are offered abroad. Migration to new countries are beset with uncertainty in terms of return or the duration of settlement in those places, making international travel and cosmopolitanism a necessary feature of contemporary times.

Afropolitanism thus becomes a primary aesthetic to describe migration from Africa. The argument that I am trying to make is that these various layers problematize the concept of Afropolitanism with reference to Asia, yet overlooking them from Afropolitan debates would be a grave exclusion because of the sheer number of Africans of Asian origin.

With reference to the Ismaili[5] community from Asia in Africa, P. K. Balachandran remarks: "The Ismailis have been the worst hit among the Asians in East Africa, particularly in Tanzania. At the instance of their leader the Aga Khan, they had taken local citizenship *en masse* but, when it came to Africanization or nationalization, they were given no special consideration". (320). It was precisely the "ethnic cleansing" agenda by Idi Amin that disrupted the identity and citizenship notions of the Asians in Africa. The commotion entailing Africanization policies disregarded their stability in the continent and they would as Balachandran suggests in his essay, start packing their bags (Ibid). Anirudha Gupta observes that "By the end of 1962, following India's military reverses at the hands of China, earlier optimism about India's international standing had begun to wane ... because the Chinese unleashed a diplomatic offensive to isolate India from the Afro-Asian camp, India found it necessary to extend effusive support to African nationalism and pan-Africanist goals". (317). Gupta's suggestion is that the Asians, in an effort to demonstrate their solidarity with the Africans participated in African nationalism and pan-Africanist movements. However, only international political developments affecting Asian participation in African national movements, is too narrow a justification. As already mentioned in this essay, the fact that Asians were born and brought up in Africa engendered notions of complete belonging and citizenship. It was their exterior that led to racialized perceptions and therefore their rejection by the African Idi Amin. Their settlements since the first wave of Asian migration made them feel African in terms of identity. Nevertheless, their Asian ancestry wasn't detachable from their memories.

Conclusion

The manifold implications of the term Afropolitanism is palpable. It appears as though scholars appropriate the term to define the theoretical position they most subscribe to. Yet, it cannot be denied that in this maze of complex definitions and multiple conceptual significations, the term is helpful in demarcating African colonial history and modern movements that take place from Africa. Within this discursive space, the presence of migrants who arrived in Africa from Asia, Europe, and Arabia, created cultural and political assimilations that cannot be obliterated or evaded. Their subsequent generations claim Africa as their home, since their ancestral homelands exist only in narrative experiences and memories. These arguments vivify in the work *And*

Home Was Kariakoo and Vassanji delineates Asian migration through Indian Ocean historical framework, making Africa the point for further migrations that Africans of Asian descent were to make, and continue to make.

Notes

1. Most narratives by M. G. Vassanji trace the migration of Gujarati Indians to Africa and represents them in terms of generations, how the people maintained their culture and traditions, yet intermingled with the host society, how African history and politics affected the lives of the Gujarati migrants, and so on. The presentation of generations portrays evolving values and hybridizing influences that collectively shape the attitudes and lives of members of the Asian descent residing in Africa.
2. M. G. Vassanji's another non-fiction work *A Place Within: Rediscovering India* (2009) deals with the author's visit to his ancestral homeland, India, where he describes the history of the country, the trials and tribulations, the ups and downs the nation went through; the places of interest in India and the architectural marvels of the country. He travels throughout the subcontinent and portrays the cultural aspects that he encounters and the implications they cast on the social and political fabric of the nation.
3. Manubhai Madhvani in his autobiography *Tide of Fortune: A Family Tale* (2009), mentions his elation at being able to return to his Kakira sugar estates in Africa after a long and painful hiatus from the African continent and life in the UK.
4. The epics the *Ramayana* and the *Mahabharatha*, became critical cultural resources for Indians to reconnect with their homeland. The characters in the mythological stories became means of understanding their roots, cultural and religious identities. For instance, the character of Rama became symptomatic of a migrant who returned to homeland after many years.
5. Interestingly, the Ismaili community has been expatiated at length in Vassanji's works and the writer mentions in his other fictional representations, how their culture and religion were recreated in places that their communities settled in. While establishing themselves, it was necessary to assimilate in the host African society and the Asians were prepared for this and willingly did so.

Works cited

Acharya, Gunvantrai P, and Kamal Sanyal (1936) 2000. *Dariyalal*. Calcutta: Dictum in association with Thema.

Balachandran, P. K. "An Embattled Community: Asians in East Africa Today." *African Affairs* 80, no. 320 (1981): 317–25. http://www.jstor.org/stable/721659.

Desai, Gaurav. 2013. *Commerce with the universe: Africa, India, and the Afrasian imagination*. New York: Columbia University Press.

Ede, Amatoritsero. 2015. "The politics of Afropolitanism." *Journal of African Cultural Studies*. 28 (1): 88–100.
Eze, Chielozona. 2014. "Rethinking African culture and identity the Afropolitan model." *Journal of African Cultural Studies*. 26 (2): 234–247.
Eze, Chielozona. 2016. "We, Afropolitans." *Journal of African Cultural Studies*. 28 (1): 114–119.
Gikandi, Simon. 2011. "Foreword: On Afropolitanism." *Negotiating Afropolitanism: essays on borders and spaces in contemporary African literature and folklore*. Eds. Jennifer Wawrzinek and J. K. S. Makokha. Amsterdam [u.a.]: Rodopi. 9–11.
Gupta, Anirudha. "Ugandan Asians, Britain, India and the Commonwealth." *African Affairs* 73, no. 292 (1974): 312–24. http://www.jstor.org/stable/720810.
Hofmeyr, Isabel. "Universalizing the Indian Ocean." *PMLA* 125, no. 3 (2010): 721–29. http://www.jstor.org/stable/25704470.
James Hodapp, Wei. 2016. "The Proto-Afropolitan Bildungsroman: Yoruba Women, Resistance, and the Nation in Simi Bedford's Yoruba Girl Dancing." *The Global South*. 10 (1): 130.
Krishnan, Madhu. "Negotiating Africa Now." *Transition*, no. 113 (2014): 11–24. doi:10.2979/transition.113.11.
Madhvani, Manubhai, and Giles Foden. *Tide of Fortune: A Family Tale*. Noida: Random House India, 2009. Print.
Makokha, J.K.S. 2011. "Introduction: In the Spirit of Afropolitanism." *Negotiating Afropolitanism: essays on borders and spaces in contemporary African literature and folklore*. Eds. Jennifer Wawrzinek and J. K. S. Makokha. Amsterdam [u.a.]: Rodopi. 13–22.
Mbembe, Achille, and Sarah Balakrishnan. "Pan-African Legacies, Afropolitan Futures." *Transition*, no. 120 (2016): 28–37. doi:10.2979/transition.120.1.04.
Nuttall, S., & Mbembe, A. (2007). "Afropolis: From Johannesburg." *PMLA*, 122(1), 281–288. Retrieved from http://www.jstor.org/stable/25501689
Oonk, Gijsbert. 2013. *Settled strangers: Asian business elites in East Africa (1800–2000)*. New Delhi: SAGE Publications.
Selasi, Taiye. "Bye-Bye Babar." *The Lip*, 3 Mar. 2005. Web. August 5, 2017.
Tveit, Marta. "The Afropolitan Must Go." November 28, 2013. http://africasacountry.com/2013/11/the-afropolitan-must-go/. Blog.
Vassanji, M.G. 2014. *And home was kariakoo a memoir of East Africa*. India: Hamish Hamilton (an imprint of Penguin).

5

"White Man's Magic"

A. Igoni Barrett's *Blackass*, Afropolitanism, and (Post)Racial Anxieties

Julie Iromuanya

Introduction

In an interview with Sarah Balakrishnan, Achille Mbembe describes Afropolitanism as "a name for undertaking a critical reflection on the many ways in which, in fact, there is no world without Africa and there is no Africa that is not part of it" (2016: 29). In other words, Africa must be recognized as playing a crucial and fundamental role in global notions of progress and modernity. Afropolitan criticism tends to focus its analysis on mapping the physical and psychic border crossings of African authors and characters who have left the continent; however, as Chielozona Eze points out, Afropolitanism "can be between one African city and another, or even within an African city" (2016: 115). Presented in this context, Lagos-based Nigerian writer A. Igoni Barrett's 2015 satirical debut novel, *Blackass*, might be read less as a parody of Franz Kafka's renowned novella, *Metamorphosis*, and more as a work positioned within and composed of a larger body of world literatures concerned with mobility in a neocolonial landscape.

Indeed, *Blackass's* Kafkaesque setup is familiar: a mundane reality and hyperreal imaginary collide in absurd fashion to magnify the demise of the psyche when a young man of the white-collar variety awakens to encounter a surrealistic dreamscape where he has been transformed—Gregor Samsa, into a vermin (Kafka 1915), and Nigerian Furo Wariboko, into a white man "full oyibo" (Barrett 2015: 4). In *Metamorphosis* Gregor's existential angst is borne of limitations imposed by his physical immobility. Imprisoned in his desiccating carcass and unable to participate in the economic machine, he loses his vitality and is unceremoniously disposed of by the narrative's end. On the contrary, reborn as "Frank Whyte," Furo enters the contemporary Lagosian landscape armed with whiteness. Instead of immobility and social demise, *Blackass*'s "cocktail of Kafka and comedy" is marked by mobility and enhanced social status (Habila 2015). The novel's eponymous *Blackass*—an allusion to Apuleius's *Golden Ass*—gets its title from Furo's sole remaindered phenotype.

Unsurprisingly, it is the Kafkaesque setup that has evoked the widest range of responses. Reviewers roundly acknowledge the novel's ambition and audacity, but fall short of calling it visionary or even relevant in larger questions pertaining to contemporary African letters or world literature. Quoting Wole Soyinka in his *Guardian* review, Helon Habila remarks, "I prefer my Kafka straight" (2015). *Kirkus Reviews* concurs, suggesting that "[t]he story doesn't quite live up to its brilliant premise" (2016: 267). Noting the "superficial and obvious similarities" with *Metamorphosis*, Rone Shavers sums that *Blackass* is less about existential alienation and more about "how the color of one's skin both connotes and denotes privilege" (2016: 19). While the racial transformation and its attendant privileges are central to the novel, read solely as mimicry of *Metamorphosis* critics overlook the intertextual dialogs at work in the narrative, from allusions to ancient Romans Apuleius and Ovid to postcolonial theorist Frantz Fanon.

At the same time, *Blackass* remains uniquely Nigerian, drawing its premise on what Nigerians colloquially refer to as "white man's magic," preferential treatment stemming from the belief that whiteness leads to "anything good" (Sydelle 2007). Still, the notion that passing as white will beget magical values and a surplus value, while wearing a black skin carries a burdensome tax is not unlike the central feature of the traditional African American racial "passing" novel. Using the "passing" novel as a critical framework opens *Blackass* to a broader literary tradition that includes African diasporic texts. Within this context *Blackass*'s musings on skin color prejudice and existentialism, rather than being read as separate or oppositional, might be interpreted as an interplay that invokes Frantz Fanon's meditations on existentialized alienation from the skin and, consequently, the nature of the racialized being, playing a crucial role in contemporary debates about mobility, space, and socio-economics as they relate to global blackness and, more specifically, Afropolitanism.

Dystopian Speculations of Afropolitanism

In its simplest incarnation, "Afropolitan," the lexical merge of "African" and "cosmopolitan," is defined in terms of location and displacement, cataloguing peoples of African descent born or living outside of Africa. Writer Taiye Selasi is often credited for the popularization of this idea. In her interview with Aaron Bady for *Transition* magazine, Selasi declares that the term emerged from a "stranded place" where her identity, and that of her friends, was not easily categorizable (2015: 160). She desired to name, recognize, and embrace an identity that best describes "an African diaspora, not the original one" (2015: 160). Her reference to the "original" African diaspora presumably speaks to the dispersal of black Africans around the world as a result of trans-Atlantic slavery and colonialism, in contrast to the "new" diaspora, which accounts for those, like Selasi, who are of African descent with more recent dispersals from the continent.

Selasi's effort to distinguish she and her ilk from descendants of the earlier diaspora has ignited critics like Cheryl Sterling to condemn Selasi's "anti-black rhetoric" and argue, "Whether they intended to or not ... [t]hey confirmed, for me, a sense of elitism of the Afropolitan stance, a need to separate themselves from the Blacks over there, i.e. ghettoized African-Americans, who are conceived of with all the stereotypes attached to blackness, whose nature and culture, they would like to believe, is fundamentally different from theirs" (2015: 127). From Sterling's standpoint, those "ghettoized African-Americans" are marked in terms of immobility. "[T]he Blacks over there" remain fixed "with all the stereotypes attached to blackness," while Afropolitans, freed from such racialized signifiers, have the ability to progress (2015: 127). If the Afropolitan's progress is necessarily dependent on discarding and deserting African Americans in a location fixed by "stereotypes attached to blackness," then the mantle of white supremacy is only maintained rather than dismantled. Ironically, as noted above, it was Selasi's desire to emerge from a "stranded place" that drew her to Afropolitanism (2015: 160). It would seem that the two perspectives are two sides of the same coin. Both Selasi and Sterling reveal how social mobility is fundamentally embedded in racial anxiety.

While Sterling's assessment of Afropolitanism illuminates the significance of mobility in metrics of race, Emma Dabiri's is decidedly economic. In "Why I'm Not an Afropolitan," Dabiri contends that Afropolitanism's "centrality of capitalism" is of concern and its "commodification of dissent" leads to a "polite, corporate, glossy" counter-culture movement which she likens to "second wave feminists who failed to identify their privilege as white and middle class while claiming to speak for all women" (2014). Dabiri presents a dystopian possibility, an Afropolitanism that shallowly performs a manufactured idea of Africa, mass produced and detached from intrinsic meaning, whether it be in the form of kente cloth handbags, or on a more insidious level, elites from remote access points parasitically exploiting and profiting from an underclass that acts as its source of capital but reaps none of its benefits.

Tracing this corporate chain to its topmost level, Binyavanga Wainaina concurs, offering Pan-Africanism as an alternative to a consumerist commodified movement "funded by the West" (qtd. in Santana 2016: 121). Wainaina's address at the 2012 African Studies Association UK imagines an Afropolitan literary world devoid of authenticity, aesthetics, and stakes. In a marketplace largely driven by the Western gaze, it would be no surprise that remnants of colonialism and white supremacy are resonant. From such a standpoint, Afropolitans "not citizens, but Africans of the world" might then be viewed as mere surrogates of neocolonialism (Selasi 2015). Critics of the "anti-black" and "anti-African" mindset are united in their contempt for a movement that they believe celebrates privilege and promotes divisiveness.

On the contrary, proponents of Afropolitanism like Mbembe, rather than centering race or corporate capitalism, frame it "in terms of movement, mobility, circulation" (2016: 35). Lagos, then, "the economic capital of Nigeria and its most cosmopolitan city" would seem like a setting rife with possibility (Barrett 2015: 9). An African metropolis of global transaction and exchange, theoretically, the college educated, technologically savvy, and Western-oriented Nigerian youth—many of whom would be classified as "Afropolitans" if they lived elsewhere—would be ideally positioned for success. Nonetheless, the Lagos of Barrett's *Blackass* is a marketplace glutted with overqualified native Nigerian applicants in the thousands, governed by "big man power" and "oga politics," and the promises of Africa-rooted cosmopolitanism are out of reach for everyday Lagosians like Furo in his pre-metamorphosis days (Murphy 2017: 292). The centrality and legitimization of the "big man" and "oga" is reproduced because specifically capitalist spaces necessarily depend on the exploitation of the "small man" (Murphy 2017: 292). Hence, progress and success are fundamentally framed in exceptionalist terms. Critic Laura Murphy contends that one way of moving into exclusive spaces is through a politics of "hustle" (2017: 292); thus, Furo's white skin becomes his hustle, his modus of mobility.

The presumption that whiteness will beget surplus value while blackness will incur debt and ransom, in, of all places, black-majority cosmopolitan Lagos is not only evidence of skin color prejudice; importantly, it runs counter to Afropolitan perspectives that seek to challenge postcolonial epistemologies of victimhood through the invocation of ideologies that overlook and minimize race. However, Bady questions the centrality of white supremacy in *Blackass*, noting that "[w]hiteness, as it turns out, is an opportunity to *be* used" (2016). Admittedly, in *Blackass* Nigerians in search of their own hustle view whites as "historical opportunists or gullible victims," and when they come across Furo, they seize upon his whiteness as a means for mobility (Barrett 2015: 10). Still, the notion that proximity to whiteness is even a means for success reveals that a white supremacist colonial past persists, even amid efforts to shed it. Moreover, only after the racial transformation does Furo's life have economic value. He becomes mobile enough to circumvent economic and social barriers as he is "inundated with job offers and propositions" (Bady 2016). Even as his claim to whiteness is repeatedly challenged—through his Nigerian accent and his remaindered ass—Furo continually reaffirms his claim to whiteness and its entitlements. Ultimately, he learns to leverage his whiteness for benefits and, in the process, becomes increasingly alienated from, not only his black skin, but all that it signifies.

To be clear, Barrett's interrogation is not as straightforward as it might seem. Whiteness isn't idealized. Frank Whyte is depicted as grotesque, red, and sweaty; moreover, he is inept. White supremacy, then, is hollow and dysfunctional; yet its power is maintained by those who promote it. Barrett satirizes the great lengths of self-degradation that his Nigerian characters will submit to in order to maintain white supremacy, if only to benefit from it; thus, his central critique is of surrogates of white supremacy. Historically, metropole colonies depended on members of the subjugated class to maintain hegemony, and *Blackass* asks if we are so far removed from that past. Rather than whites, it is Nigerians who weaponize whiteness in order to attain social mobility. While Furo, as "Frank Whyte," remains hapless, ordinary, and even childlike, other characters fail to expose him as a fraud and instead utilize his whiteness. In lieu of disrupting this bankrupt system, they perpetuate it.

Barrett is both critical of the "hustle" and the system that corrupts its actors. In invoking "white man's magic" as a central trope, he speculates that in spite of social and economic progress, latent existentialized racial anxiety persists. Thus, rather than shedding race altogether, which would signify a post-racial or deracinated future, Furo's blackness is merely *concealed* by whiteness, as evidenced by his remaindered black ass. In doing so, Barrett's speculative novel simultaneously depicts a surreal colonial past and the Afropolitan's deracinated or post-racial future as two polar opposites coexisting in tension with one another. However, *Blackass*, when read through a critical framework of racial passing, attempts to mediate these positions. By deploying "white man's magic," Barrett's novel, read as contemporary racial passing narrative, offers a complex psychosocial critique of Afropolitanism, engaging with latent racialized anxieties embedded in its elite exceptionalist framework of African identity and harkening a return to Frantz Fanon's familiar "black skin, white masks."

Being and *Becoming*: An Ontology of Racialized Existentialism

In *Black Skin, White Masks*, Frantz Fanon's reflections on racial psychopathology and ontology present whiteness as an elusive liminal state. In the colonial Caribbean and North Africa of his time, social mobility was marked by proximity to whiteness, assimilation of its values, and negation of blackness. While much has changed since the colonial period, a neocolonial landscape dependent on alliances between former colonizers and subjects presents similar challenges. Like the upwardly mobile civil servants of colonial Africa, Afropolitans might, on the one hand, be viewed as single-minded and opportunistic. On the other hand, they might be viewed as savvy, and moreover, practical, simply learning to "hustle" in a fraught socio-economic landscape. In this light, their efforts to look past race-based frameworks in favor of other measures has as much to do with the narrowness that prescriptions of race might offer and creating distance from negative associations with blackness. In a sense, it is understandable that those who might be adversely impacted by racial distinctions would prefer, both strategically and philosophically, to promote alternative categories for self-identity. Furthermore, conceptions of race are largely dependent on social context and circumstances. In many places, particularly former metropole colonies where the population is racially homogenous, ethnic, tribal, religious, or social class distinctions impact daily life more egregiously, and, thus, have more significance in identity politics. Nigerian writer Chimamanda Ngozi Adichie confirms this in her 2014 interview with Terry Gross, where she famously muses that she learned to be black when she came to America. This became a central theme in her third novel, *Americanah*.

At the same time, whiteness remains the unquestioned ideal, not only evidenced by "white man's magic" but also by the prevalence of colorism, intra-racial discrimination that manifests in preference for light skin, lank hair, and Eurocentric facial features. It remains a social and economic hindrance for darker skinned peoples in postcolonial nations throughout the world. Tellingly, as critical examinations center on race, it is blackness, not whiteness, that becomes its casualty. Deracinated whiteness remains the assumed hegemonic ideal, instead of ascribed in racialized terms that signal its constructedness; thus, race (i.e., the black), not racism (i.e., the system of white supremacy), is problematized.

Because of this, even in a majority black nation like Nigeria, the values of colonialism and white supremacy are promoted in indirect ways, often by other blacks. In *Blackass* Furo's bookseller doesn't sell Nigerian books because "We only sell world-class books" (2015: 239), and when he reflects on his education, Furo remembers his English Literature teacher pillorying, *Things Fall Apart*, Chinua Achebe's literary masterpiece: "*The white man in this book is a symbol of progress. Okonkwo fought against the white man and lost. Progress always wins that's why it's progress*" (2015: 27; italics in the original). Likewise, @_igoni/Morpheus, Barrett's authorial alter ego, reflects on "lifelong teachers who instilled in us their deep-seated humiliation over the failures of Nigeria as well as their bitter nostalgia for the administrative competence of colonial rule" (2015: 162). Each case illustrates the ways blackness is presumed to be inferior or at least counterfeit. Particularly of note is the way the system of colonialism remains an ever-present intermediary force when the actors are black. Here "world-class books" becomes synonymous with approval by the Western gaze; "the white man" and "progress" are linked to conquest; and colonial rule is viewed only in terms of "competence." Throughout his education, the lesson that is repeatedly instilled in Furo is that blackness, and likewise, Nigerianness, are sufficient if only in a provincial context; however, when committed to mobility and progress, the path is whiteness.

Few studies have examined race in black-majority former metropole colonies, preferring instead to focus on former settler colonies like South Africa and the United States where the history of Apartheid and Jim Crow-era segregation were overt and state-sanctioned. However, Pere Ayling's research on schooling in Nigeria provides insights into how white supremacy and colonialism are propagated socially and institutionally. Her findings might better help us to understand how whiteness, serving as both economic and cultural capital, is also encoded in terms of dominance and inferiority:

> Historical factors, such as colonization and imperialism, as well as the continuous perpetuation of hegemonic discourses such as West is best have not only made the West dominant and non-Western countries like Nigeria the dominated, but have also successfully constructed Whiteness and White culture as a highly valuable symbolic and cultural capital.
>
> AYLING 2015: 460

In attempts to distinguish themselves as "transnational/global elites" (2015: 455), upwardly mobile Nigerian families undertake "key micro-social processes, specifically; minority status, bodily transformation, and refined British accent, which allow parents to reproduce their social positioning as the genuine Nigerian elites while limiting entry into this group at the same time" (2015: 455). The "education" the pupils receive is that Europe is both a physical and psychic destination. Importantly, rather than crafting their own unique ideal of a Nigerian elite—composed, of, say, varying African cultures—the parents in Ayling's study are invested in what they "perceived as 'Britishness'—manifested in White British upper-class' deportment, decorum and accent—[that] will provide their children with a unique set of Western dispositions, setting them apart from the newcomers within their social field while endowing their children with highly profitable identities" (2015: 455).

Using Ayling's framework is helpful for elucidating the social processes that propagate white supremacy in a neo-colonial context, particularly how these processes may be inherently encoded in the ideals of Afropolitanism. Importantly, this process is not organic—the result of natural cultural ebbs, currents, and exchanges over time—but as a manufactured product with an overdetermined outcome, a vision reminiscent of Dabiri's speculation of a "corporate, glossy" "commodification of dissent" (2014). Moreover, the process is uni-directional as opposed to bi-directional, positioning the formerly colonized as the supplicant and the West as its benefactor rather than facilitating an exchange that goes both ways. Furthermore, it is Western-oriented without presuming—perhaps from a Pan-African standpoint—that other African nations might provide valuable social and economic capital. In *Blackass* this dystopian speculation is best illustrated when Furo discovers that Syreeta, his romantic interest, is not only attracted to him because of his white skin, but in order to access membership into an elite league of Nigerian mothers of mixed-race children sired by white European expatriates (2015: 136). Syreeta's clique is strategically engineering the Afropolitans of tomorrow.

Both Ayling and Barrett present this manufactured identity as incomplete, drawing attention to its constructedness. In her study, Ayling observes that in order to be "recognizable and accepted as local elites," some perceptible "Nigerianness" must be retained (2015: 463). Likewise, for Furo, white Europeanness is a model that he is not ever able to fully achieve. Even as he becomes more deeply embroiled in his deception, Barrett makes it clear to readers that Furo's whiteness is always under construction. This is best signified in his remaindered "robustly black" ass and Nigerian accent (2015: 255). While his Nigerian accent helps him in situations where he is under suspicion, it works as the inverse of Ayling's finding. Rather than being received as a "local elite" due to the perceptible "Nigerianness," Furo's accent, a source of "Nigerianness" within his whiteness, creates camaraderie, making what is exotic and foreign familiar and accessible. However, in order for the ruse to succeed, his whiteness must be unquestionable; thus, his black ass—his blackness—acts as both a stain, sullying his ideal of whiteness and a trace, reminding him that his white skin is only a perforated mask.

Rather than *being* white, Furo is always in the process of *becoming* white; indeed, as @_igoni/Morpheus remarks, "It is easier to *be* than to *become*" (2015: 261; my emphasis). The notion of existential "being" recalls Frantz Fanon's reflections on racial psychopathology and ontology in *Black Skin, White Masks*. Not surprisingly, among the epigraphs on transformation throughout *Blackass*, Barrett includes one from Fanon: "For the black man there is only one destiny. And it is white" (qtd. in Barrett 2015: 171). The future that Fanon disparages, and that Barrett satirizes, is decidedly white: "he becomes whiter as he renounces his blackness" (Fanon 2008: 9). This is simultaneously an act of composition and negation (Fanon 2008: 83). "Being" and "becoming" emerge from an ever-present dialectic between the self, the body, the skin, and the world.

Invoking epidermal and corporeal schemas, Fanon's racial psychopathology is informed by notions of both space and time. While the body becomes this contest's site, temporalities "in opposition to historical becoming" and "the unforeseeable" reassert the deceptions in an Afropolitan framework focused exclusively on a post-racial future without recognition of the detrimental effects from the colonial past that linger into the present progressive (Fanon 2008: 103). Citing Fanon's "notions of epidermal and corporeal schemas" in his analysis of Nella Larsen's *Passing*, Steve Pile focuses on skin, because it provides a different, and unsettling, angle on the question of the relationship between racialized bodies and racialized spaces. This is because skin refuses to settle into binary logics that code bodies and spaces as black or white. Yet skin also resolutely refuses to be colourless: despite protestations that race is socially constructed, skin determinedly asks that bodies be recognized as having a race.

(2010: 27)

Simply put, skin *both* resists the binary racial logics that Afropolitanism attempts to distance itself from *and* it affirms them. By centering Fanon's "epidermal and corporeal schemas" in his analysis, Pile engages in a *both/and* mindset that recognizes the complexity of our inherited racial history, one which Afropolitanism seeks to minimize and look beyond. However, in Barrett's use of "white man's magic," skin acts not only as a helpful way to elucidate complex latent racial anxieties, it also becomes an important narrative device as *Blackass* takes the form of a novel of "racial passing."

"White Man's Magic" and the "Racial Passing" Drama

Just as *Blackass* is conversant with Kafka's *Metamorphosis*, Barrett's deployment of "white man's magic" in the context of race and mobility has a literary counterpart in the American racial passing novel, and its influence is resonant. "Racial passing," as an act and literary conceit, evolved from the slave-era practice of granting enslaved people permission to travel unaccompanied with a document called a "pass" (Bennett 1998: 36). Undocumented blacks, free or enslaved, were considered trespassers and risked capture or arrest. As a result, blackness and mobility were inherently criminalized, while whiteness signified freedom. In *Blackass*, "white man's magic" conveys, not only power and fortune; it also speaks to a sense of elusiveness granted exclusively to whites that demarcates whites and whiteness as unrestricted in the context of contemporary Nigeria. Likewise, throughout US history, when light-skinned African Americans used their phenotypically white appearance as a "pass" to access the mobility and enhanced social status of whites, their movements were considered, not only impersonation, but also criminal trespass.

Even after the abolition of slavery in the United States, racial passing persisted in response to post-Reconstruction efforts to limit the freedom and movement of African Americans, particularly in places like Louisiana with a tertiary racial caste system that positioned mixed-race populations between whites and blacks. In terms of racial legislation, no outcome is more significant than that of the US Supreme Court's 1896 *Plessy v. Ferguson* case.

Plessy v. Ferguson is credited for widespread application of the so-called "one drop policy" which denied anyone with known African ancestry the lawful entitlement to the property and "reputation of being a white man" (1896). Thus, like material property, the performance of whiteness was regarded, not only as specious, but also as an unlawful theft of the inheritable property of white racial supremacy, among those properties, unencumbered mobility.

Racial hypodescent laws are a brutal vestige of the legacy of white supremacy, and this inheritance is most visible in sites, like former British colonies, where blatant acts of discrimination, violence, and state-sponsored or condoned miscarriages of justice reigned. Because Nigeria was not a settler colony, however, its race relations did not evolve in the same way as the United States and other settler colonies; nonetheless, traces of white supremacy remain. In Nigeria, black Africans performed roles that, while mutually beneficial, also perpetuated white supremacy. Acknowledging this, Barrett utilizes literary conventions of the American racial passing drama in order to illustrate the ways that white supremacy exists in the form of "white man's magic" despite Afropolitan post-racial sentiments.

The complex interplay of racial performance, space, and boundaries is not lost on the Lagosian backdrop of *Blackass*. "In some parts of the city it is not unusual to see a white person walking the streets (Barrett 2015: 7), but in other areas, "a good number of the inhabitants have never held a conversation with an oyibo, never considered white people as anything more or less than historical opportunists or gullible victims" (2015: 9). Thus, Furo's identity and sense of belonging are shaped by his movement through socially policed territories. Even in his own neighborhood, Furo is "seen as a freak: exposed to wonder, invisible to comprehension" (2015: 11). If inhabiting legitimate racial territories is a crucial aspect of being recognized as white, then "white man's magic" is dependent on Furo's distance from exclusively "black" spaces. Thus, like the classic racial passing figure, Furo leaves his black working-class neighborhood and absconds to the affluent Victoria Island, where, with the support of romantic interest Syreeta, an opportunist and a "kept" woman in her own right, he takes up residence.

To receive the full benefits of "white man's magic," Furo must also distance himself from blackness psychically. In a pivotal scene Furo renounces his blackness and embraces his new identity and social reality:

> Furo picked up the newspaper and gazed at the face bearing his name. . . . black skin: that's all he saw. The person wasn't him. He had moved on beyond that . . . he strode to the tall mirror over the vanity table and stared into the face of his new self . . . He knew at last he had nothing to fear. He was a different person.
>
> (2015: 155–156)

Furo's black skin causes him racial terror, and it is his Lacanian gaze in the mirror that placates him and affirms his white skin as part of an Imaginary sense of being (Lacan 1973). It is also at this moment that Furo recognizes that his whole, unitary sense of self is lacking. This is a sharp contrast from the fragmented, pre-Symbolic sense Furo experiences before gazing in the mirror (Lacan 1973). At once, Furo christens himself with the European moniker "Frank Whyte," rather than a Nigerian ethnic name. Additionally, in an effort to more wholly *become* white, he determines that he must legalize his identity by obtaining a passport bearing his new name and face. He recognizes that white identity is not only in the skin. Part of eluding detection of fraud from others requires Furo's successful performance of whiteness, and it begins with the body. Initially, Furo's performance is limited to adjusting his posture and gaze (Barrett 2015: 11), but as he becomes more alienated from his blackness, his performance includes exploiting, berating, and degrading fellow Nigerians—he, in fact, performs what he and his fellow Nigerians believe whiteness is. As a parable, *Blackass* cautions Afropolitans that "movement, mobility, circulation" at the expense of authenticity and community is morally dubious (Mbembe 2016: 35).

Like the classic "tragic mulatto," Furo's bloodline also threatens to expose him, so despite his family's frantic efforts to find him via digital and material media outlets, he cuts off all contact with them, effectively becoming a social orphan. As Furo ascends the socio-economic ladder, he goes it alone, never once offering monetary support to his family, even though his mother "counted him as her second chance to succeed in everything his father had failed at" (2015: 40). Because Furo is not committed or responsible to others, he lacks citizenship; his position as a social orphan mirrors his statelessness, and ultimately results in his mounting narcissism. Furthermore, in spite of the fact that his skin is white, Furo also fears his black African ancestry will be apparent in his progeny, so he talks Syreeta into an abortion. Because of the ongoing risk, it is presumed that he will eventually permanently sterilize himself, effectively limiting his ability to create a new family. Echoing the concerns of Afropolitanism critics Dabiri and Wainaina, *Blackass* speculates that if the sole condition of progress is for one to sacrifice his history and community in hopes of attaining the benefits and privileges of another, in the end, it will only lead to personal and social demise.

As a literary trope and rhetorical device, the tragic mulatto/a served a crucial role in the abolitionist movement illustrating that in spite of the skin, the character's black African ancestry was viewed in terms of barely perceptible taint, affirming notions of white supremacy couched in terms of purity. In antet and post-bellum America, myths about the physical stain of blood quantum on the body were historically commonplace, resulting in increased scrutiny of suspected racial interlopers. While skin color, hair texture, facial features, and even the color and shape of genitals could be sources of racial anxiety, in an absurdist comic turn, Furo's albatross is the novel's eponymous *blackass*. Furo's skin, like a "mask," conceals his "black" body, a "body" metaphorically constituted of his family, friends, history, bloodline, and ethnicity before the metamorphosis; at the same time, Furo's skin, specifically his *black ass*, also betrays his racial terror: "[T]he bigger terror was that the blackness of his buttocks would spread into sight, would creep outwards to engulf everything, to show him up as an imposter . . . He knew that so long as the vestiges of his old self remained with him, his new self would never be safe from ridicule and incomprehension" (2015: 111). Importantly, instead of interpreting his white skin as the stain, Furo considers his black skin—the vestige of his "old self [that] remained with him"—"a blemish," a source of ridicule (2015: 111), and a "problem to be solved" (2015: 119). The notion that blackness is a problem to overcome in order to progress demonstrates the folly of what Sterling describes as "anti-black" Afropolitanism.

Throughout the novel, Furo attempts to solve the problem of blackness by turning to toxic skin-whitening creams, which are pervasive throughout Nigeria and other formerly colonized nations. On Syreeta's vanity table, a variety of creams are available to Furo, of different grades and qualities, signifying both the commodification of whiteness and its appearance at all levels of the economic spectrum. As a result of the cream's corrosiveness, Furo's skin grows worryingly painful, red, itchy, and bloody, reflecting the unnaturalness, discomfort, and toxicity of effacing his black skin. When his sore forms a scab and falls away, Furo attains the white skin he so desires—but only momentarily. In an atavistic turn, hyperpigmentation occurs and his skin is "robustly black" (2015: 255). Furo's failed efforts to *become* white, by both concealing and erasing his blackness, illustrate the paradoxical construction and negation of self that Fanon illuminates in *Black Skin, White Masks* and that critics of Afropolitanism caution.

Conclusion

In closing, A. Igoni Barrett's *Blackass* appropriates Kafka's existentialist meditations and Fanon's notions of racialized existentialism to project a dystopian speculation of the dangers of an upward mobility that is formed through exclusivity, be it of the "anti-black" or "anti-African" variety. One distinction it is necessary to make is that rather than arguing that Afropolitanism *is* anti-black or anti-African, Barrett's work is speculative, presenting this scenario as a parable that informs readers of the necessary self-reflexivity involved in espousing movements, practices, and philosophies. In *Blackass*, Furo Wariboko's black skin, rather than being shed, is merely "masked" by whiteness. The "white man's magic" that he inherits when he racially passes as white, only further demonstrates local manifestation of the global system of white supremacy, propagated by European colonization, but he, like his fellow Nigerians in the novel, are so singularly driven by desire to progress that they are unable to carefully consider what is at stake. Likewise, proponents of Afropolitanism who seek to minimize or overlook the systems of white supremacy and colonialism, rather than considering them integral and insidious, risk the possibility of *becoming* colonizers.

Importantly, Barrett's use of Kafka's *Metamorphosis* as a prototype is not incidental. By satirizing a European's most recognizable work—a work that has proliferated the globe in intellectual and popular contexts—Barrett positions his novel in the larger body of world literatures. Likewise, by paying homage to the African American "racial passing" narrative, which is inherently part of an African Diasporic genre, he involves multiple literary texts in this conversation, while at the same time telling a uniquely Nigerian story. *Blackass* is an ambitious work, not only because of the risks involved in the satirical form (and the book's daring title!), but also because the novel positions itself within significant conversations about new directions for Africana literature and intellectual thought. In addition to those themes raised regarding race and Afropolitanism, many discursive questions remain regarding Barrett's utilization of identity as it relates to gender and digital environs, though I am unable to fully interrogate them due to the limitations of space. Nonetheless, A. Igoni Barrett's *Blackass* is a visionary work that looks both forward and back, and, likewise, both centralizes Africa and situates it within a global context.

Works cited

Adichie, Chimamanda Ngozi. "Fresh Air: 'Americanah' Author Explains Learning to be Black in the U.S." *NPR.org*. 7 March 2014. Accessed July 29, 2018. <https://www.npr.org/2014/03/07/286903648/americanah-author-explains-learning-to-be-black-in-the-u-s>.

Ayling, Pere. "Embodying 'Britishness': The (Re)making of the Contemporary Nigerian Elite Child." *Curriculum Inquiry*. 45.5. (2015): 455–71.

Bady, Aaron. "A. Igoni Barrett's 'Blackass' and the Afropolitan Debate." *Okayafrica*. March 10, 2016. Accessed July 5, 2018. <http://www.okayafrica.com/a-igoni-barrett-blackass-afropolitan-debate/>.

Bady, Aaron and Taiye Selasi. "From That Stranded Place." *Transition*. 117. (2015): 148–165.

Balakrishnan, Sarah and Achille Mbembe. "Pan-African Legacies, Afropolitan Futures: A Conversation with Achille Mbembe." *Transition*. 120. (2016): 28–37.

Barrett, A. Igoni. *Blackass*. Minneapolis: Graywolf Press, 2015.

Bennett, Juda. *The Passing Figure: Racial Confusion in Modern American Literature*. New York: Peter Lang, 1998.

"Blackass." *Kirkus Reviews*. 84.1. 1 January 2016: 267. Accessed August 10, 2017. Web.

Carter, Perry L. "The Penumbral Spaces of Nella Larsen's *Passing*: Undecidable Bodies, Mobile Identities, and the Deconstruction of Racial Boundaries."

Gender, Place & Culture: A Journal of Feminist Geography. 13.3. (2006): 227–246.

Dabiri, Emma. "Why I Am Not an Afropolitan." *Africa is a Country.* January 21, 2014. Accessed August 10, 2016. <http://africasacountry.com/2014/01/why-im-not-an-afropolitan/>.

Eze, Chielozona. "We, Afropolitans." *Journal of African Cultural Studies.* 28.1. (2016): 114–119.

Fanon, Frantz. *Black Skin, White Masks.* (1952). Trans. Charles Lam Markmann. London: Pluto Press, 2008.

Habila, Helon. "Blackass by A. Igoni Barrett Review—A Cocktail of Kafka and Comedy." *The Guardian.* August 14, 2015. Accessed August 3, 2017. <https://www.theguardian.com/books/2015/aug/14/blackass-by-a-igoni-barrett-review-cocktail-kafka-comedy>.

Kafka, Franz. *Metamorphosis.* (1915). Trans. Lila and Edwin Muir. New York City: Limited Editions Club, 1984.

Lacan, Jacques. *The Four Fundamental Concepts of Psychoanalysis.* (1973). Trans. Alan Sheridan. London: W.W. Norton, 1998.

Larsen, Nella. *Passing.* New York and London: A.A Knopf, 1929.

Murphy, Laura T. "The Ethics of African Studies in the Age of Oga Politics: A Response to Tejumola Olaniyan's 'African Literature in the Post-Global Age.'" *The Cambridge Journal of Postcolonial Literary Inquiry.* 4.2. (April 2017): 286–295.

Pile, Steve. "Skin, Race and Space: The Clash of Bodily Schemas in Frantz Fanon's *Black Skins, White Masks* and Nella Larsen's *Passing.*" *Cultural Geographies.* 18.1. (2010): 25–41.

Plessy v. Ferguson. 163. US Supreme Court. 537 (1896).

Santana, Stephanie Bosch. "Exorcising the future: Afropolitanism's Spectral Origins." *Journal of African Cultural Studies.* 28.1 (2016): 120–126.

Selasi, Taiye. "Bye-Bye Babar?" *The LIP.* 3 March 2005. Accessed. August 8, 2016. <https://thelip.robertsharp.co.uk/?p=76>.

Shavers, Rone. "Identity Crisis." *American Book Review.* 37.6. (Sept/Oct 2016): 19.

Sterling, Cheryl. "Race Matters: Cosmopolitanism, Afropolitanism, and Pan-Africanism via Edward Wilmot Blyden." *The Journal of Pan African Studies.* 8.1. (June 2015): 119–145.

Sydelle, Solomon. "White Man's Magic." *Nigerian Curiosity.* February 24, 2007. Accessed August 10, 2017. <http://www.nigeriancuriosity.com/2007/02/white-mans-magic_24.html>.

6

Toward an Environmental Theory of Afropolitan Literature

Juan Meneses

To write about Afropolitan literature is to face a number of critical challenges rooted in the coining and development of the notion of Afropolitanism. As multiple critics of the term have suggested, Afropolitanism, especially when it is understood as a discourse of high mobility and globalization, legitimizes a certain detachment between Africa and the African (or descendant of Africans) that seems to do more damage to the relationship of individuals and communities to the realities of the continent than invigorate or re-envision them. My own skepticism stems from the fear that Afropolitanism may end up "partak[ing] of the negation of 'the political,'" as Chantal Mouffe has stated about certain operations of the idea of cosmopolitanism (Mouffe 2005, 90). Understanding Afropolitanism as a free-floating form of global citizenship can be detrimental to the politics of the local, regional, national, and transnational connections it aims to construct. Yet I think that, like cosmopolitanism, which can be deployed in ways that do not foreclose the political charges of world citizenship, a critical examination can also offer ways to understand Afropolitanism as a global form of African citizenship that brings to the fore the tensions and complexities of those connections. As the still inchoate theoretical discourses around it are currently shaping its meaning and nuances, it is worth considering how other dimensions that are not central to extant debates can shed light onto it. One of them, and the focus of this chapter, concerns questions about its environmental imbrications.

As the term's morphological makeup suggests, Afropolitanism designates a form of African cosmopolitanism[1] that places an emphasis on an individual's claims about her subjectivity as determined to her belonging to one or several places. Its main departure from cosmopolitanism, however, resides in its paradoxical relationship between the openness on which the latter rests and the differential ontology that the former registers. Afropolitanism operates as an index of citizenship in the world that is nonetheless contained by the boundaries of (the idea of) Africa and hinges, to quote Achille Mbembe and Sarah Nuttall, on a reassessment of "the frontiers of commonality and the potential of *sameness-as-worldliness*" (Mbembe and Nuttall 2004, 351; italics original). What makes Afropolitanism an extremely productive category is the negotiative power that its geographical and historical grounding bestows upon the individual who chooses to be an Afropolitan. The varieties of this "sameness-as-worldliness," further, are infinite yet they are underpinned by a continental affiliation that exceeds the individualism that governs certain understandings of cosmopolitanism, thus revealing ethical and political dimensions inherent to this choice as it inscribes an individual's being in the world within the parameters of his Africanness.

The study of Afropolitan literature as world literature, therefore, must include analyses of the rich and often paradoxical connections that Afropolitanism generates. Certain definitions of Afropolitanism, especially those that figure it as a form of highly mobile, transnational, and self-stylized sense of self with a strong emphasis on personal background and heritage, such as Taiye Selasi's, deem that "the Afropolitan must form an identity along at least three dimensions: national, racial, cultural" (Selasi 2005). Others putting a stress on history and difference as the basis for a critical form of African subjectivity, such as Achille Mbembe's, stem from the individual's claim to a certain transnational sovereignty, looking to Africa as a vehicle to express the interconnections between "the here and there," to make sense of the tensions between "primary roots and memberships," and to reconcile one's familiarity with "strangeness, foreignness and remoteness" (Mbembe 2007, 28). Afropolitanism is also, in Mbembe's theorization, "an aesthetic and a particular poetic of the world" that is based, as in Selasi's, on a "political and cultural stance in relation to nation, to race and to the issue of difference in general" (Mbembe 2007, 29). To be Afropolitan, thus, is both to connect and be connected to the world via Africa, and the work of current critical debates lies therefore in exploring how these connections manifest in literature.

Questions concerning the environment must be at the forefront if we want to understand fully this new way of being African in the world. Some general ideas about geography that feature in almost any discussion of Afropolitanism easily set the stage for this kind of exploration, although more work needs to address ecology in explicit and nuanced ways. As Achille Mbembe and Sarah Nuttall have suggested, "One of the more potent ways of disrupting and 'jamming' the dominant imaginings of Africa," to which Afropolitan literature is often thought to contribute, "is . . . to concern ourselves anew with *space* and with *discontinuities*, to revisit our *topographical imagination* when it comes to this vast *geographical landmass* made up of a multiplicity of *social forms* and *interlaced boundaries*" (Mbembe and Nuttall 2004, 352; my italics). These are questions of import for the study of Afropolitan literature as world literature and, consequently, require much more attention than they have so far received. Notions that are commonly associated with Afropolitan discourse such as migrancy and mobility as well as related ones such as place, affiliation, and the environmental registers of culture and belonging warrant analyzing Afropolitan literature from an explicitly ecocritical perspective.

Yet, as Pheng Cheah has convincingly argued, an important dimension of the political work of world literature resides in its temporal operations if we understand the former as a figuration of the historical processes in which the phenomenology of being in the world is rooted. As he puts it, one of the defining aesthetico-political attributes of world literature is to be found in its "worlding" capacities—that is, in the ways it sheds light onto "how a world is held together and given unity by the force of time," while "temporalization constitutes an openness of a world, the opening that is world" (Cheah 2016, 8–9). This means that, to our investigations of the Afropolitan's claim to Africa's specific spaces and environments, a temporal dimension needs to be incorporated. The Afropolitan's experience of the world is the result of a series of historical processes, be it in the sense of the conditions and circumstances that allow an Afropolitan to refer to herself as such or, at a more personal level, as the passage of time that reveals his relationship to (the African) space. Thus, if to declare oneself Afropolitan is to submit one's self-determination as irresolutely linked (from close quarters as well as from the distance) to the materiality of the continent, this can only be registered as expressions of temporality, as events linking the individual and the world his Afropolitanism configures. The literary representation of this temporal dimension of being, then, must be considered as an analytical question of a first order.

In conjunction, these two aspects reveal how, as Simon Gikandi has put it, Afropolitanism "embraces movement across time and space as the condition of possibility of an African way of being" (Gikandi 2011, 10). In order to understand the environmental underpinnings of the relationships that Afropolitanism promotes, therefore, the formulation of a literary theory of environmental Afropolitanism or, as I will call it, eco-Afropolitanism, can be understood first and foremost as a way to imagine it as a situated cosmopolitanism. What is more, given the critical questions that emerge from the tensions between the mobility of the Afropolitan, her will to imagine herself as attached to the heterogeneous and multilayered entity of the African continent, and the latter's geographical and ecological features, the situatedness established by those physical and temporal coordinates is bound to generate a productive critical apparatus. Eco-Afropolitan literature is, to borrow Pascale Casanova's terminology, a "world literary *space*," that is, "not an abstract and theoretical construction, but an actual—albeit unseen—world made up by the lands of literature; a world in which what is judged worthy of being considered literary is brought into existence; a world in which the ways and means of literary art are argued over and decided" (Casanova 2004, 3–4, emphasis mine). By investigating this literary space as superimposed on Africa's environmental material reality, then, we will be able to understand how meaning is produced and ascribed to the continental network of spaces, social relations, and peoples.

In the following two sections, I want to explore in more detail the contours of this environmental understanding of Afropolitanism and its operation in the realm of literary invention. I do not intend, however, to present a prescriptive blueprint of the environmental tenets of Afropolitan literature but, in light of the dearth of discussions from an ecocritical perspective, I intend it as an exploratory incursion that might serve as an initial contribution to future critical debates. After doing so, I will offer an examination of one literary example, Zakes Mda's 2000 novel *The Heart of Redness*, with the purpose of illustrating the analytical application of this approach. My ultimate goal is to shed light onto the kinds of questions that an eco-Afropolitan literary analysis might need to tackle. I want to turn now to what I consider to be the three main questions at the core of any discussion of eco-Afropolitanism.

Toward a Theory of Eco-Afropolitanism

In beginning to formulate a theory of eco-Afropolitan literature, it is important to establish its properties as a critical discourse that is different from the larger question of African environmentalism.[2] To do so, we can address separately the ecological implications of three main notions upon which it rests: African identity, the idea of a continental kind of cosmopolitanism, and the political undertones of this form of global citizenship. In doing so, we will be able to begin mapping out the main questions that an ecocritical analysis can answer in interrogating Afropolitanism and the complexities of the Afropolitan's identity claims both inside and outside of Africa.

The first component is the African identity that gives the discourse of Afropolitanism its substance. This question, as Achille Mbembe has suggested (Mbembe 2007, 28–29), must be broached not with the intention to produce an exhaustive catalog but in attending to the kinds of networks and flows that constitute it. Were we to try and enumerate the main characteristics of this identity, we would be undertaking an exercise that would be as impossible—due to the infinite permutations that compose the notion of identity—as theoretically unproductive—given that we would ultimately be assailed by a fruitless essentialism that would run counter to the expansive and open-ended identity that Afropolitanism registers. Instead, we can think of the claims that the Afropolitan makes to construct such an identity and explore their specific role in revealing "the limitations of current means of understanding African environments and environmental problems" so as to "develop alternatives" (Caminero-Santangelo and Myers 2011, 11). Governing them, above all, is the fact that the Afropolitan declares to have a bond with a whole continent via certain environmental affiliations that operate at the national, regional, and local levels and determine both the networks of identification that can ultimately be called Afropolitan and the aesthetics that (re-)imagine them.

As a twenty-first-century phenomenon, Afropolitanism must be considered an identity construction with unavoidable postcolonial roots and, therefore, impregnated with a global sense of history. This means that the ecologies subtending the idea of Africa are prominently shaped by the historical place of colonialism and the processes of liberation and nation-building that, implicitly or explicitly, reside in the Afropolitan's imagination. Questions of land tenancy, sovereignty, and access to resources, for instance, are intimately linked to this history and connect it to other important global issues of our time. The emergence of the idea of the Global South as a transcontinental network of solidarities in which Africa plays such a crucial role, for instance, as well as the channels of global exchange that connect the continent with the rest of the planet—from the flows of capital and their important ecological repercussions to the religious and secular discourses of conservation—are essential factors to bear in mind. Eco-Afropolitanism must also be studied in light of the tensions between urban and rural spaces to which the Afropolitan claims an attachment, with a variety of questions at the forefront, from industrial pollution and the importance of flora and fauna to specific communities to the transit of migrating species across the countryside as well as through its cities. And if violence, conflict, and war play a crucial role in the formation of certain iterations of Afropolitanism, so does the environmental material destruction that emanates from them. Given that Afropolitan identities are also intimately linked to specific cultural practices (traditional as well as those produced by modernity), the environmental ramifications of food, work, and leisure, amongst many others, must be central to the analytical scope of this critical approach. Africa's diverse landscapes and seascapes, and the various climates and weather phenomena related to them, finally, contribute to the construction of this eco-Afropolitan consciousness and should be explored through the lens of Afropolitanism's most common inflections (i.e., nostalgia, detachment, celebration, amnesia, etc.)

The second aspect to consider is the kind of cosmopolitanism that Afropolitanism figures. One can begin with the observation that Afropolitanism is a form of "modulated" cosmopolitanism that, with the expansive attributes of its continental scope, denotes an understanding of being in the world that is nonetheless situated along a set of geo-historical parameters. These parameters can be understood first and foremost, following Chielozona Eze, as a "universal" kind of relationality (Eze 2016, 118) whose purview nonetheless remains within the boundaries of a continent and its ecological particularities. A specifically environmental ethical commitment to others, therefore, would translate this way of being in the world into a web of relationships that manifest in the concrete terms that I briefly outlined above. Ultimately, if finding "different ways of speaking about the environment" can be a vehicle to ground cosmopolitanism "in our relationships to each other" instead of "the categorical equivalence of human beings," as Craig Calhoun suggests, the same can be said about the work of eco-Afropolitanism (Calhoun 2017, 196–197). Eco-Afropolitanism can build structures of attachment that, moving beyond the elitist impulses that are often associated to Afropolitanism, situate the Afropolitan as an individual who stylizes his identity in environmental terms while forming relationships with others by way of those same structures. However, this kind of commitment does not necessarily need to manifest as exclusive to the African context. Instead, it signifies a discourse that reifies the individual's ethical fidelity toward the other, African or not, from an African perspective.

At the same time, if what has been called "eco-cosmopolitanism" articulates an "ecological awareness and environmental ethics" that is "not so much a sense of place as a sense of planet—a sense of how political, economic, technological, social, cultural, and ecological networks shape daily routines" (Heise 2008, 55), an ecocritical approach can offer productive insights that reveal the worlding potentiality of Afropolitanism. Whether as a mobile global citizen or an individual with deep roots in Africa, in reclaiming a distinctly African identity, the Afropolitan grounds herself in the idea of place against the backdrop of a planetary form of being. As Simon Gikandi argues, Afropolitanism allows us to "think of African identities as both rooted in specific local geographies but also transcendental of them" (Gikandi 2011, 9). This bears a connection with the ways in which environmental consciousness is expressed materially. As Lawrence Buell defines it, place is "space that is bounded and marked as humanly meaningful through personal attachment, social relations, and physiographic distinctiveness" (Buell 2005, 145). The Afropolitan's relationship to place, however, defies most accounts of a material understanding of being in the world, as the attachment to the socialized space that Africa becomes is experienced in a variety of ways, including from the distance afforded by global mobility. Buell asks, "Is a place-responsive ecoliterature of global scope an impossibility, then?" (Buell 2005, 92). An eco-Afropolitan literary approach answers this question in the negative. It is the task of critics to untangle the different ways in which Africa-as-space and this global form of citizenship are visualized in particular literary works. As Gikandi puts it, "what makes Afropolitan literature interesting is that ... instead of celebrating transnationalism, it creates a new space" (Rask Knudsen and Rahbek 2016, 51).

Finally, as a situated form of cosmopolitanism, Afropolitanism addresses one of the main challenges of cosmopolitanism, namely the danger that it may operate as an abstract—and therefore apolitical—form of citizenship. In environmental terms, this materializes as an agenda that maps out and provides responses to some of the most urgent questions with regard to what has been called "earth democracy"[3] in the continent and the ability for Africans to develop a relationship with the environment that permits them to pursue a fair, dignified, and good life. The formulation of eco-Afropolitan literary theory I am offering here, thus, establishes a number of bridges with the global political drive that one finds in articulations of Afropolitanism by Achille Mbembe, Chielozona Eze, and others. Many aspects define this agenda, but we can isolate some of the most important. The discourse of eco-Afropolitanism is useful to shore up the efforts of the environmentalisms emerging from the Global South.[4] Similarly, it tackles questions of inhabitancy and environmental justice, offering a strong response to the current predominance of neoliberalism in the processes of global governance. If, as Jean Comaroff has claimed, "In Africa ... agents of structural adjustment have labored to make democracy synonymous with privatization and minimal government, as well as with constitutionalism and an almost obsessional reliance on legal regulation" (Comaroff 2005, 133), additionally, an eco-Afropolitan approach offers ways to think about an alternative politics that reinforces the progressive goals of most environmentalisms. Modernization and development are key, as are partnerships ranging from local alliances to continental coalitions.

This political inclination, further, offers a partial answer to the important issues raised by those who remain critical of the discourse of Afropolitanism, and especially those who see it as a signifier for a transnational neoliberal identity and those who argue that Africans living in the continent, particularly the poor and immobile, are not represented by it.[5] Eco-Afropolitanism has the potential to build new, more inclusive alliances. An eco-Afropolitan literary theory will, therefore, theorize the lives of those highly mobile, urban, sophisticated, hyper-educated citizens as well as intra-continental migrants of means, struggling itinerant families traveling across the world in search of a place to settle, and people who have spent their entire lives in the continent in remote, rural areas and those living in opulent sky scrapers in complete isolation from the hustle and bustle of the city. This critical gesture also addresses Kwame Anthony Appiah's concern that Afropolitanism might privilege sub-Saharan Anglophone Africa (Rask Knudsen and Rahbek 2016, 149–151). In this sense, eco-Afropolitanism breaks with such imbalances by prioritizing analyses of the continent's material reality against the grain of entrenched socio-political configurations that limit the scope of certain extant discourses of Afropolitanism. Eco-Afropolitan literary theory, thus, can act as an expansive and corrective apparatus that connects the historical, geographic, social, and economic forces that impact the continent's multiple environments.

Having proposed this admittedly broad outline, I want now to offer an example of this kind of literary analysis. I will focus my discussion on the protagonist of Zakes Mda's 2000 novel *The Heart of Redness*. Whereas

Mda is hardly the first name that comes to mind when one thinks of Afropolitanism and its literary manifestations, his work in fact sheds light onto the kinds of interventions that eco-Afropolitanism can exert. Yet I do not mean to claim that Mda's narrative or its protagonist, are examples of an appropriate or even politically ideal discourse of eco-Afropolitanism. Instead, I want to show how the novel explores the notion of Afropolitanism from an environmental point of view given that, in the words of Rita Barnard, it involves "a kind of territorial micropolitics" that, while crucial to "grassroots emancipation," is "neither spatially nor temporally confined" but "multidimensional and culturally porous" (Barnard 2007, 148).

Land Matters and Afropolitan Mediation in Zakes Mda's *The Heart of Redness*

The Heart of Redness is structured on two temporal levels. This narrative form enables Mda to connect the pressures of both colonialism and neoliberalism onto the relationship of the Xhosa people with the land they inhabit, underscoring the historical links between their anti-imperial struggle in the nineteenth century and their response to the irruption of capitalist development ventures into the village of Qolorha-by-Sea, in South Africa, in the present. With this transhistorical structure, the novel examines the disagreement that exists at the heart of the community.[6] It is the portion of the plot set in the present, however, that I want to address here for it offers an interesting reflection on Afropolitanism and its relation to the human–land relations that the novel explores through its protagonist, a man named Camagu.

Camagu enters the plot very early as he contemplates in Hillbrow, Johannesburg, returning to the United States after four years of no luck trying to find a job that matches his qualifications and professional experience. Having lived for nearly thirty years in the US, where he gets his PhD in communications and subsequently works in the private sector, Camagu decides to come back to newly democratized South Africa, dramatizing with his return one of the most common and productive themes in Afropolitan literature. As Rask Knudsen and Rahbek argue, the trope of the return reveals how "the politics of any (re)connection to Africa would have to be constructed as … open to negotiation" (Rask Knudsen and Rahbek 2016, 142). It is the distance created by his protracted time abroad, I want to argue, that allows Camagu to adopt an Afropolitan stance that determines the way he renegotiates his relationship with South Africa in particular and with the whole continent more generally. As he struggles to settle in Johannesburg, Camagu realizes that there is no place for him in the new, post-apartheid society in which he is considered a virtual foreigner. His unsuccessful return, however, is quickly re-routed as he is drawn to Qolorha, a small village in the Eastern Cape, where he recuperates a sense of belonging by combining his 30-year-long experience in the capitalist democracy that dictates the tempos of the global order with which South Africa must now catch up (Camagu describes the US in rather critical terms a number of times) with an attachment to the village's local politics. The more he feels detached from the bureaucratic and urban post-apartheid South Africa, the more he feels at home in Qolorha, where his affiliative impulses become less national and, as a result, more Afropolitan.

Camagu's Afropolitan inclinations are revealed early in the novel by a mobility that is driven, in large part, by his sexual desire, which pulls him away from the unwelcoming city. After a night out drinking, Camagu ends up in a wake for a deceased Qolorha man at the top of a building. There he sees a girl by the name of NomaRussia, with whom he is instantly infatuated, and decides to chase her to Qolorha, where he loses track of her. His unsuccessful quest to find NomaRussia, however, draws him close to two other women: Xoliswa Ximiya and Qukezwa. Xoliswa Ximiya is the daughter of Bhonco (a descendant of the detractors of Nongqawuse's prophecy, or Unbelievers). A recently promoted, snobbish teacher who once spent a short time in the United States, Xoliswa has several conversations with Camagu about the need for modernization in the area. On the other hand, the daughter of Zim (a descendant of the followers of the prophecy, or Believers), Qukezwa is a young woman with great knowledge of and respect for the village's flora and fauna and with whom Camagu later has a baby. Camagu's not unproblematic desire,[7] thus, acts as the motivator of a mobility that, while it once allowed him to seek a better future abroad, brings him now to find a sense of belonging in the rural South African community, where he ends up settling down.

Camagu's connection with Qolorha quickly takes on environmental overtones. Shortly after arriving in the village, he is "filled with a searing longing for an imagined blissfulness of his youth," while he remembers "his home village up in the mountains in the distant inland parts of the country," its "fruit trees," and the "lush plants that grew in his grandfather's garden" (Mda 2000, 59). Connected to this nostalgia are other experiences of an ecological nature that draw him closer to the village, such as a series of dreams in which he becomes the river and the snake he finds in his bed, which he interprets as a visit from Majola, the totem of his amaMpondomise clan. Camagu, therefore, develops a newfound attachment with Qolorha that replaces his failed attempt to re-connect with South Africa upon return from the US. His efforts to establish "a fundamental connection to an elsewhere" (Mbembe and Nuttall 2004, 351), thus, allow him to circumvent the pressures of the structures of the State as figured by Johannesburg's hostile urban setting—where nepotism and favoritism get in the way of his finding a decent job and where his status as a quasi-foreigner is revealed by his inability to catch up with the latest professional conventions—and enter the politically open space of Qolorha—where he is only taken as a stranger insofar as he is not recognized as a local, an estimation that nevertheless becomes less apparent over time.

From this position, Camagu sets out to understand the long-lasting disagreement between Believers and Unbelievers by observing their confronted positions on virtually any matter. This disagreement crystallizes most emphatically in their opposed views with regard to whether the village should let a company build a casino and a holiday resort. The most representative instantiation of this tension occurs in the numerous *imbhizos*, or public meetings, during which they discuss, amongst other issues, the impending construction plan. It is during these *imbhizos* that Zim and Bhonco, the main voice of the local movement for the conservation of Qolorha and the leader of the village's faction in favor of allowing investors to develop the area respectively, engage in rather acrimonious discussions, often recriminating each other's positions by appealing to their ancestors' history.

Interestingly, the political alignments of Believers and Unbelievers are inverted in this part of the narrative. Whereas in the colonial era the Believers sacrifice their land in compliance with the prophecy, they argue today for the protection of their cultural and environmental legacy from the development plan. This attachment to the land and its wildlife is manifest, for instance, in Zim's cherished bond with "the gigantic fig tree" outside his home: "The wild fig tree knows all his secrets. It is his confessional. Under it he finds solace, for it is directly linked to the ancestors—all of Twin's progeny who planted it more than a hundred years ago" (37–38). On the other hand, the Unbelievers, who once spurned the prophecy, now argue with fervor that the construction plans will bring jobs and development to the village. As Xoliswa Ximiya argues in a circle of Unbelievers: "Cape Town is now becoming a celebrity paradise. Qolorha can be one too if these conservative villagers stop standing in the way of progress.... We cannot stop civilization just because some sentimental old fools want to preserve birds and trees and an outmoded way of life" (67). This inversion of political alignments signals, as Byron Caminero-Santangelo has argued, a particular effort on the part of Mda to bring "into question clearly bounded idealist categories" while encouraging "critical distance from its own romantic lapses.... The novel suggests that the local, the natural, and the indigenous must be seen as emerging and remerging from specific, messy interrelationships with their supposed opposites" (Caminero-Santangelo 2011, 296). Camagu, then, operates as a mediator between the two sides who, as neither a local nor an urban cosmopolitan, can propose an Afropolitan approach to the question of the village's development.

Camagu is not only often treated as an outsider (sometimes people even take him to be an American) but, more importantly, he also insists on placing himself as a neutral figure despite the efforts of Bhonco's and Zim's families to either recruit him or reproach him for siding with the other clan. As Mike Kissack and Michael Titlestad assert, this status "enables him to assess the traditional conflicts of the region with a certain detachment" despite the fact that "he is simultaneously incorporated into the skein of intrigue, suspicion and recrimination that defines the local politics of the area" (Kissack and Titlestad 2009, 157). Even after settling down in Qolorha and starting a fishing business that employs a handful of local women, Camagu insists on not taking sides, although he soon becomes invested in proposing an alternative development plan that protects Qolorha's against the construction prospect on the grounds that the kind of tourism it will attract will be extremely detrimental to the wellbeing of the community.

Camagu's role as a semi-assimilated, Afropolitan middle-man, however, presents certain political complications. His presence in Qolorha has indeed been criticized for contributing to the external interference in the village's inhabitants' political efforts to determine their relationship with the land. James Graham, for instance, has argued that "Mda can only attribute agency to those in certain privileged social positions," suggesting that it is only characters like Camagu himself and John Dalton, a white merchant and descendant of British colonizers, who can actually do something to preserve the political status of the Qolorha inhabitants in the face of the neoliberal pressures exerted by the developers (Graham 2009, 166). Grant Farred, further, has taken Camagu's politics to task, arguing that his ultimate objective is to pursue local consensus via the "bridging of difference... [and] the reconciliation of the newly reopened split between Believers and Unbelievers," making him the embodiment of "the voice of post-apartheid South Africa's representative, accountable democracy: the privileging of unity over dissent" (Farred 2009, 268). I agree with these assessments. Camagu's arrival in the village as an urban, liberal denizen of the world with renewed ties to Africa, his position in between the village's two factions, and his romantic notions about preserving the environment based on nostalgic memories of his childhood do interfere with the sovereignty of the locals. However, an alternative interpretation, or perhaps a complementary reading to Graham's and Farred's, can construe Camagu's interference as a way of working out the challenges derived from the new consensual order and not as the root of the village's depoliticization. In other words, Camagu's attitude might be read not as the typification of the new status quo but as a possible course of action with an eye to the future of the local environmentalism of villages like Qolorha. This would explain Camagu's avowed intention not to decide for the inhabitants of Qolorha.

In a key conversation with John Dalton, Camagu argues that the political agency of the Qolorha people over an environmental matter as important as the availability of water in the village cannot be established from the outside but must emerge from inside the community. Shortly after the creation of a project to bring water to the homes of Qolorha, the managing committee decides to stop the service because some villagers have failed to pay the maintenance fees despite the fact that, in the words of a local woman, "some of us have been paying regularly ever since communal taps were constructed"

(164). Dalton is frustrated by this situation. He is convinced that the community as a whole has failed not only him, who wanted to help them improve their living standards, but themselves, as they were incapable of overcoming their disagreement to work together. However, Camagu shows to Dalton how the problem resides in a major flaw in his plan: "You went about this whole thing the wrong way, John. The water project is failing because it was imposed on the people. No one bothered to find out their needs. . . . They should be active participants in the conception of the project, in raising funds for it, in constructing it. Then it becomes their project. Then they will look after it" (179). Whereas both want to help the villagers prosper in their own terms, Dalton seems to be bound to fall victim to his own altruistic aspirations. He has worked hard to solve the question of the communal water management, yet he is incapable of seeing how he has ultimately imposed the development project onto the locals. Camagu's attitude, on the contrary, exceeds the depoliticizing pressures of local programs like Dalton's as well as global capitalism (at one point we are told that the "big company" behind the plans "owns hotels throughout southern Africa") and the State's connivance with it (66). It is in these terms that Camagu, revealing the political and environmental inflections of his newly acquired Afropolitan affiliation to the village, seeks to re-deploy the disagreement at the core of the community.

Camagu's involvement as an insider-outsider in the village's dispute reaches a critical point when, later in the novel, Qolorha needs finally to decide whether or not to accept the developers' offer to build the casino and resort. When the developers arrive to hold a public meeting with the villagers, the company's coercive approach is hardly disguised in its executive's words. The villagers are told

> how lucky they are to be living in a new and democratic South Africa where the key word is transparency. In the bad old days such projects would be done without consulting them at all. So, in the same spirit in which the government has respected them by consulting them, they must also show respect to these important visitors, by not voicing the objections that he heard some of the villagers were having about a project of such national importance.
>
> (198–199)

Whereas the novel has presented internal disagreement as a major force that maintains Qolorha's communal cohesion, it now underscores its co-optation by the developers into a form of national treason. According to this view, resisting the entrance of neoliberal competition to exploit Qolorha's land is rejecting the government's efforts to empower the rural areas of the country of the new South Africa. It is Camagu, however, who immediately lays out the exploitative ramifications of the casino plan in a passionate objection:

You talk of all these ... wonderful things ... but for whose benefit are they? What will these villagers who are sitting here get from all these things? Will their children ride on those merry-go-rounds and roller coasters? On those cable-cars and boats? Of course not! They will not have any money to pay for these things. These things will be enjoyed by rich people who will come here and pollute *our* rivers and *our* ocean. ... It is a project of national importance only to your company and shareholders, not to these people! ... I tell you, people of Qolorha, these visitors are interested only in profits for their company. This sea will no longer belong to you. You will have to pay to use it.

(200; my italics)

In his capacity as an Afropolitan with strong local affiliations and an acute awareness of the devastating consequences of letting capital intrude the land-related disputes of the village, Camagu can appeal to both Believers and Unbelievers while exposing the motivations behind the developers' plan. The democratic spirit to which the governmental authorities and investors appeal is revealed as nothing more than a method with which the Qolorha inhabitants are estranged from their own land. Local politics are in danger of being superseded by an aggressive global strand of capitalism backed by the country's governance bodies. In this sense, the failure that James Graham sees in the novel, as it can speak "to the nation: demanding a redefinition of the terms of postcolonial, post-apartheid national development" yet "it is unwilling to speak *for* the nation in the same vein," can in fact be construed as a success (Graham 2009, 164, emphasis original). It is precisely the novel's inability to provide an intervention at the national level that unveils the incompatibility between South Africa's new democracy and Qolorha's politics. Camagu's Afropolitanism, thus, acts as a catalyst for an emancipatory environmental politics that, wedged between the realms of the local and the national, has the potential to revitalize the political agency of Qolorha's inhabitants.

Indeed, this intervention does not occlude the internal conflict that defines the village's core political foundations. After a succession of heated disputes between Believers and Unbelievers over the developments, Camagu and Dalton devise a plan to have the Qolorha land declared a national heritage site, which prevents the construction project from being carried out for the time being and allows for each of them to develop alternative plans for local development. The construction plans are called off and, in their place, Camagu creates a collectively managed backpackers' hostel that later becomes a holiday camp, whereas Dalton constructs a "cultural village," a problematic historical reenactment site in which live actors perform "traditional" life scenes that nonetheless fuels widespread disapproval, including that of Camagu himself (274). A temporary determent against the disruptive presence of unbridled capitalism, this is then far from a conclusive settlement of the ongoing disputes between Qolorha's two factions. The fact that they continue to shape the state of local politics proves this point. Thus, following Zin's death, Bhonco personifies a persisting resentment towards the cancellation of the casino and resort scheme, which is no doubt bound to give rise to further local tensions that will open up a new phase in the communal relationships of affiliation and opposition that give structure to Qolorha's polity.

The novel, however, ends on a cautionary note, warning the reader of the danger that the forces of capitalism shored up by the State might overturn the very empowerment that the villagers have gained in preventing the casino project from coming to fruition. The narrator tells us of Camagu's reflections on Qolorha's future:

> He feels fortunate that he lives in Qolorha. Those who want to preserve indigenous plants and birds have won the day there. At least for now. But for how long? The whole country is ruled by greed.... Sooner or later the powers that be may decide, in the name of the people, that it is good for the people to have a gambling complex at Qolorha-by-Sea. And the gambling complex shall come into being. And of course the powers that be or their proxies—in the form of wives, sons, daughters, and cousins—shall be given equity. And so the people shall be empowered.
>
> (277)

Camagu's apprehension, which is rooted in the new perspective that his Afropolitanism affords him, highlights the underside of the terms in which the new democratic governance has been established in South Africa. The outlook is not very auspicious, not least with regard to the villagers' relationship with their own environmental milieu, as their agency is bound to be perennially compromised, threatened by the country's embrace of global neoliberalism as a vehicle to bringing development to its most rural parts.

Whither Eco-Afropolitanism?

The Heart of Redness offers a critical reflection of human–land relationships from a historico-ecological point of view that puts into perspective the threat that modern democratic governance poses to local political organization. Camagu arguably personifies the cosmopolitan's urge to get "back in touch (as much as a modern, urbanised person can) with his roots in a pre-capitalist culture" (Vital 2005, 310). Yet his motivations are as much located in the past as they are in the future. Whereas his plans for the holiday camp seek to keep foreign investors at bay (if only temporarily), its construction is a way to resist the irruption of global capitalism in the community because it occupies the mechanisms of land use that more aggressive ventures seek to capture. Camagu's plan is ultimately a realistic response to the flows of global capital that works toward maintaining the disagreement defining the village's political culture.

Camagu's Afropolitanism, thus, seems to offer ways for Qolorha to face the pressures of global capitalism through the intermediary worlding process of his newly developed attachment to the village. The eco-Afropolitan tonalities of *The Heart of Redness*, consequently, provide an important meditation on the valences of an African ontology that disputes a unilateral understanding of local environmentalism, the State, and the economic and social forces of modernity and progress. Camagu's position between the local disagreement that energizes Qolorha's inhabitants' sovereignty and State-sponsored, corporate economic intervention opens up a space to practice an environmentalism that de-emphasizes the dictates of administrative and territorial politics in favor of a reactivation of a sense of locality intimately linked to the village's natural surroundings. Understanding Qolorha as an African space, thus, Camagu can satisfy his need to establish new nodes of affiliation upon his return from the United States while, at the same time, re-casting the community's historical tensions as a productive background against which the relationships amongst the villagers—and between them and their environment—manifest rather than a justification for such relationships to disintegrate.

Mda's novel is but one example of the kind of eco-Afropolitan literary theory I have sought to explore in this chapter. As I have shown, it has promising potential and it is a productive approach to read other Afropolitan texts. How are we to interpret, for instance, the environmental significance of the omnipresent guavas in NoViolet Bulawayo's *We Need New Names* (Bulawayo 2013) or Julius's wandering through the city and his relationship to the "bird migrations" he observes from his apartment in the opening of Teju Cole's *Open City* (Cole 2012, 3)? There are also much larger questions that I have not addressed but are of crucial importance for this theory and its future development. I want to conclude by mentioning briefly some of them. I have considered here a specific reading of eco-Afropolitanism in relationship to the political imbrications of the return to the continent and the internal dynamics of a community's relationship to the land. However, other analytical agendas are key too, such as romantic techniques of representation or the role of the pastoral in Afropolitan literature. The modes of writing that eco-Afropolitan literature may prioritize must be accounted for: what are the specific attributes of, say, "eco-Afropolitan realism" or "eco-Afropolitan utopianism"? Conceptual questions arise too. How can theories of post- and transhumanism illuminate humans' relationships with the non-human animal and vegetal worlds in texts belonging to the Afropolitan literary corpus? What do works of eco-Afropolitan women's writing look like, and what are the characteristics of queer eco-Afropolitanism? On a different register, what would be the main questions that a post-political analysis of this kind of environmental literature would raise? These are among the most important concerns that future lines of inquiry might seek to explore.

As I mentioned in the opening of this essay, the discourse of Afropolitanism is still relatively new and it is, therefore, open to a variety of theoretical explorations that will surely give rise to important critical debates. In responding to the cosmopolitan politics that currently govern globalization while offering a new lens through which to explore an African way of being in the world, Afropolitan literary theory has immense potential. An environmental approach, thus, seems to be worth exploring in much more detail and in several different directions so as to expand the boundaries of Afropolitanism and its literary expressions. Most importantly, eco-Afropolitan literature, as I have called it, provides a valuable framework to investigate its worlding valences and can, consequently, make an important contribution to the main debates in the discipline of world literary studies.

Acknowledgments

The author would like to thank Jennifer Wenzel and Robert Marzec for their comments on a much earlier draft that presented a radically different argument.

Notes

1. See Chielozona Eze (2014) for a discussion of Afropolitanism in the context of cosmopolitan theory.
2. See, for instance, Anthony Vital's "Toward an African Ecocriticism: Postcolonialism, Ecology and *Life & Times of Michael K*."
3. See Shiva.
4. For an exploration of this question, see Guha and Martinez-Alier.
5. See, among others, Santana, Dabiri, and Tveit.
6. The historical part of the narrative, which focuses on Nongqawuse's 1856–1857 cattle-killing prophecy, opens up important questions about the Xhosa people's sovereignty and their anti-colonial struggle, providing an important parallel with the context of present-day, post-apartheid South Africa. As Jennifer Wenzel has argued, "the Xhosa cattle killing and its afterlives" play a crucial part "in imagining national communities and transnational networks of affiliation" (Wenzel 2009, 3). For a comparative study of the past and present plot lines, see Oliveira Gonçalves Pires.
7. As Meg Samuelson points out, the women "enter the plot as love interests of Camagu," and while the latter "becomes the spokesman for Mda's strongly worded critique of the 'new' South Africa," the novel's critique rests on an "essentialised gender politics" (Samuelson 2009, 237).

Works cited

Barnard, Rita, *Apartheid and Beyond: South African Writers and the Politics of Place*. Oxford: Oxford University Press, 2007.

Bulawayo, NoViolet, *We Need New Names*. New York: Little Brown, 2013.

Calhoun, Craig, "A Cosmopolitanism of Connections," in Bruce Robbins and Paulo Lemos Horta (eds), *Cosmopolitanisms*. New York: New York University Press, 2017: 189–200.

Caminero-Santangelo, Byron, "In Place: Tourism, Cosmopolitanism, and Zakes Mda's *The Heart of Redness*," in Elizabeth DeLoughrey and George B. Handley (eds), *Postcolonial Ecologies: Literatures of the Environment*. Oxford: Oxford University Press, 2011: 291–302.

Caminero-Santangelo, Byron and Garth Myers, "Introduction," in Byron Caminero-Santangelo and Garth Myers (eds), *Environment at the Margins: Literary and Environmental Studies in Africa*. Athens: Ohio University Press, 2011.

Casanova, Pascale, *The World Republic of Letters*, trans. M. B. DeBevoise. Cambridge: Harvard University Press, 2004.

Cheah, Pheng, *What is a World? On Postcolonial Literature as World Literature*. Durham: Duke University Press, 2016.

Cole, Teju, *Open City*. New York: Random House, 2012.

Comaroff, Jean, "The End of History, Again? Pursuing the Past in the Postcolony," in Ania Loomba et al. (eds), *Postcolonial Studies and Beyond*. Durham: Duke University Press, 2005: 125–144.

Dabiri, Emma, "Why I am (Still) Not an Afropolitan," *Journal of African Cultural Studies* 28.1 (2016): 104–108

Eze, Chielozona, "Rethinking African Culture and Identity: The Afropolitan Model," *Journal of African Cultural Studies* 26.2 (2014): 234–247.

Eze, Chielozona, "We, Afropolitans," *Journal of African Cultural Studies* 28.1 (2016): 114–119.

Farred, Grant, "A Politics of Doubt," in David Bell and J. U. Jacobs (eds), *Ways of Writing. Critical Essays on Zakes Mda*. Scottsville: University of KwaZulu-Natal Press, 2009: 255–275.

Gikandi, Simon, "Foreword: On Afropolitanism," in Jennifer Wawrzinek and J. K. S. Makokha (eds.), *Negotiating Afropolitanism: Essays on Borders and Spaces in Contemporary African Literature and Folklore*. Amsterdam: Rodopi, 2011: 9–11.

Graham, James, *Land and Nationalism in Fictions of Southern Africa*. New York: Routledge, 2009.

Guha, Ramachandra and Joan Martinez-Alier, *Varieties of Environmentalism: Essays North and South*. London: Earthscan, 1997.

Heise, Ursula K., *Sense of Place and Sense of Planet: The Environmental Imagination of the Global*. Oxford: Oxford University Press, 2008.

Kissack, Mike and Michael Titlestad, "Invidious Interpreters: The Post-Colonial Intellectual in *The Heart of Redness*," in David Bell and J. U. Jacobs (eds), *Ways of Writing. Critical Essays on Zakes Mda*. Scottsville: University of KwaZulu-Natal Press, 2009: 149–168.

Mbembe, Achille, "Afropolitanism," trans. Laurent Chauvet, in Njami Simon (ed.), *Africa Remix: Contemporary Art of a Continent*. Johannesburg: Jacana Media, 2007: 26–30.

Mbembe, Achille and Sarah Nuttall, "Writing the World from an African Metropolis," *Public Culture* 16.3 (2004): 347–372.

Mda, Zakes, *The Heart of Redness*. New York: Picador, 2000.

Mouffe, Chantal, *On the Political*. London: Routledge, 2005.

Oliveira Gonçalves Pires, Ana Luisa, "From Neglected History to Tourist Attraction: Reordering the Past in Zakes Mda's *The Heart of Redness*," *Ariel: A Review of International English Literature* 44.1 (2013): 127–151.

Rask Knudsen, Eva and Ulla Rahbek, *In Search of the Afropolitan: Encounters, Conversations, and Contemporary Diasporic African Literature*. London: Rowman & Littlefield, 2016.

Samuelson, Meg, "Nongqawuse, National Time and (Female) Authorship in *The Heart of Redness*," in David Bell and J. U. Jacobs (eds), *Ways of Writing. Critical Essays on Zakes Mda*. Scottsville: University of KwaZulu-Natal Press, 2009: 229–253.

Santana, Stephanie Bosch, "Exorcising Afropolitanism: Binyavanga Wainaina Explains Why 'I Am a Pan-Africanist, Not an Afropolitan' at ASAUK 2012." *Africa in Words*. February 8, 2013. http://africainwords.com/2013/02/08/exorcizing-afropolitanism-binyavanga-wainaina-explains-why-i-am-a-pan-africanist-not-an-afropolitan-at-asauk-2012. Accessed November 22, 2017.

Selasi, Taiye, "Bye-Bye Babar." *The LIP Magazine*. March 3, 2005. http://thelip.robertsharp.co.uk/?p=76. Accessed November 30, 2017.

Shiva, Vandana, *Earth Democracy: Justice, Sustainability, and Peace*. Cambridge: South End Press, 2005.

Tveit, Marta, "The Afropolitan Must Go." *Africa is a Country*. November 28, 2013. http://africasacountry.com/2013/11/the-afropolitan-must-go. Accessed December 2, 2017.

Vital, Anthony, "Situating Ecology in Recent South African Fiction: J. M. Coetzee's *The Lives of Animals* and Zakes Mda's *The Heart of Redness*," *Journal of Southern African Studies* 31.2 (2005): 297–313.

Vital, Anthony, "Toward an African Ecocriticism: Postcolonialism, Ecology and *Life & Times of Michael K*," *Research in African Literatures* 39.1 (2008): 87–106.

Wenzel, Jennifer, *Bulletproof: Afterlives of Anticolonial Prophecy in South Africa and Beyond*. Chicago: University of Chicago Press, 2009.

7

How Afropolitanism Unworlds the African World

Amatoritsero Ede

Introduction: Afropolitanism in the New World

It is now common knowledge that modern African literature's founding moment was a reaction to colonialism; it was a conversation with, a response and a "writing back" to, Empire (Griffiths et. al., 1989; Msiska, 2016). After official decolonization and flag independence, this body of writing then entered a Commonwealth phase as a precursor to becoming world literature. In cultural material terms the Western publishing industry, largely British Heinemann Educational Publishers—and others like UK's Three Crown Press—was instrumental to that diffusion through its African Writers' Series (Hill 1971, Lizarribar 1998, Currey 2003, Clarke 2003, Ibironke 2008). It is noteworthy that, in this discussion, oral literature and the "manuscript" stages of African verbal arts have been deliberately backgrounded to focus on the natural progression of literacy from reading to writing. This is especially significant for a literary corpus that is still relatively very recent. Moreover, literature in this chapter denotes writing in a European language—English in this instance. Moreover, it refers to only creative writing. This is in consonance with that understanding of literature as 'imaginative' writing, a notion of the literary which African and other writing inherited from the Romantic literary period in England (Eagleton 1983:16).

This chapter establishes a continuity between the global consecration of foundational African literature and the framing and possibility of its derivative Afropolitan writing as world literature. Apart from literary history, I pay attention to the cosmopolitanism evoked in the idea of the

Afropolitan, to complex identity formations, to commodity fetishism, to changing trends in Western academic criticism, as well as to material conditions of literary production and reception and the question of audience (Adesokan 2012, Julien 2006), in locating how Afropolitan writing becomes world literature. However, I also submit that contemporary Afropolitanism's futuristic (Gikandi 2011) "Post-Colonial," as distinct from postcolonial, gaze (Shohat 1992, McClintock 1992) is problematic because it ideologically distances any Afropolitan body of work away from Africa's global geopolitical, social and economic history (Parry 1999).

For example, new African writing considered to be Afropolitan does not engage itself with the historical effects of colonialism on the continent. It is in this negative sense Post-Colonial or "Past-Colonial." The resulting generic postcolonialism performs a scission between the past and the present, resulting in "an astonishing sense of weightlessness with regard to the gravity of history" (Said 1993: 366–367). A close reading of such Afropolitan-inclined works as *We Need New Names* (Bulawayo 2013)), *Open City* (Cole 2011) or *Ghana Must Go* (2013) preponderantly engages themes of migration, cosmopolitanism, and diasporization as the horizon to which characterisation tends. While plot, theme, and narration might engage the existential struggles of characters in a cultural materialist manner, the larger colonialist ontology behind these are never focalized; they are eclipsed in favor of an immediate, text-bound, rather than an historical verisimilitude.

To highlight the ideological disconnection between Afropolitan aesthetics and a heretofore universal African literary ethics, I juxtapose the idea of the Afropolitan with the concept of the Afropean in Francophone African literary scholarship. I conclude that it is because of an Afropolitan literary futurism—which corrupts the ontological "worlding" potential of Afropolitan writing as world literature due to a lack of an ideological commitment to the African continent—that the existential query then arises, "what is a world"? (Cheah 2016). That is the question this chapter concludes with in relation to Africa's place inside and outside of globalization.

In other words, I apprehend the "world" in "world literature" in two ways. One sense is that of the usual literal understanding of it as "all literary works that circulate beyond their culture of origin, either in translations or in their original languages" (Damrosch 2003: 4). The other sense is that of an existential permutation of the literal one and begs the questions—what "ontological worlding," that is, what world-making or positive ideological impact—does the global circulation or "literary worlding" of the Afropolitan text have? Does such a text change the subject's perception of the objective world or impact the history of ideas on the continent and in the African and Black Diaspora at all or in any significant way? These are questions central to this chapter's consideration of Afropolitanism itself as an idea.

Perhaps it is useful to briefly consider why the Afropolitan is implicated in the burden of a traumatic African past for which he or she is not directly responsible. The distant history of slavery and a relatively immediate colonialism both indirectly and directly resulted in an African textual contestation of Euro-modernity in novelistic and essayistic-critical forms. Present day continental Africans and those in the old and new African diasporas of the Euro-Americas are implicated, willy-nilly, in that history. This is because it has had a great impact on, and continues to shape, their present. Repressed pasts return into the present as slippages of global and local economic, social, cultural, and political domination of Africa and its diasporas. This is immediately tangible in the form of a proliferation of right-wing parties in the EU or an anti-Black racism in the metropolis—so much so that there is, for example, a renewed civil rights struggle in contemporary USA referred to as the Black Lives Matter Movement (Sterling 2015). In the case of Africa's immediate colonial history Leela Ghandi has this to say:

> Postcolonial nation states are often deluded and unsuccessful in their attempts to disown the burdens of their colonial inheritance. The mere repression of colonial memories is never, in itself, tantamount to a surpassing of or emancipation from the uncomfortable realties of the colonial encounter.
>
> (1998: 4)

The neurotic repression of the past referred to above is discernible in the Afropolitan or Afropean writer. The writer, scholar, or thinker, as a moulder of public thought and social reality, would be irresponsible to refuse to engage such a past. This is why Chinua Achebe insists that an African writer (and by extension the Afropolitan or Afropean) cannot afford the indulgence of art-for-art's sake unlike his British or American counterpart with a radically different past (1975:19). Otherwise, the result will be a perpetuation of that crisis of consciousness which has informed African literature from its inception (Onoge 1974) and now invades Afropolitan writing. That crisis of consciousness, it can be argued, is at the root of the double-consciousness, which overdetermines the identity crisis of Afropolitan or Afropean subjectivity.

Before I proceed, there is a need to delimit the range of the discussion here. I reiterate that the term *world literature* as applied to Afropolitan writing vis-à-vis other world literatures is not understood in a hierarchical or comparative literature framework. It merely signifies the traveling text as a cultural object dis-embedded from its initial site of literary production and bridging local and global readerships. Or put differently, the emphasis in this chapter is about how Afropolitan writing becomes world literature in largely "world-making" terms. Otherwise, any kind of juxtaposing will be in relationship to how contemporary Afropolitan writing compares in ideological worlding terms to its precursor in the Black Atlantic. In short, the objective is not to provide proof that Afropolitan literature is world literature because it obviously now is—as witnessed by the recent wealth of academic and popular engagement of the topic. Since 2005 when Taiye Selasi first deployed the neologism, "Afropolitan," in her online article in the *Lip* magazine, there has been an explosion in popular discussions and academic criticism of the phenomenon. This has been accompanied and exacerbated by an increasing production of celebrated novels which demonstrate and give credence to the subjectivity and consciousness referenced by the term.

An important corollary to the major world-making concern above is this chapter's thesis that any contemporary Afropolitan literary worlding process, resulting from transnational publishing and print capitalism as it does, is shadowed by the cultural producer's conscious or unconscious ideological unworlding of the African world due, I argue, to an apolitical, market-driven self-positioning within the field of cultural production. I proceed by positing and historicizing the original Afropolitan figure as the enslaved or formerly enslaved Black New World writer, intellectual, artist, citizen and—by dint of her or his erudition and cosmopolitan 'worldliness' —renaissance woman or man. This is, for example, the freedman or emancipated slave in Europe and the Americas, who foreshadowed his or her contemporary incarnation—the twenty-first century Afropolitan writer of a relatively more recent African and Black diaspora and with a more immediate continental genealogy. That proposition will be much clearer presently.

After Europe imagined Africa in the medieval period as a place of fantasy and desire (Hochschild 1998:1), the latter's unwilling insertion into modernity began in 1441 with slave raids on the African coast by Portuguese sailors, Antão Gonçalves and Nuno Tristão.[1] They captured twelve free African men in Cabo Branco, modern Mauritania, and took them to Portugal as chattel slaves. Another Portuguese, a tax collector called Lançarote de Freitas, formed a company in Lagos, a city in Portugal, in 1444. His goal, in the seminal euphemistic language for European invasion of Africa was to "trade"—in this instance again with coastal Mauritania. He initiated this "trade" by, again, kidnapping 235 Africans on August 8 the same year and bringing them to Lagos in Portugal. It is presumable that this initial European vigilantism on the African coast then created and fueled the oxymoron, "slave trade," which seized the European imagination and exacerbated original medieval fantasies about the continent.

The subterfuge of "trade" was legitimized when a sitting Pope, Nicholas V, decreed through two papal Bulls—the *Dum Divas* on June 18, 1452 and the *Romanus pontifex* on January 8, 1454—the enabling of Portuguese enslavement of "non-Christians," on the one hand, and the conferring of a "trade" monopoly with Africa to the Portuguese, on the other. However, that "native Africa" that Europe desired in the language of trade was a dehumanized and an enslaved non-partner initially oblivious of any trade agreements, or of the fact that it was being traded with. How does one go into a trade agreement with, or as, a "commodity"? And long after slavery was "officially" abolished (in 1807 in the UK and 1863 in the USA) or rather when it ended due to a complex of political and economic forces as well as to a changing social order and mode of production (Fogel and Engerman 1974), the rhetoric of "trade" intensified and was a subterfuge for the colonial desire and actual physical colonialism that succeeded slavery.

The historic conspiracy between capitalism—in so far as "trading" in slaves was for the purpose of generating capital (Williams 1944)—and Christianity was consolidated by the church's embrace of a "Hamitic principle" (Goldenberg 2003), which declared African people to be the descendants of the cursed biblical Ham. That pervasive, dehumanizing, Judeo-Christian medieval European sentiment "authorized" by Papal Bulls (Hood 1994) prefigured the Ur-Afropolitan as a cosmopolitan personage in the New World metropolis, an article of the "trade" in "slave trade," who was initially spirited across the Trans-Atlantic Ocean in the belly of the slave ship.

It must be noted that an "Out of Africa" thesis by Paleoanthropologists such as Mary Leakey and Louis Leakey (see Johanson et. al. 1990), Egyptologists (Obenga 2004), Historians (Bernal 1987 Vol. 1–3; Diop 1974), Anthropological Geneticists (Cheng[2] et al. 2005), and Black Historians (Sertima 1994; Rashidi 1992) could infinitely defer the beginning of an Afropolitan worldliness. However, the Trans-Atlantic slave trade was the first recorded massive movement of people out of Africa antecedent to the modern period. Moreover, it is significant that this particular migration was accompanied by prodigious literary production. The kind of cosmopolitanism or worldliness in question at the intersection of world literature is one that is enlarged by Black Atlantic Letters, of which there was a proliferation during slavery as exemplified in the Slave Narrative, in moral criticism, in private letters or in Philosophical and legal disquisition.[3]

The significance of the history of African deracination above is that the forced and violent displacement of that Ur-Afropolitan figure from the continent to the New World and the ensuing dispersal across the Northern Hemisphere is symbolic of an "unworlding" of the Black or African world. It is noteworthy that in this chapter, the qualifiers, "Black" and "African" will be deployed interchangeably as synonyms due to their continuous and very much intertwined historical identities. The one emphasizes an initial six-centuries-old New World diasporization beginning in 1441 and, the other, an unbroken continental presence or a more recent and unforced emigration, of which today's Afropolitans an Afropeans are a product.

It might now be apparent that I will be deploying the term "unworlding," and, by extension, its corollary "worlding," in two respective senses in turn—one material and, the other, symbolic. That is this chapter's primary understanding of them. In these arguments a worlding is any obviously positive historical, organic, that is, material denaturing or alteration process, which progressively changes the environment, and thereby, physical reality and the social life-world in a slow but drastic and permanent manner. A similar material process that is nevertheless negative in its physical and environmental effects constitute an "unworlding." Such a denaturing or alteration process through ideological, aesthetic, or means other than the organic and material, which affects subjectivities and their perception of objective reality in a permanent fashion, is a measure of a symbolic worlding or unworlding respectively, depending on whether the effect is positive or negative.

In Africa's *Longue durée* both a material and symbolic unworlding is remarkable in the historical deterritorialization of bodies and objects involved in slavery and colonialism, on the one hand, and in the psychic alienation and temporal unyoking of Africa from its original existential trajectory, on the other. In my usage these phenomena are also connoted in the contemporary results of modern African history: in a material unworlding sense, continental geographical fragmentation, dislocation, and dispersal of peoples as well as a broad and current economic over-dependency on the West—and more recently on China; and in a symbolic unworlding sense, an internalized alienation in the modern African subject. He or she is, for example, Christianized or Islamized to the detriment of original spiritualties and generally de-cultured—it can be argued—in certain important areas of psychic and material life.

It is possible to consider especially Islam (or even Christianity) as having been long domesticated in Africa. Nevertheless, both religions were, and still are, conquering, disruptive, and domineering forces—and particularly so when juxtaposed with traditional African religions which they have violently demonized and repressed. This, of course, is a purview beyond the fact that cultures are, indeed, never in isolation nor are they hermetically sealed away from each other (Friedman 1997, 15). The contention is that it is only in instances of a super-ordination of one culture over and above another one, which subsequently becomes (therefore) alienated from itself, that such excesses of a cultural encounter become remarkably negative and insidious in its effect on self-constitution, resulting in an unworlding of the subject and host world. It is due to the alienating effect of modern African history that this chapter's immediate consideration of Afropolitan literature is in relation to its (im)possibilities as an agent of self-recovery and continental re-worlding. In other words, I consider whether Afropolitanism possesses symbolic worlding effect in terms of its ideological and aesthetic appeals.

The hallmark of contemporary Afropolitanism in the metropolis is that it enables social and class mobility through the human agency accruing from the symbolic capital of the Afropolitan writer's work (Ede 2016). This is, indeed, a worlding event even if it is on a personal, apolitical and individualized rather than a universal level. However, there is a larger historical sense in which it can be suggested that the freedman or emancipated slave was the original Afropolitan—in terms, not only of those personages' worldliness or cosmopolitanism but—especially due to the universal rather than personal, humanizing force of their creativity. I refer to such cosmopolitan New World writers (Potkay and Burr 1995) in the Black Atlantic like Oluadah Equiano (1745–1797), Ignatius Sanchos (1729–1780), Quobna Otobah Cugoano (c. 1775), Phyllis Wheatley (1753–1784), Anton Wilhelm Amo (1703–c.1759), James Africanus Bearle Horton (1835–1883), James Weldon Johnson (1871–1938), Edward Blyden (1832–1912), Joseph Ephraim Casely-Hayford (1866–1930), Adelaide Casely-Hayford (1868–1960) or Samuel Johnson[4] (1846–1901).

The works of the above-mentioned Black Atlantic writers and artists of the eighteenth century (Gates Jr. and Andrews 1998) was far-reaching and universal in their politically liberating and humanizing effect across the Black and, subsequently, African world. Slave narratives and, eventually, other artistic forms such as Jazz, created a Black human agency through what I refer to as an aesthetic abolitionism (July 1968: 35).

There is a clear and poignant contemporary example of the representational force of human agency vis-à-vis Blackness conveyed through the very recent American film, *Black Panther*, which re-worlds the African or Black subject and world positively as differentiated from a historically demonizing and static or progressively negative perennial media representation in most publics around the globe (Kanneh 1998, 31). Irrespective of any representational short-comings in the Black Panther film—its cinematic over-compression of space, for example—what is crucial here is the fact of its desperate longing for an African Utopia.

The urgency and upsurge of that humanizing aesthetic tradition and counter Euro-modern symbolic Black worlding, which began with Black Atlantic Slave narratives in the eighteenth century—and was long preceded by the material worlding of slave rebellions in previous epochs—enabled twentieth century Black internationalism (Edwards 2001; Erbune and Braddock 2005). This was an overarching cultural mass movement along and across the original Transatlantic slave routes but in a reverse direction—from the Black Atlantic into Africa in this instance. In other words, that umbrella movement localized itself in the Western hemispheric nexus of France, America, the Caribbean, and Britain, with the city of Paris as its confluence, and with its influence reaching into the continent and engendering a liberating politics. Black Internationalism's Black micro-politics and cultural network flowed into Africa and ignited the black consciousness movement (Fatton 1986) and anti-colonial agitation, both of which re-worlded Africa in their material and symbolic aspects, with the symbolic informing a foundational decolonizing, politically conscious, first-generation African writing.

This meant that the triangular trade came full-circle with a triangular repossession—at least of physical land (through flag independence), of body to a large extent, and of mind (but in a fragmented, ambivalent manner). With Paris as the cultural capital of the Western world in the nineteenth century (Benjamin 1968), it was also naturally the cultural capital of the Black Diaspora in the twentieth due to the presence of a large congregation of the old Black Diaspora with new world linkages and new ones made up of the colonized drawn massively by educational and other assimilationist attractions of the French "mother" country. Hence the expression in Francophone African studies, "Black Paris," (Jules-Rosette 1993) announces that historic European city as a centripetal locus for early twentieth century Black Atlantic and African counter-cultural movements like Negritude (Irele 1965a, 1965b), the Harlem Renaissance (Huggins 1975), and Indigeneity and Negrismo (Jahn 1968).

Premised on the assertion above that Afropolitanism began in an eighteenth century New World, proliferating within early twentieth century Black Internationalism and that it is not just a completely new phenomenon, an overview of the prevailing contemporary popular and theoretical understanding of Afropolitanism as praxis and lived experience is pertinent. From the moment of what I will like to refer to as a "resurgence" of an Afropolitan consciousness through that phenomenon's annunciation with Taiye Selasi's 2005 online article, "Bye-Bye Babar," and Achille Mbembe ([2006] 2007; 2010) as well as Simon Gikandi's (2011) theoretical deepening and reconfiguration of that rather journalistic beginning, Afropolitanism as a form of self-consciousness has been presented as if it were a totally new experience. Nevertheless, the question of subjectivity that is central to every single popular interpretation or scholarly disquisition on Afropolitanism all insinuate a very basic human condition—movement and migration, consequent upon which the subject's self-consciousness about, and experience of, foreignness results in an identity politics. That idea of movement is discernible in the sub-text of, for example, the very important intervention on the topic in a special issue of the *Journal of African Cultural Studies* (28.1, 2016) or in Jennifer Wawrzinek—and J.K.S. Makokha-edited *Negotiating Afropolitanism* (2011), directly in Simon Gikandi's introduction to the latter volume and very clearly in Mbembe's seminal theoretical contribution.

Movement involves endless human migration and mixing, diasporization, alienation and dislocation to varying degrees across human history. Mbembe mirrors that condition with the expression, "worlds in movement" ([2006] 2007: 26). He is specifically discussing Euro-Asian movement into Africa over centuries and the question of the ambivalence and instability of African settlers' cultural self-identity—this is an aspect of a modern continental Afropolitanism that still needs much future discussion. The kind of movement relevant to this reflection is that one which led to Africa's first major and modern Diaspora. It is the result of a continentally outward—and not the inward-bound movement simultaneously emphasized in the 2007 English translation, "Afropolitanism," of Mbembe's 2006 essay. An invariably self-willed or colonial-capitalist, invading or conquering, Africa-bound migration is still benign in juxtaposition with the epic trauma of the New World deracination that is in question.

Deracination to a transatlantic environment presupposes the effects of migration enumerated above but, more positively, a historically concomitant Pan-Africanism that should be central to the Afropolitan experience rather than the embracing of routes without a commitment to roots that is one of the signatures of contemporary Afropolitanism. Were it not for its elitism, and its staunchly ahistorical mood, Afropolitanism would wholeheartedly embrace it if only because Pan-Africanism "is a movement predicated on the construction of blackness and African-ness that presupposes a commonality in suffering faced by all Black peoples due to slavery, racial discrimination, colonial exploitation, and the movements for decolonization, which in turn, allows for a common form of identification that nullifies geographic, ethnic, social, cultural, and class differences" (Sterling 2015: 129).

In view of the violent removal involved in slavery, the "movement" in Mbembe's "worlds in movement" when applied to an African deracination beginning in 1441 becomes tantamount to an "unworlding" of the African world, which is defined above as a forced deterritorialization of bodies and objects. It is also in the same sense of their materiality that New World slave rebellions and, African material and symbolic anti-colonial activities respectively, would constitute historical efforts at a material or symbolic worlding.

From the foregoing, Africa's first modern Diaspora consisted of the slave in the New World. This translates into the fact that a massive movement of black peoples across the Atlantic Ocean created the first African cosmopolitans in modern times. And especially after abolition and emancipation these cosmopolitans became Ur-Afropolitans due, not just to their African self-identification, but—more importantly—to an enduring Pan-African sensibility reflected in eighteenth and nineteenth century Black Atlantic metropolitan letters. These writers made sure to announce their Africanness as paratexts in the prelims or in the titling, of their works. Oluadah Equaino's attestation is bold in the titling of his autobiography as *The Interesting Narrative of the Life of Olaudah Equiano, or Gustavus Vassa, the African* (1789). Other examples are *Thoughts and Sentiments on the Evil and Wicked Traffic of the Slavery and Commerce of the Human Species, humbly submitted to the inhabitants of Great-Britain by Ottobah* Cugoano, *a native of Africa* (1787), *Letters of the Late Ignatius Sancho: An African, to which are Prefixed, Memoirs of his Life*, (1782). In all these writings there is an affirmation of the authors' "Africanness."

That is an historical contradiction in relation to the contemporary Afropolitan who is quick to apologize, as it were, for his or her Africanness and declare fervently that "I am not an African Writer!" (Adesokan 2012)—irrespective of high-sounding excuses for such declarations. In equal weight to the above subjective African self-identification, Black Atlantic Ur-Afropolitan Pan-Africanism also objectively pervades the spirit and thematic concern of the slave narrative—that of the equality of the African as human being and a contestation of an ironic anti-enlightenment, anti-rationalist institution of slavery.

Afropolitan Writing as World literature?

The significance of the above arguments in relationship to Afropolitan writing as world literature is that Afropolitanism in the New World possessed a nascent Pan-Africanist consciousness while contemporary Afropolitanism is not necessarily Pan-Africanist, if not totally against the idea. That detachment is only further underscored if, in different contexts, Biyanvanga Wainaina, Chimamanda Adichie (Santana 2016:120–121), and Yewande Omotosho (Fasselt 2014) reject the Afropolitan interpellation. They eschew the identity politics that has become part of the new Western consecrating rubric for contemporary African writing.

New writers have instinctively internalized the narrative expectation of Western literary establishments and produce corresponding work. This could be, on the one hand, in the mode of a "strategic exoticism" (Huggan 2001: 32). Graham Huggan (2001) explains it as "the means by which postcolonial writers/thinkers, working from within exoticist [Western] codes of representation, either manage to subvert those codes ... or succeed in redeploying them for the purposes of uncovering differential relations of power" (32). On the other hand, it could be in the semblance of a strategic exoticism steeped in narratives of migration, diasporization, cosmopolitanism, estrangement, dislocation, and alienation typical of most Afropolitan fiction.

Pan-Africanism has a significance for the ability of either Ur-Afropolitan writing or its contemporary variation to world the Black and African world. I referred above to New World's Pan-Africanism as "nascent" because it predated the organized and formal Pan-Africanism of the mid-nineteenth to early and late-twentieth centuries, which united Black Atlantic (including African-American, Caribbean, Black British) and continental African intellectuals, politicians as well as anti-colonial activists and visionaries within the Black cultural movements discussed previously, with Paris as their "cultural capital" in the twentieth century. A nascent New World Pan-Africanism is what became a highly organized, visible, centralized and documented variation with a clear cultural mandate in other eras.

In foregrounding the worlding possibilities of an erstwhile Pan-Africanist-inflected writing—without necessarily prescribing it as a formula for the present—the significance of the descriptive, "world literature" in relationship to contemporary Afropolitanism will then be African writing that ideologically signifies a positive material, existential, or symbolic re/worlding of the world it encounters towards Black agency. Such writing's reconstructive and rehabilitative effect would reconfigure the subject's consciousness and apprehension of things, thereby reducing the alienating effect of history, re-ordering a normalized perception of objective reality and lead to a revolution in ideas and a general socio-political, cultural and, in indirect relation, economic, transformation.

My argument is that contemporary alienated Afropolitan writing does not reflect any potential for that worlding possibility described immediately above. However, New World Afropolitan writing achieved it and is in this sense a "world literature"—a literature that positively re/worlds the world it encounters. It is equally a world literature in the sense of its literary-historical provenance—wide-spread, consecration, circulation, dissemination, and expansive readership in the Atlantic world, all these emphasised by its endurance as celebrated slave narrative text in contemporary times. New Afropolitanism is synonymous with world literature not in the sense of a symbolic worlding but only in the sense of a very recent twenty-first century literary circulation.

Moreover, as proof of its remarkable worlding efficacy and the universality of its humanizing Black agency, Black Atlantic Writing contributed in large part to a radical New World social contract. It aided the abolition of slavery and, in historical succession via Black internationalism, distantly ushered in a decolonial era in Africa. In a manner of speaking then, decolonization, arguably, has its provenance in New World aesthetic abolitionism. It is an irony of history that aesthetic abolitionism was largely responsible for, and enabled, in the *Longue durée*, the political freedoms and ease of access to the cultural capital, and in effect also the symbolic capital, now enjoyed by an ideologically uncommitted contemporary Afropolitan; freedoms which slaves won with great personal sacrifice:

> Education for slaves was generally proscribed and after the slave rebellions of the 1820s and 1830s, especially Nat Turner's rebellion in 1831, most of the Southern states passed codes explicitly prohibiting the teaching of reading and writing to slaves. Nat Turner was literate and the connection between reading and writing and rebellion was well recognized.
>
> LIVINGSTON 1976: 247

The material worlding suggested in the slave's physical agitation, rebellions and struggle to acquire an ability to read and write was a prerequisite for transitioning to a symbolic worlding through aesthetic form. In this instance that form was writing and, the eventual literary consecration that imbued the freed slave with human agency and destroyed the rationalist fallacy that the slave could neither think nor had cognition. This was one of the pro-slavery arguments during the abolitionist debate of the 1800s as it is evident in the literature.

For example, in the introduction to a special issue of *Critical Enquiry* on the interweaving between racial (in)equality and writing, Henry Louis Gate Jr. eloquently recounts the politics of literacy and human agency in the Black Atlantic. He underscores this by recalling the very public examination of an adolescent Phyllis Wheatley (1753–1784), whose first collection of poetry, *Poems on Various Subjects, Religious and Moral* (1773), was met with incredulity by the white "metropolitan public" (Ede 2016:), whose leading political and intellectual representatives now interviewed the 18-year-old in a town hall towards the purpose of ascertaining that she was not a literary fraud and, more importantly, that a slave could indeed possess the specialized rational skills and high faculty required for creative writing. Gates' explanation for a Western valorization of reason in relationship to being human or less—that is, being a "slave," is worth quoting at some length:

> Why was the creative writing of the African of such importance to the eighteenth century's debate over slavery? I can briefly outline one thesis: after Rene Descartes, reason was privileged, or valorized, above all other human characteristics. Writing, especially after the printing press became so widespread, was taken to be the visible sign of reason. Blacks were reasonable, and hence men, if-and only if-they demonstrated mastery of the arts and sciences, the eighteenth century's formula for writing. So, while the Enlightenment is characterized by its foundation on man's ability to reason, it simultaneously used the absence and presence of reason to delimit and circumscribe the very humanity of the cultures and people of color which Europeans had been discovering since the Renaissance.
>
> (1985: 8)

The public assessment of Phillis Wheatley was, in a manner of speaking, a literary competition involving only one candidate—herself as representative of Blackness. After passing her "test," the metropolitan, agency-inducing consecration and literary prestige which accrued to Wheatley is part of what makes her an Ur-Afropolitan alongside new Afropolitan writers such as Taiye Selasi, Teju Cole, Kofi Effoui or Jean Luc Raharimanana.

I have argued elsewhere that "consecration is a precondition for the effectiveness of agency" (Ede 2016). Wheatley was imbued with consecration after her "examination" and possessed agency, in the sense of Michael E. Bratman's, idea of "individual autonomy, self-governance and agential authority" (2007: 4). As a matter of course, that individual autonomy for a slave or freed man or woman was inversely proportional to the level of their freedom; however, possessing literary consecration and its accrued symbolic capital gave leverage to the slave's political project of freedom and self-determination in a progressive manner as is now historically evident. That humanizing progression is what WEB Dubois most likely referenced in his 1903 essay where he insists, in a direct and related African-American context, that the advancement of the "race" would depend on a "talented tenth" of educated Black people. This is a small population who would be imbued with the necessary cultural capital that would translate into its cognate symbolic capital, with the combined effect being the accruing of agency and a positive material and symbolic worlding of the Black world.

The New World "talented tenth"—in retrospect—Wheatley as well as other New World writers such as the aforementioned Equiano or Ignatius Sanchos, Quobna Otobah Cugoano or Anton Wilhelm Amo all wrote works that possessed illumination and were consecrated purveyors of human agency in the same sense in which contemporary Afropolitans' works possesses these qualities too. Robert July (1968) has referred to New World writers as the "Eighteenth-century forerunners" (35) of African literature and intellection. As I have maintained here, these New World writers are also the forerunners of the contemporary Afropolitan writer. However, what differentiates the Ur-Afropolitan from the contemporary Afropolitan is that the former's literary work has an historically poignant worlding effect on the Black or African world while the latter's writings constitute a symbolic unworlding in its ideological rejection of roots and a Pan-Africanist lack—even when the writers do personally embrace, and novelize, routes. For new Afropolitanism, roots exist in the form of a self-distancing affiliation. A brief example will suffice in order keep within the limited scope of this chapter.

The Afropolitan protagonist of Teju Cole's *Open City*, Julius—psychiatrist, intellectual, and Renaissance man—embodies that self-distancing affiliation. Even though he accepts his African worldliness and acknowledges other Africans or Blacks in his peregrinations across New York city, that affirmation is couched in a demonstrated cynicism and superiority complex. So obvious it is to the young African-American street he encounters that it mugs him in his Afropolitan superciliousness, even though that street otherwise still ironically considers him a "brother." "Somehow it was clear that they did not intend to kill me. There was an ease to their violence [. . .]. I was being beaten, but it was not severe, certainly not as severe as it could be if they were truly angry" (212–213).

When Julius encounters Kenneth, a Black immigrant from the island of Bhabuda, who recognizes himself in the protagonist and sort solidarity in a normally informal restaurant environment, Julius is distant and haughty. This is because Kenneth, although Black like Julius, is not necessarily "Afropolitan" due to the former's lack of any specialized artistic skills and accompanying metropolitan consecration as well as symbolic capital. This is insinuated in the novel's sub-text, I suggest. As a janitor at the Folk-Art museum, Kenneth has a lower-class status imposed, as it were, by Julius, who discountenances this "brother's" humanity. This is similar to, if not as drastic as, that dehumanized ontological condition, which New World Afropolitan writing focalized as unjust, as an unfreedom and a lack of agency that needed to be re-worlded. In denying him coeval-ness, in imposing an outward standard of being human in which Kenneth is "less-than," Julius unhinges and unworlds Kenneth's world; and a less-human self-perception is forced upon difference. "Kenneth was by now starting to wear on me, and I began to wish he would go away. I thought of the cabdriver who had driven me home from the Folk Art Museum—hey, I 'm African just like you. Kenneth was making the same claim" (53).

In contradistinction to Afropolitan literature, foundational African writing, that is, first-generation African writing—for example those by Wole Soyinka, Chinua Achebe, Ngugi Wa Thiong'o, Hampate Ba, Leopold Senghor, or David Diop—maintained the worlding possibilities inherited from the Black Atlantic. It was directly instrumental to decolonization and led to the protest tradition—especially in Francophone African literature—against a self-legitimizing, post-independence African political bourgeoisie and its "presidents-for-life" syndrome (Ekeh, 1975; Adesanmi 2010). Those works contest, an attendant, and still, pervasive unworlding corruption of the postcolonial state (Bayart 1989, Chabal and Daloz 1999). It could be taken for granted that the contemporary African writer is not interested in being counted as one of Dubois' talented tenth. He or she is individualized in the extreme and is apparently not enamored of a New World, Black Atlantic, or early-twentieth-century African group cohesion. This is due to the alienation induced by a distant and recent history.

Afropolitan Writing as Commodity

If, as already emphasized, contemporary Afropolitan writing is not world literature in symbolic worlding terms, then its material globalizing element is necessarily indistinguishable from its value as a commodity, both for the writer and the publisher—but especially for the Western reader, whose self-constitution, it seems, depends on a perennial negative othering—especially of African difference. Kadiatu Kanneh frames that historical confrontation between European self and African Other thus: "Africa's historical role in the formation of modernity, particularly as a discursive site for ideologies of race, humanity and progress, is one that helped to forge Europe's idea of itself, as well as to lay the foundations of modern Black identities" ("History Africa and Modernity" 32). In contemporary times, that perennial Self/Other dichotomy is at the heart of a demonizing variety of Western media representation. "The [twentieth century] anticolonial struggles and internecine strife that characterize Africa's place in the media and the frequent footage of famine, AIDS and 'natural' disasters perpetuate the image of the Dark Continent" (31).

It is then not surprising that what has become the prize-winning staple for Western literary establishments are the "extroverted" (Julien 2006) negatively unidimensional stories about Africa sold to a willing primary target-audience in the Western metropolis. Such "single stories" include those of an exaggerated African patriarchy in Chimamanda Adichie's *Purple Hibiscus*; the "exceptional" African "criminality" reflected in Tricia Nwaubani's *I Do Not Come to You by Chance*, in NoViolet Bulawayo's Caine-Prize-winning short story "Hitting Budapest"-'s (2005) hyper-focalization of poverty, child abuse, and neglect as well as its elaboration in that story's novelization, *We Need New Names* (2011).

The significance of a sensationalizing narration, uni-dimensional plotting and an ideological void in the Afropolitan novel is that such works become mere raw materials for the transnational publishing industry. These writers' first audience becomes the Western reader as represented by the Western literary agent (Nwaubani 2014). In a macabre re-enactment of original African unworlding occasioned by the Slave Trade and colonialism, the relationship of writer and publisher to the continent becomes one in which Africa is objectified as mostly a source of raw material—with stories being the raw material in this instance.

The significance is that having abandoned a traditional New World, Black Internationalist and early and late twentieth-century African ethical approach to literary representation, contemporary Afropolitan writing appeals to the Western reader's consumption of Africa in an ocular regime (Adesanmi 2005: 270) in which Africa is an exotic and a strange spectacle. As a matter of course, there are exceptions to this stylistic trend such as Wainaina's story, "Discovering Home" (2001) or Moses Isegawa's novel, *Abyssinian Chronicles* (2001). Wainana's story for example is set in Africa; its plot follows the trajectory of an internal exile as he navigates his way towards home across the continent. However, the market-driven stylistics of most new fiction genuflects to the commodification charge of some critics of Afropolitanism like Wainaina. The postcolonial exotic market logic of contemporary Afropolitan writing has been much discussed in the literature and bears no repetition here (Huggan 2001, Brouillette, Adesokan 2012, Ede 2015). The unworlding and commodifying relationship of the Afropolitan writer to his object is exacerbated in the Francophone African writer, that is, in the even more radically alienated "Afropean" based in Paris.

An overt Afropean, as opposed to covert Afropolitan, rejection of roots is detailed in Odile Cazenave and Patricia Célérier's 2011 study of commitment in Francophone African literature. They note that Afropeans are "weary of the label of 'African writer' and dissociate themselves from the notion of [ideologically or politically] engaged writing" (183). Importantly, this preference and valuing of aesthetics over ethics rather than their marriage as in foundational African literature is not necessarily a result of a postcolonial amnesia (Gandhi 1998). Rather it is reducible to a studied affectation that the Afropean, especially, cultivates and loudly celebrates as witnessed by Jean Luc Rahimanana. In his own words:

> We were only promising young authors ... filled with revolt, with a desire to abscond from the legacies of our elders, a legacy that was hard to bear, the whole continent's pain in fact. Our only wish was to write, to be good writers, to play with aesthetics or just tell a story, and here we were, twenty years old, and summoned to save Africa!
>
> CAZENAVE AND CÉLÉRIER 97

Perhaps the alienation and strong rejection of roots expressed in the above quote could be explained by John Nimis' (2014) globalizing conception of the Afropean—the French-speaking African variation of the English-Speaking Afropolitan:

> Afropean points to a group with dual cultural and political identities without any basis or investment in the national, either as a source of legitimacy or a target of resistance. The absence of a hyphen in the term therefore registers the integrity of human subjects, thus designating a seamless mixture and crossing, across distance and across imagined categories of humans (black and white).
>
> NIMIS 49

It is hard to quarrel with Nimis' view and celebration of the transnational. However, it needs to be qualified by the fact that cultural hybridity is no buffer against observable negative political interpellation of blackness in the Western metropolis, that the novel is an ideological form and that an anti-national, alienated, de-politicized Afropean self-positioning is therefore a political act and leads to an unworlding of the African world, willy-nilly. This is ironic given the history of Black Paris as an early-twentieth-century locus of Black Atlantic struggle for emancipation and agency.

Clearly, Afropolitan and Afropean writing are not world literature in symbolic worlding terms, as this chapter has been arguing. Their world literature status resides only in a global circulation that is invariably yoked to the literary worlding of foundational African literature as well as to the vicissitudes of the transnational literary market. The moment of the literary worlding of both Afropolitan and Afropean writing is therefore worth a brief overview.

Rise of the Afropolitan Novel

As a summary,[5] first generation African literature's rise as world literature is invariably interwoven with the political urgency of decolonisation and that oeuvre's international dissemination by William Heinemann publishers in the UK. Beginning in the early 1950s African writing's literary worlding started as a flow into global circulation of "Third World" textual contestations of Euro-modernity from Africa (Msika 2016), the Caribbean (Nair 2016), and Latin America. Olakunle George (2003) refers to the aggregate of early twentieth century African intellection, which empowered and gave agency to the African world, as "African Letters." The Europhone literary aspect of that tradition began in 1958, exactly 60 years ago, with the publishing of *Things Fall Apart* as a founding Anglophone text of Heinemann Publishers' African Writers' Series (Hill 1971). Translated Francophone texts such as Mongo Beti' *Mission to Karla* (1964) and Ferdinand Oyono's *Houseboy* (1966) later joined the oeuvre under the same series, which "was initially founded on Nigerian fiction" (Hill 20).

Although Amos Tutuola's *The Palwine Drinkard* (1952) and Cyprian Ekwensi's *People of the City* (1954) preceded Achebe's work, they—especially the former—were hardly instrumental to that literary worlding and agency that began properly with *Things Fall Apart*'s direct contestation of Euro-modernity (Achebe 1972, 7). For example, Faber and Faber's assessment of Tutola's linguistically "strange" and necromantic work (Low 2006: 15), which "provoked acute anxiety over how to manage [its] meaning" (21), was purely market-oriented. The publisher, Geoffrey Faber's, prevailing concern was that the work should satisfy a Western exotic consumption of an "authentic" anthropological Africa (Lindfors 1975 in Low 22). In his view "publishing is a business and like all businesses must be made to pay" (Low 22).

Faber and Faber's hard-nosed pragmatism was in direct contradistinction to Heinemann's admixture of market dynamics with vision, and a local cultural advocacy on behalf of a home-grown African literary corpus (Currey 2003: 576). This is in spite of any criticism of Heinemann's near-monopoly or the half-hearted and hurried ghettoization[6] charge leveled against its series by Wole Soyinka. And history and context has proven Heinemann right. According to James Currey (2003): "When Soyinka was in prison in Nigeria, his wife agreed to let André Deutsch finally sub-lease the novel for the Series. Deutsch's story was that she said she needed food for the family, while Wole Soyinka in prison was at least being fed" (585).

By the 1980s when Heinemann's African Writer's Series died due to a continental economic downtown and the vicissitudes of transnational capital as dictated by the company's new ownership, the series had created a permanent niche for African literature in the so-called Western Canon. That aura of consecration was inherited by Afropolitan writing—which is simply writing by that group of writers who have come to be identified as the "third generation" (Adesanmi 2005) of African writers. It seems that, after 60 years, it is Faber and Faber's erstwhile commodifying market imperative rather than Heinemann's admixture of vision and practical business, which has re-established itself in the transnational literary establishment's re-engagement with contemporary African literature.

Due, amongst other reasons, to the same African economic lull (Griswold 2000) that led to the continental exit of Heineman international in the 1980s, there was a brief literary interregnum—a period of quiescence—when it appeared that African writing's global circulation had been arrested. While some of those who would later join metropolitan Afropolitan and Afropean ranks remained on the continent, the economic depression of the 1980s led to a mass exodus of young Africans to the literary capitals of the West—usually the USA and UK for Anglophones and France or Belgium for Francophones—in search of publishing opportunities[7] (Garuba 1987: xv). In a prescient ironic expression and referring to objects—artworks—Harry Garuba opines that what was once forcibly taken away was now willing going into exile (1). That historical unworlding applied as well to black bodies—once forcibly removed (during slavery) but now willingly boarding ships and planes for the Western hemisphere.

In a similar fashion to the burgeoning of Caribbean literature in the 1950s due to the arrival of the Windrush Generation in London in 1948 (Brown 2016), a group of young Africans, who would later flow into a nascent metropolitan Afropolitan and Afropean pool, willingly arrived in Western Capitals in the 1980s into the late 1990s. This movement was very dissimilar to the coerced uprooting of their distant New World ancestors. It resulted in a renaissance of African literary production and an international publication unfettered by ideological concerns. In other words, the social condition of their presence in the metropolis as economic and literary exiles, not as slaves or the colonized, meant that they would naturally have a different relationship to roots compared to a romantic Black Atlantic. More importantly, these young generations full of levity lived, and still live, in a relatively humane condition and radically different socio-political dispensation beside the servitude and brutality of the "old" New World, the continued injustices of the later Black Atlantic after the First World War, the racialized interpellation of blackness in the colonial metropolis or the violent decolonial upheaval in Sub-Saharan African in the 1960s (Jameson 1987). There was therefore, and still is, an existential and historical disconnection which led to the new Afropolitans and Afropeans emphasising routes and discountenancing roots as joyously celebrated in Taiye Selasi's "Bye-Bye Babar" (2005).

Nascent Afropolitans and Afropeans were ushered into global "literary capitals" synonymous with enormous resources for literary illumination as understood by Pascale Cassanova (2004). These metropolitan locales were already conversant with African literature as a corpus with an established literary worlding capacity based on the work and metropolitan consecration of first and second generation African writers. This is exemplified in the "hyper-canonization" (Hassan 2001: 298) of Chinua Achebe, Ngugi Wa Thiongo and others; the awarding of the 1986 Nobel Prize to Wole Soyinka, or Ben Okri' winning of the Booker prize in 1991. This elaborate illumination pointed to a ready metropolitan market and audience, both synonymous with, and indistinguishable from, one another.

The relationship of the new Afropolitan and Afropean as subject to their object—literature—is therefore necessarily mediated by the dynamics of the metropolitan book market itself as an institution. Although Richard Peterson (1985) identifies six limitations to literary production, "technology, law, industry structure, organizational structure, the market and occupational careers" (45), I want to submit that all these factors are largely subsumed under the "Institution" of the market and are symptoms and functions of it. This is much in the same way that the eighteenth century Romantic Artist's relationship to its audience or literary patrons became mediated by the institution of the Market after the discovery of the printing press enabled mass production. And the contemporary African writer is more market-oriented than ever before.

It is then instinctive that most Afropolitan and Afropean writers today would tailor their writing to suit the literary taste of the metropolitan market—prize-awarding bodies such as the Caine Prize for African Writing in London, established in 1999 towards harnessing the new metropolitan influx of talents, or the much older Prix Goncourt in Paris. This is apart from the British Commonwealth short story prize, the Commonwealth Writers Prize, and the Booker Prize. The market also includes, as a matter of course, metropolitan publishers, book reviewers, literary agents, readers, and other general literary administrative bodies and facilitators such as PEN International—"agents of legitimation" (Huggan 2001:5) of which Graham Huggan (2001) considers the writer himself or herself as one (5). These all constitute an amorphous market, which the Afropolitan or Afropean writer appeals to in his or her aesthetics—plot, story, and narrative strategies that aligns with the fetishized image of Africa redolent in the Western imaginary since the medieval period. The question of ethics, which engaged previous generations of African and Black writers going back to the 1700s thus becomes superfluous in the ideologically vacuous, market-ruled, individualistic, and impersonal metropolitan publishing Socious into which the new Afropolitan/Afropean writer is thrust.

The literary worlding of the Afropolitan or Afropean novel is literally and literarily a twenty-first century phenomenon, beginning around the end of the twentieth century and being consolidated through international literary prizes by the year 2000 forwards. The London publication of the

Nigerian Biyi Bandele-Thomas' *The Sympathetic Undertaker and Other dreams* [1991], *The Man Who Came in from the Back of the Beyond* [1991] to literary acclaim and academic canonization in the UK, Canada and the USA alerted the metropolitan literary establishment to a resurgence of African literature. The British establishment responded to the promise of an African literary renaissance in the metropolis, especially after the long demise of the African Writers' Series, by establishing the aforementioned Caine Prize in 1999.[8] Doseline Wanjiru Kiguru's 2016 PhD dissertation is a detailed and elaborate discussion of the role of international literary prizes in the worlding of contemporary African writing and therefore bears no repetition here. Suffice it to say that Western literary agents of legitimation have had a major role in the global circulation and canonization of Afropolitan and Afropean writing.

Conclusion: What is a World?

If Afropolitan writing is only world literature in literary rather than sociopolitical world-making terms, in what shape does such writing then leave the world it comes into contact with? Pheng Cheah's 2016 critic of European time and its subordination of all other local temporalities to a Greenwich Mean Time exemplifies the constructedness of the globe, that is, of maps and their inscriptions and the ways of reading them. Moreover, the efficacy of aesthetic abolitionism in the Black Atlantic suggests that literature is a kind of social map, an inscription with political valence and social transformative power. However, most Afropolitan writings do not coincide with such a view of literature due to their refusal to have a much more socially relevant impact on the black and African world. New Afropolitan writing is in a supply-and-demand economic relationship with the Western literary establishment. It is rather more responsive to the vicissitudes of the global literary marketplace than to any world-making imperatives.

To continue the cartographic analogy, Afropolitan literature like Black and African writing before it could be a kind of map for re-reading and making meaning of the objective world, for repositioning the self to that world that has been already constructed by older hermeneutical maps. As it is presently, Afropolitanism fails to reshape our old ways of seeing the African world and engaging or interacting with it. This lack of a symbolic worlding is a twenty-first century perpetuation of a millennial African crisis in which the continent seems to move forwards only to stand still, trapped in a socio-economic, political, and developmental morass.

The Afropolitan and (similar) Afropean refusal to engage Africa on a cultural materialist level in terms of its colonial past and neocolonial present recalls Benita Parry's materialist critique of theories which ignore the sociopolitical and economic realities of Africa for a formalist reading of text.

Afropean and Afropolitan writing seems to be performative of a creative equivalent of such formalist textual exegesis. Perhaps this serious hermeneutical omission has as its goal a projection of the continent into a utopic future. However, such impatient futurism will merely consolidate, rather than help surpass, the challenges of the past while enlarging and normalizing an equally problematic and neo-colonial present.

Notes

1 For slavery timeline see: http://www.brycchancarey.com/slavery/chrono2.htm
2 See Cheng, K.C. et. al. *SLC24A5 affects Pigmentation in Zebrafish and Humans* (2005). This ground breaking DNA research by a group of Pennsylvania State University anthropological geneticists has effectively resolved the eternal argument about the biological validity of the sociological category of "race." Keith Cheng and his group of twenty-four scientists have proven that whiteness is due to a gene mutation which occurred between 20,000 and 50,000 years ago as Homo Sapiens Sapien migrated northward and eastward away from Africa as the original home of the human species. This supports archaeological, ancient historical, and anthropological accounts of the negroid antecedents of man.
3 Some of the works produced by these freed African slaves are *Thoughts and Sentiments on the Evil and Wicked Traffic of the Slavery and Commerce of the Human Species, humbly submitted to the inhabitants of Great-Britain by Ottobah Cugoano, a native of Africa* (London: T. Becker, 1787); *The Interesting Narrative of the Life of Oluadah Equiano written by Himself* (London, 1789), *Letters of the Late Ignatius Sancho: An African, to which are Prefixed, Memoirs of his Life* (London: John Nichols, 1782); *Tractatus de arte sobrie et accurate philosophandi* (Germany, 1729); and *Disputation De jure Maurorum in Europa* (Germany, 1739), both philosophical and legal writings by Amo. There is evidence of much earlier writing by Juan Latino (1516–1606). He published works in 1573, 1576 and 1585. See Jahnheinz Jahn (1968:30).
4 He was an emancipated slave of Nigerian stock and is not to be confused with the British lexicographer and writer of the same name often referred to as Dr. Johnson and who lived during the eighteenth century (1709–1784).
5 Simon Gikandi's introduction to *The Novel in Africa and the Caribbean since 1950*, also edited by him, gives a detailed and elaborate analysis of the worlding of African literature; as such an overview is sufficient here.
6 Allan Hill reports that when Soyinka refused to have his novel, *The Interpreters*, re-issued in the Heinemann Series while in prison, his wife at the time quipped that the family needed to eat and that at least Soyinka was being fed in prison.
7 There is the unusual example of Moses Izegawa who moved to the Netherlands. However, his work, *Abyssinian Chronicles*, is not conceived in the Afropolitan spirit. This is one of several exceptions to the rule of Afropolitanism.

8 See Doseline Kiguru's 2016 Stellenbosch University PhD dissertation, "Prizing African Literature: Awards and Cultural Value," for a detailed history of late twentieth century establishment of the Caine and the Commonwealth prizes and their impact on African literature.

Works cited

Achebe, Chinua. *Things Fall Apart*. London: Heinemann, 1958.
Achebe, Chinua. "Africa and her Writers." *The Massachusetts Review* 14.3 (1973): 617–629.
Adesanmi, Pius. "Colonialism, Ecriture, Engage, and Africa's New Intellectuals." *The Dark Webs of Remembrance*. Toyin Falola ed.. (North Carolina: Carolina Academic Press, 2005): 269–285.
Adesanmi, Pius. "Third Generation African Literatures and Contemporary Theorising." *The Study of Africa* vol. 1 Paul Tiyambe Zeleza (Senegal: Codesria, 2006): 101–115.
Adesanmi, Pius. "Reshaping Power and the Public Sphere: The Political Voices of African Writers" in *Reframing Contemporary Africa: Politics, Economics and Culture in the Global Era*. Peyi Soyinka Airewele and Rita Kiki Edozie Eds. (2010): 258–274.
Adesokan, Akin. "I Am Not an African Writer, Damn You!" *SLIP* blog. Stellenbosch Literary Project, 2014. Accessed August 20, 2018. http://slipnet.co.za/view/blog/im-not-an-african-writer-damn-you
Adesokan, Akin. "New African writing and the question of audience." *Research in African Literatures* 43.3 (2012): 1–20.
Ashcroft, Bill, Gareth Griffiths, and Helen Tiffin. *The Empire Writes Back: Theory and Practice in Post-Colonial Literatures*. London: Routledge, 1989. Print.
Bandele-Thomas, Biyi. *The Man who Came in from the Back of Beyond*. Heinemann, 1992.
Bandele-Thomas, Biyi. *The sympathetic undertaker and other dreams*. Heinemann International, 1993.
Bayart, Jean-Francois. *The state in Africa. The politics of the belly*. Paris, Fayard, 1989.
Benjamin, Walter. "Paris: Capital of the Nineteenth Century." New Left Review. Vol. 1.48. March-April 1968.
Bernal, Martin. *Black Athena: Afroasiatic Roots of Classical Civilization, Volume I: The Fabrication of Ancient Greece, 1785–1985*. Rutgers University Press, 1987.
Bernal, Martin. *Black Athena: The archaeological and documentary evidence*. Vol. 2. Rutgers University Press, 1987.
Bernal, Martin. *Black Athena: The linguistic evidence*. Vol. 3. Rutgers University Press, 1987.
Bratman, Michael E. *Structures of Agency: Essays*. Oxford: Oxford University Press, 2007.
Brouillette, Sarah. Postcolonial Writers in the Global Literary Marketplace. Basingstoke; New York: Palgrave Macmillan, 2007.

Brown, Dillon J. "Geographies of Migration in the Caribbean Novel." *The Novel in Africa and the Caribbean since 1950 Vol II*. ed. Simon Gikandi. (2016): 120–134.
Bulawayo, NoViolet. *We need New Names:* A Novel. Hachette UK, 2013.
Casanova, Pascale. *The World Republic of Letters*. Cambridge: Harvard University Press, 2004.
Cazenave, Odile, and Patricia Célérier. *Contemporary African Francophone Writers and the Burden of Commitment*. Charlottesville: University of Virginia Press, 2011.
Chabal, Patrick, and Jean-Pascal Daloz. *Africa Works: Disorder as Political Instrument*. African issues. James Currey, Oxford, 1999.
Cheah, Pheng. *What is a World?: On Postcolonial Literature As World Literature*. Durham: Duke University Press Books, 2016. eBook Collection (EBSCOhost). Web. December 26, 2016.
Cheng, Keith C. et al. "SLC24A5, A Putative Cation Exchanger, Affects Pigmentation in Zebrafish and Humans." *Science* 310.5755 (2005): 1782–1786.
Clarke, Becky. "The African Writers Series: Celebrating Forty Years of Publishing Distinction." *Research in African literatures* (2003): 163–174.
Cole, Teju. *Open City*. New York: Random House, 2011.
Cugoano, Ottobah. "A Native of Africa." *Thoughts and Sentiments on the Evil and Wicked Traffic of the Slavery and Commerce of the Human Species, Humbly Submitted to the Inhabitants of Great-Britain* (1787).
Currey, James. "Chinua Achebe, the African Writers Series and the Establishment of African Literature." *African affairs* 102.409 (2003): 575–585.
Dabiri, Emma. "Why I Am (still) Not an Afropolitan." Journal of African Cultural Studies 28.1 (2015):104–108.
DuBois, William Edward Burghardt. *The talented tenth*. New York, NY: James Pott and Company, 1903.
Eagleton, Terry. *Literary Theory: An Introduction*. UK: Blackwell, 1983.
Eburne, Jonathan P. (Jonathan Paul) and Braddock, Jeremy. "Introduction: Paris, Capital of the Black Atlantic." Project Muse. Modern Fiction Studies, 51.4, Winter (2005): 731–740.
Ede, Amatoritsero. "Narrative Moment and Self-Anthropologizing Discourse." Research in African Literatures 46.3 (2015): 112–129.
Ede, Amatoritsero. "The politics of Afropolitanism." *Journal of African Cultural Studies* 28.1 (2016): 88–100.
Edwards, Brent Hayes. *The Practice of Diaspora: Literature, Translation, and the Rise of Black Internationalism* (2003). Harvard University Press, 2003.
Ekeh, Peter P. 1975. "Colonialism and the Two Publics in Africa: A Theoretical Statement." Comparative Studies in Society and History 17 (1): 91–112.
Ekwensi, Cyprian. *People of the City*. Dakers, 1954.
Equiano, Olaudah. *The Interesting Narrative of the Life of Olaudah Equiano; Or Gustavus Vassa, the African*, 1789.
Eze, Chielozona. "Rethinking African Culture and Identity: The Afropolitan Model." *Journal of African Cultural Studies* 26.2 (2014): 234–247. Accessed October 2, 2018. http://dx.doi.org/10.1080/13696815.2014.894474.
Fabre, Michel. From Harlem to Paris: Black American Writers in France, 1840–1980. Urbana: University of Illinois Press, 1991.

Fasselt, Rebecca. "'I'm not Afropolitan—I'm of the Continent': A Conversation with Yewande Omotoso." *The Journal of Commonwealth Literature* (2014): 1–16.
Fatton, Robert Jr.: *Black consciousness in South Africa*. New York: State U of NYP, 1986.
Fogel, Robert W., and L. Stanley, Engerman. *Time on the Cross: The Economics of American Negro Slavery* Vol. 1 & 2. Boston: Little, Brown, 1994.
Friedman, Jonathan. "Global Crises, the Struggle for Cultural Identity and Intellectual Porkbarrelling: Cosmopolitans versus Locals, Ethnics and Nationals in an Era of De-hegemonisation." *Debating Cultural Hybridity: Multi-cultural Identities and the Politics of Anti-Racism* (1997): 70–89.
Gandhi, Leela. *Postcolonial Theory: A Critical Introduction*. New York: Columbia University Press, 1998.
Garuba, Harry. *Voices from the Fringe: An ANA anthology of New Nigerian Poetry*. Lagos; London: Malthouse, 1988.
Gates, Henry Louis, Jr. "Editor's Introduction: Writing, 'Race' and the Difference it Makes." *Critical Inquiry* 12.1. "Race, Writing, and Difference." (1985): 1–20.
Gates, Henry Louis, and W. Andrews. *Pioneers of The Black Atlantic: Five Slave Narratives, 1772–1815*. New York: Basic Civitas, 1998.
Gehrmann, Susanne. "Cosmopolitanism with African Roots. Afropolitanism's Ambivalent Mobilities." Journal of African Cultural Studies 28.1 (2015): 1–12. (Accessed August 8, 2018). http://dx.doi.org/10.1080/13696815.2015.1112770.
George, Olakunle. *Relocating Agency: Modernity and African Letters*. New York: SUNY Press, 2003.
Gikandi, Simon. "On Afropolitanism." In *Negotiating Afropolitanism: Essays on Borders and Spaces in Contemporary African Literature and Folklore*, edited by Jennifer Wawrzinek and J. K. S. Makokha, 9–13. Amsterdam/New York: Rodopi, 2011.
Gilroy, Paul. *The Black Atlantic: Modernity and Double Consciousness*. Harvard University Press, 1993.
Gilroy, Paul. *Against Race: Imagining Political Culture beyond the Color Line*. Harvard University Press, 2000.
Goldenberg, David M. *The curse of Ham: Race and slavery in early Judaism, Christianity, and Islam*. Princeton University Press, 2003.
Griswold, Wendy. *Bearing Witness: Readers, Writers, and the Novel in Nigeria*. Princeton Studies in Cultural Sociology. Princeton, N.J.: Princeton University Press, 2000.
Hassan, Salah Dean Assaf. "Canons after 'Postcolonial Studies.'" Project Muse. Pedagogy 1.2 (2001): 297–304.
Hill, Alan. "The African Writers Series." *Research in African Literatures* (1971): 18–20.
Hitchcott, Nicki, and Thomas Dominic. *Francophone Afropean Literatures*. Liverpool: Liverpool University Press, 2014.
Holgado, Miasol Eguíbar. "Transforming the body, transculturing the city: Nalo Hopkinson's fantastic Afropolitans." *European Journal of English Studies* 21.2 (2017): 174–188.
Hood, Robert. 1994. *Begrimed and Black: Christian Traditions on Blacks and Blackness*. Minneapolis.

Horowitz, Evan. "London: Capital of the Nineteenth Century." Project Muse. New Literary History 41.1 (2010): 111–128.
Huggan, Graham. 2001. *The Postcolonial Exotic: Marketing the Margins*. London: Routledge.
Huggins, Nathan Irvin. *Harlem Renaissance*. New York: Oxford University Press, 1973.
Ibironke, "Olabode. Between African Writers and Heinemann Educational Publishers: The Political Economy of a Culture Industry." Diss. Michigan State U, 2008.
Irele, Abiola. "Négritude or Black Cultural Nationalism." *The Journal of Modern African Studies* 3.3 (1965): 321–348.
Irele, Abiola. "Negritude—Literature and Ideology." *The Journal of Modern African Studies* 3.4 (1965): 499–526.
Jahn, Janheinz. *A History of Neo-African Literature: Writing in Two Continents*. Trans. Oliver Coburn and Ursula Lehrburger. London: Faber, 1968.
Jameson, Fredric. "Periodizing the 60s." *Social Text* 9/10 (1984): 178–209.
Johanson, Donald, Maitland Edey, and Maitland Armstrong Edey. *Lucy: The beginnings of Humankind*. Simon and Schuster, 1990.
Jules-Rosette, Bennetta. *Black Paris: The African Writers' Landscape*. Urbana: University of Illinois Press, 1993.
Julien, Eileen. "The Extroverted African Novel." *The Novel* 1, edited by Franco Moretti, 667–700. Princeton: Princeton University Press, 2006.
July, Robert W. *The Origins of Modern African Thought*. Faber, 1968.
Kanneh, Kadiatu. "History, 'Africa' and Modernity." *Interventions: International Journal of Postcolonial Studies* 1.1 (1998): 30–34.
Kiguru, Doseline Wanjiru. *Prizing African literature: awards and cultural value*. Diss. Stellenbosch: Stellenbosch University, 2016.
Lindfors, Bernth. *Critical Perspectives on Amos Tutuola*. Critical Perspectives. Washington: Three Continents Press, 1975.
Livingston, Thomas W. "The Exportation of American higher Education to West Africa: Liberia College, 1850-1900." *The Journal of Negro Education* 45.3(1976): 246–262.
Lizarribar Buxo, Camille. "Something Else Will Stand Beside it: The African Writers Series and the Development of African Literature." Harvard University, PhD Dissertation, 1998.
McClintock, Anne. "The Angel of Progress: Pitfalls of the term 'Post-Colonialism.'" *Social text* 31/32 (1992): 84–98.
Mbembe, Achille. "Afropolitanism." *Africa Remix: Contemporary Art of a Continent*. Ed. Simon Njami, 26–30. Johannesburg: Johannesburg Art Gallery, [2006] 2007.
Msiska, Mpalive-Hangson. "The novel and Decolonization in Africa." *The Novel in Africa and the Caribbean since 1950 Vol II*. Simon Gikandi, ed. (2016): 37–54.
Nair, M. Supriya "The Novel and Decolonization in the Caribbean." *The Novel in Africa and the Caribbean since 1950 Vol II*. Simon Gikandi ed. (2016): 55–68.
Ngwane, George. "Cameroonian Literature in Transition." Interview with George Ngwane. *African Writing*. Available online: http://www.african-writing.com/ngwane.htm Accessed October 22, 2018.

Nimis, John. "Corps sans Titre: Fleshiness and Afropean Identity in Bessora's 53 cm." In *Francophone Afropean Literatures*, edited by Nicki Hitchcott and Dominic Thomas, 48–63. Liverpool: Liverpool U P, 2014.

Nwaubani, Adaobi Tricia. "African Books for Western Eyes." *The New York Times*, 28 November 2014. Available online: http://www.nytimes.com/2014/11/30/opinion/sunday/african-books-forwestern-eyes.html?_r=0. Accessed November 3, 2018.

Obenga, Theophile. *African Philosophy: The Pharaonic Period: 2780-330 BC*. Trans. Ayi Kwei Armah. Popenguine Senegal: Per Ankh, 2004.

Onoge, Omafume F. "The Crisis of Consciousness in Modern African Literature: A Survey." Jstor. *Canadian Journal of African Studies/Revue Canadienne des Études Africaines* 8.2 (1974): 385–410.

Oyono, Ferdinand. *Houseboy*. Oxford: Heinemann, 1966.

Parascandola, Louis J. "'What Are We Blackmen Who Are Called French?': The Dilemma of Identity in Oyono's Un vie de boy and Sembène's La Noire de . . ." Project Muse. Comparative Literature Studies 46.2 (2009): 360–378.

Peterson, Richard A. "Six constraints on the production of literary works." *Poetics* 14.1–2 (1985): 45–67.

Pitts, Johny. "An Afropean Travel Narrative." *Transition: An International Review* 113 (2014): 44–51.

Potkay, Adam, and Sandra Burr. *Black Atlantic Writers of the Eighteenth Century: Living the New Exodus in England and the Americas*. 1st ed. ed. New York: St. Martin's Press, 1995.

Rashidi, Runoko. *Introduction to the Study of African clasical [sic] Civilizations*. Karnak House, 1992.

Said, Edward. *Culture and Imperialism*. London: Chatto and Windus, 1993.

Sancho, Ignatius. *Letters of the Late Ignatius Sancho, An African: To Which Are Prefixed Memoirs of his Life*. 1782.

Santana, Bosch Stephanie. "Exorcizing the Future: Afropolitanism's Spectral Origins." *Journal of African Cultural Studies*. 28.1 (2015): 120–126.

Selasi, Taiye. "Bye-Bye Babar." The Lip blog. *The Lip Magazine*. 2005. Available online: http://thelip.robertsharp.co.uk/?p=76. Accessed August 7, 2018.

Selasi, Taiye. "Stop pidgeonholing African Writers." The Guardian Newspapers, 2015. Available online: http://www.theguardian.com/books/2015/jul/04/taiye-selasi-stop-pigeonholing-african-writers. Accessed August 4, 2018.

Sterling, Cheryl. "Race Matters: Cosmopolitanism, Afropolitanism, and Pan-Africanism via Edward Wilmot Blyden." *Journal of Pan African Studies* 8.1 (2015): 119–145.

Thomas, Nicholas. *Colonialism's Culture: Anthropology, Travel, and Government*. Princeton, N.J: Princeton University Press, 1994.

Tutuola, Amos. *The Palm-wine Drinkard and His Dead Palm-wine Tapster in the Dead's Town*. Faber & Faber, 1952.

Van Sertima, Ivan, ed. *Egypt: Child of Africa*. Transaction Publishers, 1994.

Waberi, Abdulrahman. "Les enfants de la postcolonie. Esquisse d'une nouvelle génération d'écrivains francophones d'Afrique noire." *Notre Librairie* 135, sept/dec (1998): 8–15.

Wawrzinek, Jennifer, and Makokha, J.K.S. *Negotiating Afropolitanism: Essays on Borders and Spaces in Contemporary African Literature and Folklore.* Amsterdam/New York: Rodopi, 2011.

Wheatley, Phillis. *Poems on Various Subjects, Religious and Moral.* WH Lawrence & Company, 1887.

Williams, Chancellor. *Capitalism and Slavery.* Chapel Hill, USA: University of North Carolina Press, 1944

8

Afropolitan Aesthetics as an Ethics of Openness

Chielozona Eze

What is Africa to Me?

"What is Africa to me?" This question, posed in the poem "Heritage" by the African American poet Countee Cullen, is still as pertinent today as it was in the early decades of the twentieth century, for it engages the issues of being and representation, of identity and existence. Like the dominant thinkers and writers of the Harlem Renaissance, such as W.E.B. Du Bois and Alain Locke, who sought to infuse nobility into blackness, or the poet Langston Hughes, who highlighted the Africanness of blacks at the time, Cullen affirmed Africa, the supposedly legitimizing trope of black identity in America. Cullen's affirmation, however, served to complicate this identity. The question is subversive and deconstructive; it is also path-breaking in regard to the moral demands of group identity. Cullen acknowledged his African ancestry and, like most of his contemporaries, subscribed to the force of the Negritude movement that was gathering steam in the 1930s. However, resisting the temptation to resort to an exclusively abstract conception of Africa, the speaker in the poem acknowledges less flattering images of Africa. Charles Molesworth (2012) states that "Cullen insisted on his African American identity, and at the same time, on his freedom and pleasure in writing on what he hoped was a plane of experience and expression that went beyond—even as it included—race." (p. 77). Recognizing that identity is always born of a synthesis of opposites, Cullen wrote in a brief self-description that he had to find a way to reconcile his "Christian upbringing with a pagan inclination" (quoted in Molesworth, p. 77).

Cullen's question is pertinent not only because of the speaker's spatial and temporal distance from Africa, but also because of the moral space it opens up to the African on the continent. Thus, it is worth repeating today even as we hold some of the supposed tropes of African identity in our hands or pound our feet to the rhythm of the songs of our African villages. What does the presence of these forms of art mean for my identity? Am I less African if violin or cello can express my emotions better than a drum?

The African village is a construct upon which the notions of purity and innocence are projected. That is a myth, very much like the Small Town America that is praised by American Conservatives. It is a utopia, and just as utopia is not an actual place, the identity it is supposed to preserve is non-existent. If it ever did exist, it surely crumbled on the very moment of the first encounter between Africa and the West. This raises the question of how much space the notion of African identity gives a person to respond to his or her experience of the world. When does African identity conceived in the above format become an albatross?

I engage the issue of what it means to be African in the globalized world of today, a world in which hitherto structural barriers between people have fallen apart, making the movement of people and information much easier. Through the notion of Afropolitanism, an experimental idea designed to introduce the African imagination to the contours of cosmopolitanism, I explore the ethical promises of worldliness in the African literary imagination. What makes Afropolitan literature world literature? How does Africa liberate itself from the imposed need to defend Africanity or Africa, which is mostly an abstraction? I endorse Nelson Mandela's claim that in this age, when people have raised fractional forces and the tribe into desirable forms of social organizations (thereby setting one national group against the other), cosmopolitan dreams are not only desirable but a bounden duty; dreams that stress the special unity that holds the freedom forces together—[in] a bond that has been forged by common struggles, sacrifices and traditions (2010, p. 17). Openness to otherness is not a choice, but a necessity in Africa. Openness indeed is a liberatory moral imperative and it exposes the supremacy of existence (that is, worldliness) over essence, of ethics over ontology. To apprehend the need to open the African artistic imagination to the world, it is important to understand the degree to which it had been overdetermined by its provenance.

Oppositional Identity and Aesthetics Imagination

The impetus to frame African art in the idioms of the village, or in oppositional paradigm, is a relic of the notion of authentic Africa, inherited from the pioneering thinkers of postcolonial African culture, who were themselves influenced by Africans in the diaspora. The influence of African

American self-writing in African self-perception cannot be overemphasized. As V.Y. Mudimbe (1988) has argued, Africa was invented and reinvented in the West. Indeed, the contemporary African identity rooted in the constructs of nationalism was shaped in the West by such thinkers and activists as Edward Wilmot Blyden, popularly known as the intellectual father of pan-Africanism (Appiah 1993). He gave Africa the notions of "African personality" and the exceptionality of the "African race" (Lynch 1970). The notion of African personality, together with Marcus Garvey's slogan, "Africa for Africans," had a noble nationalist-political goal; however, it bequeathed Africa a nativist ideology that has seeped into various schools of thought about African identity. W.E.B. Du Bois' conception of African nationalism (Gikandi 2005; Kendhammer 2007) had a strong impact on African self-perception; the African American cultural nationalism of the Civil Rights era produced different and often wild versions of Afrocentrism, as Tunde Adeleke (2009) shows.

The counter-narrative invention of the image of the black person in America such as the New Negro was necessary given the history of racist stereotypical depiction of blacks during the Jim Crow era in particular; however, it led to the production of equally fantastical images of the black person in the arts (Henry Louis Gates Jr., 1988). More dangerously, it produced the specter of an ascribed identity that cast its shadow over the reaches of African liberation thought. This was especially notable in the writings of the first-generation postcolonial African writers and thinkers who saw their role, as pioneering intellectuals, as challenging the European epistemic shaping of African personhood. The unrealistic images of self that Africans produced about themselves in turn created artificial barriers for the imagination. One such barrier is the notion of equating victimhood with being in the right. Focusing on the need to preserve its essential nature, the mind becomes fixated on what it is against rather than what it is for. What it is against is rather well known; what it is for is unclear, and the lack of clarity is subsumed within nationalist concepts that are believed to represent Africa, such as Pan-Africanism, Negritude, and *authenticité*. All these terms constitute the core of *Africanity*, which Léopold Sédar Senghor defines as the values both common to all Africans and permanent at the same time; these values are inherent in African humanity, personality, and identity (Rabaka 2009).

Marcus Garvey's poem "The Black Woman" (1927) might have provided inspiration for African poems that celebrate Africa in the abstract and in opposition to Europe. A look at the first four lines of the poem reveals not only the degree of abstractness in the image of Africa that was invented in the West, but also its function as a legitimator of oppositional identity.

Black queen of beauty, thou hast given color to the world!
Among other women thou art royal and the fairest!

Like the brightest of jewels in the regal diadem,
Shin'st thou, Goddess of Africa, Nature's purest emblem!

It is, of course, curious that the queen, who is identified as black in the first line, becomes the "fairest" in the second. Perhaps Garvey's ideological frame of mind prevented him from noticing the impossibility of his black queen being the fairest, purest, and brightest—not even in a figurative sense. These impossible hyperboles are usually the result of engagement with abstraction rather than with reality. To be fair, it is also possible that Garvey might not have thought of fair as being pale-skinned. That, however, does not mean that he had not become subject to the aesthetic ideology which English language carries. Leopold Sedar Senghor follows Marcus Garvey's example in his poem, "Black Woman" (1945), showering praises on Africa as a personification of a woman. David Diop's (1927–1960) "Africa" (1956) shares the same attributes as Garvey's "The Black Woman."

Africa my Africa
Africa of proud warriors in ancestral savannahs
Africa of whom my grandmother sings
On the banks of the distant river
I have never known you

These first five lines establish the speaker's honesty about the absence of a direct experience of the subject of his song (we assume it is the author). It also a profession of affinity and solidarity. Nostalgia for the land he had never been to heightens the force of solidarity with that land. It appears in a more robust form in the speaker's allusion, in the subsequent lines, to African slavery and Africa's undying quest for liberty. To be sure, Diop does not need to have experienced Africa to express his solidarity with her, especially given that most African countries were still under colonial oppression. Yet the enduring nostalgia insinuated in the poem has become a powerful trait in Africa's self-definition. His "beautiful black blood" fulfills the obligation to contrast himself and Africa with Africa's white colonizers. Some of the equally well-known writers of the first-generation African writers and their works whose imagination was shaped by the oppositional conception of identity include Chinua Achebe (*Things Fall Apart*, 1958) Camara Laye, *The African Child 1959*). Ngugi wa Thiong'o (*The River Between*, 1965), Okot p'Bitek (*Song of Lawino* and *Song of Ocol*, 1966). Space would not allow me to engage in a close reading of these works. It suffices to state that the characters in the narratives were decidedly influence by the pan-African ideology and identity born of resistance and opposition to the West. There is a palpable evasion of true engagement with African reality in these narratives because of desire to put the white man in the dock of the global moral court.

I return to Cullen, who for me, stands as a symbol of African American cultural influence in Africa. He foresaw some of the dangers of the ineffectual moral posturing about Africa and the refusal to engage Africa realistically. He ruminates further about Africa:

> Africa? A book one thumbs
> Listlessly, till slumber comes.
> Unremembered are her bats
> Circling through the night, her cats
> Crouching in the river reeds,
> Stalking gentle flesh that feeds
> By the river brink; no more

Cullen does not paint an idyllic Africa. On the contrary, he mixes danger with love. He subtly urges openness to reality while we thumb that book called Africa. Openness to reality means admitting to one's vulnerability, or as Francis B.Nyamnjoh (2015) beautifully puts it, embracing the fact of "incompleteness." I locate the notion of Afropolitanism within the context of incompleteness and the requisite reaching out for completeness even if it is never fully achieved. In my discussion of Afropolitanism, I am more interested in the fates and fortunes of actual humans, especially as reflected in the works of the two contemporary writers chosen. I look for ways through which people's lives could be enhanced by some degree of openness to otherness. I do this in the belief that Africa must conceive of its reality in pluriversal rather than in universal, diverse, rather than in monolithic formats. Walter Mignolo (2011) uses the term pluriversality to designate the world which can no longer be (if ever it had been) explained from one normative standpoint. It is an entanglement of many cosmologies connected today in a power differential. Essentially, it denotes the many ways of conceiving of reality, which assumes a fundamental openness to reality. Afropolitanism offers us a way to that.

Afropolitanism: Being African of the World

In the introduction to this essay, I referred to the dominant strain of African art that presents idyllic representations of Africa. I return to African aesthetics, but of a different kind; one that does not take recourse in African idyll or the past, but rather fuses with the present to create a world that is in tune with the structure of being human today. In 2005, Taiye Selasi coined a new word, Afropolitanism, which adds to our understanding of African identity in this global age. To be sure, the notion of openness to the world has always been present in African thinking. Thinkers such as Kwame Anthony Appiah (2006) and Achille Mbembe (1992, 2001) have consistently argued for a cosmopolitan attitude in Africa. Selasi is of Nigerian and Ghanaian ancestry, and describes herself as born in London, raised in Boston, and living in New York, New Delhi, and Rome. How does one characterize an African of such a mix of influences, ancestry, worldliness, and consciousness? Echoing Cullen, we ask: What is Africa to her? Selasi describes a particular aesthetic moment in the life of young people of African ancestry in London, those who share the same complex ancestries, influences, and ultimately, identities. She writes:

> It's moments to midnight on Thursday night at Medicine Bar in London. Zak, boy-genius DJ, is spinning a Fela Kuti remix. The little downstairs dancefloor swells with smiling, sweating men and women fusing hip-hop dance moves with a funky sort of djembe. The women show off enormous afros, tiny t-shirts, gaps in teeth . . . The whole scene speaks of the Cultural Hybrid: kente cloth worn over low-waisted jeans; African Lady over Ludacris bass lines; London meets Lagos meets Durban meets Dakar.
>
> (2005 no page)

This aesthetic scene gives us nearly everything we need to know about the condition of Africans as citizens of the world. To be sure, they are Africans in the diaspora. In London, they carry with them Fela Kuti, arguably the most cosmopolitan of African musicians. But it is not just Fela Kuti; it is a remix, that is, a recreation, a revised version of him. Fela was known to have fused different elements of Yoruba music and jazz, West African highlife and funk. He is already essentially a mix. But in London he is being remixed. We therefore get a glimpse of the state of modern Africa as represented by the group mentioned above. Later on, we would learn that the DJ himself is a mix, "an ethnic fusion: Nigerian and Romanian" (Selasi 2005). Thus, we see a person of mixed racial parentage mixing African music (already a mix) to suit his London audience, who are themselves a cultural and racial mélange. One thing is therefore certain in this constellation. All those for whom the DJ mixes Fela Kuti are engaged, in their different ways, in self-creation, being fully aware that they are cultural hybrids, or as Kwame Anthony Appiah (2006) states, in a different context, examples of "a cosmopolitan contamination."

In his discussion of cosmopolitan contamination, Appiah tells the story of Publius Terentius Afer, a Roman slave of North African origin who established himself as a Roman playwright. He was known for using elements of Greek plays in his own for the Latin audience. He was then accused of contaminating Latin drama. Terentius gave an answer: "*Homo sum, humani nihil a me alienum puto*"—I am a human being; I consider nothing that is human alien to me. Appiah adapts Terence's philosophy to explain the cultural mix in our time owing to globalization, a mix that renders all attempts at achieving authenticity oxymoronic (2006, 101). The

DJ, who is himself a mix and who happily mixes what was mixed, and in so doing, produces joy, gives credence to the idea that the foundation of the human condition is the pursuit of happiness. Nothing human is foreign to humans regardless, or perhaps because, of the inevitability of mixture. I consider Francis Nyamnjoh's notion of imcompleteness as an integral aspect of Afropolitan identity conceived in the foregoing paradigm. According to Nyamnjoh, conviviality is possible only if we are aware of, and conserve, our incompleteness:

> conviviality invites us to celebrate and preserve incompleteness and mitigate the delusions of grandeur that come with ambitions and claims of completeness. Conviviality encourages frontier Africans to reach out, encounter and explore ways of enhancing or complementing themselves with the added possibilities of potency brought their way by the incompleteness of others, never as a ploy to becoming complete.
>
> (253)

Every mix or cosmopolitan contamination underscores the facticity of our incompleteness, and the unavoidability of conviviality. The awareness of our incompleteness keeps us from repeating the mistakes of European modernity that saw Europeans as model humans and others as inferior. African identity, understood as incomplete, engenders conviviality.

I return to Selasi's scene above. We imagine the people she describes providing answers to Cullen's question: What is Africa to me? Perhaps a preliminary answer is that they are Africans who take the whole world as their village or city. Selasi gives a more defined answer: "There is at least one place on The African Continent to which we tie our sense of self: be it a nation-state (Ethiopia), a city (Ibadan), or an auntie's kitchen" (Selasi 2005 no page). Yet they do not lose the awareness that they are ethnic mixes and cultural mutts. So, then, like Cullen, they admit their connection to Africa, but they are willing "to complicate Africa—namely, to engage with, critique, and celebrate the parts of Africa that mean most to them" (Selasi 2005). They are of African ancestry, but they do not derive the impetus for self-definition exclusively from that. Selasi declares unapologetically, "We are Afropolitans: not citizens, but Africans of the world" (Selasi 2005). A citizen is literally a member of a city or state (*polis*) who exercises the rights and privileges provided by that city or state. That citizen is answerable to the government, which controls the geographical boundary of that state; the citizen is therefore vested with rights, privileges, and duties, and enjoys the status of citizenship. Hannah Arendt (2003) brings into focus a problem associated with global citizenship: "a citizen is by definition a citizen among citizens of a country among countries" (p. 352). Understood in this way, global citizenship (cosmopolitanism) is unrealizable, because unitary, global government is impossible. Perhaps the awareness of the problem with citizens of the world (cosmopolitan) prompted Selasi to emphasize consciousness. For her (2005),

> [it] is the refusal to oversimplify; the effort to understand what is ailing in Africa alongside the desire to honor what is wonderful, unique. Rather than essentialising the geographical entity, we seek to comprehend the cultural complexity; to honor the intellectual and spiritual legacy; and to sustain our parents' cultures.
>
> (2005)

In Selasi's thinking, therefore, consciousness makes the difference between being an Afropolitan and not being one; it informs the Afropolitan's ability to form "an identity along at least three dimensions: national, racial, cultural – with subtle tensions in between" (Selasi 2005). In establishing the traits of Afropolitanism, Selasi outlines some of the qualities of modernity. These include the recognition of the complexity of modern cultures and the rejection of essence or tradition; above all, Afropolitanism recognizes the liminality of identity today. Afropolitanism, therefore, is a rejection of the conventional postcolonial notion of African identity rooted in opposition; it is an expression of African modernity.

It is true that Selasi emphasizes mobility. Spatial mobility, however, is only suggestive of interior mobility, which she also characterizes with her emphasis on change in consciousness. It turns out that what counts for the identity of Afropolitanism is what I, for lack of a better characterization, call flexibility of consciousness; more simply, it is the rejection of essentialism and fixity. Interior mobility points to the readiness to negotiate the world. To achieve this, one does not need to have crossed geographical boundaries; one need only cross the psychic boundaries erected by nativism, autochthony, heritage, and other mythologies of authenticity. Afropolitans are so not because they move from one city to another, but because they are capable of occupying several cultural spaces and relations in which to define who they are. Their self-definition does not seek to exclude; rather, it seeks to include.

As Simon Gikandi states, Afropolitanism is best conceptualized as "a new phenomenology of Africanness" that constitutes "an attempt to rethink African knowledge outside the trope of crisis" (Gikandi, Simon (2010), and Achille Mbembe (2007, 28) argues forcefully for an expansive understanding of the concept. He states:

> Awareness of the interweaving of the here and there, the presence of the elsewhere in the here and vice versa, the relativisation of primary roots and memberships and the way of embracing, with full knowledge of the facts, strangeness, foreignness and remoteness, the ability to recognise one's face in that of a foreigner and make the most of the traces of remoteness in closeness, to domesticate the unfamiliar, to work with what

seem to be opposites—it is this cultural, historical and aesthetic sensitivity that underlies the term Afropolitanism.

Inspired by Mbembe's rich interpretation, I argued in (Eze 2014) that it is to be understood as an ethical gesture of openness to the world.

Not everyone believes that Afropolitanism is a positive development in African thought. Emma Dabiri argues that it is no more than a "collusion with consumerism" (104). Amatoritsero Ede (2016, 88–89) suggests it is elitist "a transnational material and ideological condition, which leads to an inherent individualism and identity politics when it is confronted by metropolitan racial/class tensions and politics of difference." Grace Musila argues that "Afropolitanism seems to promise Africa lite: Africa sans the 'unhealthy' or 'intoxicating' baggage of Africa." (2016, 110). I think that the above concerns are some of the weaknesses of Afropolitanism as an interpretive model of African experience. I do not believe that the weaknesses therefore negate the concept's usefulness, especially regarding its ability to open new vistas for examining Africa's moral spaces.

Afropolitan Aesthetics and Openness

This far in the discourse of Afropolitanism, attention has been paid to its political dimension and less on the aesthetics. Even when attention is given to aesthetics, it is usually about novels (Eva Rask Knudsen & Ulla Rahbek, 2017, Miriam Pahl, 2015). I focus on the poetry of Romeo Oriogun and poetry and fiction of Chris Abani, paying particular attention to how their works help to expand the horizon of the African axis of meaning, that is, how they project Afropolitan values.

In the early months of 2014, Nigeria enacted a law banning homosexuality (AP 2014). Since then, there have been numerous cases of violence against homosexuals, often ending in death (Human Rights Watch 2016). The opponents of modernity or of the LGBTQ community define African reality quite narrowly to fit their ideological or moralistic bent. They argue that it is un-African (McKaiser 2012). Africans are different from Westerners. In the face of this defense we must raise Countee Cullen's questions yet again: What is Africa to me? What does it mean to be African in the twenty-first century? A new perception of self and the world is of urgent necessity to liberate Africa from the constricting oppositional conception of identity; this perception should reorient the imagination toward reality, beginning with the body. Essentially, then we conceive of the body as an open city.

Romeo Oriogun provides us with materials with which to substantiate this quest for new and expanded identities. Oriogun is a Nigerian queer poet, who describes his parentage as a mix of Yoruba and Edo. He is the winner of the 2017 Brunel International African Poetry Prize. Some of his poems are obviously hewn from his life as a gay person in a largely heterosexual and obviously homophobic society. One of the consequences of such an approach, that is, of conceiving of African identity in a pluriversal and diverse manner, is to consider humanity as complex and multidimensional and therefore not reducible to just one notion of the human nature. One of the many areas of contention in this respect is that of human sexuality, especially regarding queer sexual orientation. Oriogu's poems urge us to adopt a pluriversal approach to understanding the human person.

The title of the poem "Invisible Man" is obviously a nod to Ralph Ellison's famous novel of the same name. With this poem, Oriogun identifies the speaker in the position of Ellison's narrator, who speaks from his underground hideout in the basement of a whites-only apartment. Ellison's story is, in turn, a tribute to Dostoyevsky's existentialist novel, *Notes from Underground*. Well situated in the tradition of both novels, Oriogun's poem gestures to the undying question of the place of the individual in an absurd world, a world that has no place for difference. Ellison's protagonist lives in a world dictated by the whims of white racist imagination; he is invisible, but desires to be seen. The same goes for Oriogun's speaker, whose world has been relegated to the coal cellar of a homophobic society, and who cries to be heard. The first two lines bring a boy and a bird together to create a potent metaphor for entrapment and the desire for liberation: "And the voice was a lost bird embedded in a boy / like a word stranded between pages." Unlike in Marcus Garvey's poem, "The Black Woman" and David Diop's poem "Africa" Leopold Sedar Senghor, "Black Woman" Oriogun presents an actual body, who ironically, is more complex and pluriversal than the abstract one. We are given a glimpse into the psyche and emotional state of the speaker, especially in the third stanza:

> The radio said, a father shot his son for loving another man.
> Marvin Gaye lives in the heart of a black drag queen
> and to be a song of pebbles and water is to run into a city of light
> and surrender your throat to the song of a bird.
>
> ORIOGUN 2017

We have thus two principles clashing against each other: freedom and death, each as strong as the other. We are reminded of the tragedy of Marvin Gaye's death, by his own father Rev. Marvin Gaye Sr., 70, an apostolic minister. The speaker is crammed between these two worlds, just as a word is stranded between pages and as is the caged bird in Paul Laurence Dunbar's poem, "Sympathy." If we have not already divined what torments the bird (that is, why that caged bird sings), then the seventh stanza makes it more than clear:

> Wet dreams:
> a boy hears the whisper of another boy deep in his bones
> and wonders about the origin of stars,

his body is a lamp learning how to give light
in a place where a boy opens his mouth
from the door of a tomb;
where a boy takes his first breath.

ORIOGUN 2017

It is not surprising that the speaker above wants to know the origin of stars. He is yearning for a boundless freedom and boundary-transcendent solidarity. Paul Laurence Dunbar and Ralph Ellison, of course, wrote about the cage to which African Americans had been consigned. In making subtle allusions to both, Oriogun exposes an existential and universal yearning for a boundless world, a yearning to escape a closed system.

The poem "Elegy for a Burnt Friend" (Oriogun 2017) powerfully expresses the condition of Africa understood as a closed system. It is a one-stanza poem in which the powerlessness of the speaker is powerfully expressed in the following lines:

There is nowhere to say enough,
nowhere to breathe in the open sea
without salt stinging your throat;
nowhere to wash our body in water and become free.

It is heartrending to realize that the speaker desires only to be allowed to be free and human. This is obviously impossible or very difficult, given the narrow conception of being in society. He is not seeking to redefine Africa; he is asking people to accommodate his difference. Afropolitanism understood as an ethical gesture (Eze, 2016a) seeks to achieve just that; it encourages a pluriversal reading of the human body.

Oriogun's poem "How to Survive the Fire" (2017) has one dominant idea, expressed in the last two lines: "before you understand why God turned // his face from Christ and whispered, run." The idea is the fragility of life, which is expressed in the conundrum of God telling a nailed Christ to run for his life. Where would Christ have run to when he was already nailed to the cross? The fitting metaphor of Christ being abandoned, or not being helped by God despite God's omnipotence, completes the picture of a closed system that is markedly against life, a system in which love of life and human flourishing had been extinguished in people by a corrosive mix of traditional lifestyles and Christian fundamentalist ideologies. In painting the picture of a closed world, Oriogun urges the need for a more expansive reality, or at least for a redefinition of the known world. He urges a rethinking of the contours of being as an African, or rather, a person of African ancestry. What I have said about Oriogu's poems goes for Chris Abani's poems and works of fiction. Specifically, apprehending the body as a space of limitless possibilities and surprises is one of the central ideas that Oriogun has in common with Chris Abani.

Chris Abani was born on December 27, 1966 in Afikpo, Nigeria, to a Scottish mother and a Nigerian Igbo father. Like Selasi, he grew up on at least two continents, Africa and Europe; he now lives in America, where he is the Board of Trustees Professor of English at Northwestern University. Abani's *The Virgin of Flames* (2007) is set in the cosmopolitan city of Los Angeles; more specifically, it is set in East L.A., where predominantly Hispanic and African Americans live. It centers on a struggling young Nigerian American artist named Black, who is in search of his identity. He is a quintessential mix of races and influences. His father is an Igbo atheist who is a NASA scientist, while his mother is a devoutly Catholic Salvadoran. The narrator hints at one of the Afropolitan moments in the story: "With an Igbo Father and Salvadoran mother, Black never felt he was much of either" (p. 37). Rather than hold allegiance to one ethnicity, Black sees himself as "a shape-shifter able to occupy several identities, taking on different ethnic and national affiliations as though they were seasonal changes in wardrobe, and discarding them just as easily" (p. 37). He is more interested in becoming than in settling with what is. This is perhaps necessitated by the structure of Los Angeles as the "city of angels," that is, a city of beings that are not encumbered by materiality. In this way, Los Angeles is a city of shape-shifters because people are not hampered by the weight of their past. Los Angeles is a space of transgression, one in which tradition or allegiance is less likely to hold a person from becoming what he or she wishes to become than a small town or a village would. Saskia Sassen (2008) argues that:

> Cities are the terrain where people from many different countries are most likely to meet and a multiplicity of cultures come together. The international character of major cities lies not only in their telecommunication infrastructure and international firms; it lies in the many different environments in which these workers exist.
>
> (p. 89)

Los Angeles provides Black the condition that makes him aware of the fact that he is more than his past and that there are many possibilities in him. He is aware of the fullest potentials of the city, and he states, "This city wasn't a city. And if it was, it was a hidden city. There are several cities within it, and you had to yield to it, before it revealed any of its magic to you . . . it forced you to find the city within you" (p. 177). The notion of finding a city within oneself gives credence to Black's search for more possibilities to qualify who he is. Like the speaker in Oriogun's poems, Black sees his world as characterized by yearning, which is both a symbolic and actual proof of diversity within. He wants more than the present and the given; he reaches out for the Afropolitan state of being. His mobility is to be perceived as a trope of the ability to create himself and this manifests itself even in his moments of confusion.

Of course if hard pressed Black couldn't say what it was exactly that he yearned for. The nearest thing he could say was that he didn't want to be himself. Or maybe that he was looking for who he should be. But he had no idea who he wanted to be.

(p. 39)

Black's confusion is to be understood first as consequent upon his refusal to settle with an ascribed identity. His choice of avowed identity does not come without a price. But he is ready to pay it, for it is the price of being human and being it fully. Black has a friend, Iggy, who is Jewish. These two are Abani's tropes of cosmopolitanism, for they represent two of the most mobile, if not uprooted, ethnicities in the history of mankind. In this regard, Black is an Afropolitan who is aware of his parents' ancestry. But his identity is not defined in a conventional way.

Afropolitanism and Human Flourishing

In *The History of Sexuality*, Michel Foucault (1978) explains that the body is the means through which society displays its power and control. This is done through the control of pleasure, especially in sex: when it is exercised, how, and with whom. Strictly speaking, therefore, to control sexual practice and relations is to control relations in society. Through its diverse ideological apparatuses, including religious institutions, the state creates a barrier between the individual and his body by controlling the individual's exercise of sexual acts; once that is achieved, the individual surrenders his will to the state. Colonists also targeted the African body. In order to entrench their hegemony, they had to invent Manichaean allegories that demonized the black body while apotheosizing the white body. The issue is about the body of the African, what it means to the individual and to the community in which it lives, and how other individuals relate to it. The first generation of African writers understandably invested their effort in delivering Africa from the control of the colonial masters; the generation following them sought to reconstitute the nations after the disillusionment of the struggles for independence. Within these contexts it seemed inevitable to ignore any attention to the body. It was understood that the body was an integral part of the struggle and whatever fate the nation faced was invariably the fate of the individual. Thus, the individual was subsumed within the ideological conditions of national politics.

After colonialism, which built its ideology of hate on the African body, and after decades of experimentation with Africanity, which sadly ignored the human condition of that body, it is time to return to the African body. Every effort at theorizing must be practiced from the standpoint of the African body. All discourse must issue from the body as a thing that lives and feels pain and pleasure. It must engage the body from the perspective of vulnerability, that is, of care and being-with as defining traits of identity. From the foregoing therefore, it is only fitting to talk about aesthetic theory in regard to postcolonial Africa. The goal of art is not to preserve an imagined pure identity or to fight the enemy, perceived or real. The test of every art is simply the degree to which it is true to its form, the degree to which it provides joy to the sense (aesthesis). Out of this derives its ability to enhance human well-being by paving ways for the expansion of the human imagination.

According to the *OED* (Simpson and Weiner, 122), wellbeing is "the state of doing well in life; happy, healthy or prosperous condition; moral or physical welfare (of a person or community)." It is generally understood as human flourishing, which is an extension of the Greek notion of *Eudemonia*—good spirit. It occupies a central place in Aristotle's philosophy and refers to the highest human virtue, a condition for living a life of enduring happiness and fulfillment. Human flourishing also refers to the condition in which every individual achieves optimal well-being in freedom; it is also a condition of belonging to communities, helping others, and benefiting from them (Aristotle 1999, 1–8). I use wellbeing and human flourishing interchangeably to denote the condition of a good life marked by happiness and self-fulfillment and guided by the awareness and the pursuit of the common good.

Oriogun's poem "The Origin of Butterflies" is just about human flourishing. It is a one-stanza poem whose core discourse is made explicit in these lines (2017):

> Last night I saw a butterfly
> break darkness with the colours of her wings,
> she rose gently to the moon with songs
> within her body.
>
> ORIOGUN 2017

Oriogun situates the speaker's mood on the brighter side of life. It is important that what breaks the darkness surrounding the speaker's world is something as dainty, vulnerable, and harmless as the wings of butterfly. Equally important is that the butterfly rises to the moon "with her body." It is the resurrection of the body, not of the soul. Oriogun is interested in the triumph of the body, or simply in human flourishing. This is made more explicit in the last ten lines of the poem:

> There is a place where butterflies live – mother
> said happiness can come from sadness.
> On the next page of my life
> I wrote only one word: Happiness.

I watched it grew from my book
and broke the night into fragments of stars.
Someone once said, when the sun is dead
we take light in small sips.
I do not know what it means,
I only saw stars falling as butterflies.

ORIOGUN 2017

The core of the speaker's life is seen in the pursuit of the very idea, put in his head by his mother: happiness. In Oriogun's understanding, human flourishing must be like butterflies in the field which destroy nothing, but which live as fulfilled a life as they can. A fulfilled life is lived in the present, not in the abstraction of collective identity or in the thereafter.

Whereas in Oriogun the body aspires to heaven, which is a signifier of freedom, in Abani, that body brings down heaven in the gesture of complete control of the present. Like Oriogun, Abani believes in the triumph of the body. His poem "The New Religion" symbolizes the philosophy of Afropolitanism and anticipates the affirmation of the African body (2006):

The body is a nation I have not known.
The pure joy of air: the moment between leaping
from a cliff into the wall of blue below. Like that.
Or to feel the rub of tired lungs against skin-
covered bone, like a hand against the rough of bark.
Like that. The body is a savage, I said.
For years I said that: the body is a savage.
As if this safety of the mind were virtue
not cowardice. For years I have snubbed
the dark rub of it, said, I am better, Lord,
I am better, but sometimes, in an unguarded
moment of sun, I remember the cowdung-scent
of my childhood skin thick with dirt and sweat
and the screaming grass.
But this distance I keep is not divine,
for what was Christ if not God's desire
to smell his own armpit? And when I
see him, I know he will smile,
fingers glued to his nose, and say, "Next time
I will send you down as a dog
to taste this pure hunger.

(p. 56)

It is revealing of Abani's Afropolitan sensibility that this poem begins by juxtaposing the body and the nation. "The body is a nation I have not known." It is intriguing that the speaker refers to what is probably his (we take the speaker to be the author) body as an unknown entity. At the same time, that entity is where he resides and from which he derives his identity. His body is to him what that geographical (or imagined) space called "nation" is for people with common descent, history, culture, language, or life. His body is the source of his history, culture, aspiration, language, and lifestyle. Yet, he does not know that body. We are also encouraged to think of the nation in pluriversal formats. In a twenty-first century nation, heterogeneity rather than homogeneity, is the norm.

The speaker's joy of pure air parallels that of his knowledge that his tired lungs rub against his bones. This undeniable tactility of his body is part of what assures him of his citizenship of his body. But the speaker does not come to this knowledge per chance. Indeed, he had lived in the denial or demeaning of that body, taking refuge in the safety of the mind, without being grateful to the body for housing that mind. We do not know the history behind this denial. We can only assume that as a postcolonial subject and as one who had enjoyed the epistemologies issuing from Christian-colonial education, steeped in the Platonic world of ideas, the speaker must have been taught to despise his body. It is a relief that the speaker reaches the epiphany that the body is a source of joy; it is his nation. The realization comes to him "in an unguarded moment of sun," that is, in the open, when the scales of colonial and Christian education have fallen from his eyes, in the open in which reality has been laid bare. At that moment, when he does not need to hide anything or to pretend to be what he is not, he remembers his true, ordinary self, the self that had not acquired false consciousness, the self of his "childhood skin thick with dirt and sweat." What is truly amazing and even more convincing is the part of nature that he remembers at the same time that he recalls his childhood skin. It is the "cowdung-scent," the most ordinary, stinky thing, a thing as normal as life. The ordinariness of life that is perceived through the senses of touch and smell, as has been demonstrated thus far in the poem, is the location of life. It is also what the speaker has in common with God, whose deepest desire was to smell himself. The desire to become a body prompted God to incarnate in a human body, to "smell his own armpit."

One might be tempted to equate smelling one's armpit with navel-gazing. It is true that both acts focus on the individual, but the former refers specifically to egomania while the later suggests the individual embracing the less flattering part of self. Armpits remind us of our bodies as ever-decomposing entities. They must therefore be accorded attention. Chris Abani's reference to incarnation not only reveals the anthropomorphic conception of God; according to Christian belief, it signifies God reaching out to humans in order for humans to do the same to one another, incarnate in one another, care for one another. Incarnating in one another is only possible through the power of imagination, through empathy, which enables us to put ourselves in the position of the other, especially those suffering gratuitous pain. This is the locus of the new ethics of being and becoming that Afropolitanism seeks to capture.

Afropolitan Literature as World Literature

My choice of Oriogun and Abani does not imply a privileging of their works over those of contemporary African writers that gesture toward openness. Indeed, in terms of liberating the African body from forms of ideologies, contemporary African women writers and activists are inimitable trailblazers. They are no longer obsessed with writing back to the center of the empire. They write back to their bodies as a locus of their existence, their bodies as situated in the world, rather than in abstract concepts of African identity. They demand that their bodies be respected as entities that feel pain and deserve respect. That is why many of them no longer shy away from the tag of feminism. Selasi belongs to this generation of African women writers. Their writing can be justifiably tagged Afropolitan, especially in the terms I have mapped out above. I have discussed these contemporary writers in my book (Eze 2016b). Selasi is one of them; in their critique of patriarchy and their focus on the body, they call for multidimensional thinking, which is an integral part of Afropolitanism. As Selasi states, without "multi-dimensional thinking, we [Afropolitans] could not make sense of ourselves" (Selasi 2005). Thanks to the embrace of multidimensionality, Afropolitanism is to be understood as the first step toward the difficult task of cleaving the African imagination from its obsession with the past as a legitimizing principle of identity in the present; it is a step away from the indigenist and nativist rhetoric of Africanity. What Selasi says about Africans in the diaspora who move between Africa and the West applies to Africans who move between places in Africa, between one African city and another, between one African village and another. The concept therefore points to a fundamental shift in conceptions of African identity, especially in the twenty-first century; this shift highlights the fluidity in African self-perception and visions of the world. It is on this basis that the concept has been interpreted as an African inflection of cosmopolitanism, or Afro-cosmopolitanism (Eze 2014). Within that context, it offers a new ethics of being for Africans.

While the notion of Afropolitanism as a thing of consciousness, or the embrace of multidimensionality, is profoundly ethical (Eze 2016 a), it is so only to the degree that the Afropolitan reaches out to others and sees in them the same freedom she sees in herself; only then can it claim to be world literature. That is, it is oriented toward the world as unbounded. On the African continent, it reveals itself as the audacity to stake moral claims to Africa and the world and, conversely, to admit that others can lay the same claim to Africa. Within this perimeter, the Afropolitan believes that being

African is not reductive to color, heritage or autochthony; rather, being African is expansive. Thus, Afropolitanism operates from the belief that to be is to relate. It is only in relating to others that the Afropolitan consciousness incarnates itself in the world, becoming worldly. The more expansive Afropolitans' spheres of relations are, the deeper their humanity.

The philosophical basis of Afropolitanism is that the traditional notion of African identity, rooted in opposition to the West, is no longer adequate to capture the complex structure of being human today. It is at this point that Afropolitanism can be understood as a manifestation of the philosophical premises of wider horizons of meaning and being African in the world. These horizons of meaning emerge in the moments of encounter, in being with others; it is not based on where those others come from. Encountering others does not mean the abdication of Africa, or the rejection of African identity. On the contrary, it is the full acceptance of the worldliness of Africa; that is, Africa the way it is. Accepting Africa thus paves the way to relate to it realistically, rather than in the abstract. The central moral attitude of this new world is the rejection of the oppositional frame of being.

Based on the impulse derived from the exercise of the imagination to include the other or otherness in its sphere, the Afropolitan disposition toward the world understands universality to mean that one cannot consider a particular thing to the exclusion of others. An idea has meaning only in relation to other ideas. So do humans. I am human because I relate to other humans. Others affirm me; they provide the context within which my story has meaning. In this context, I am who I am not because I am opposed to someone else. This is true in every African society of today, the Africa in which socio-historical contexts have shifted. The issue therefore is no longer how different we are from others, but rather what we can learn from them, what we have in common with them. This implies a conscious effort to affirm something in others and to seek to relate to them. Let it be the starting point of encounter. Any literature from Africa or by a person of African ancestry that embodies this spirit of openness, any literature that gestures toward the world as a limitless space is, by definition, a world literature.

Works cited

Abani, Chris. 2004. *Graceland*. New York. Farrar, Straus and Giroux.
Abani, Chris. 2006. *Hands Washing Water*. Port Townsend, Washington: Copper Canyon Press.
Abani, Chris. 2007. *The Virgin of Flames*. New York: Penguin Books.
Achebe, Chinua. 1958. *Things Fall Apart*. London, Heinemann
Adeleke, Tunde. 2009. *The Case Against Afrocentrism*. University of Press of Mississippi.

AP. 2014. "Nigeria passes law banning homosexuality." *The Telegraph*. http://www.telegraph.co.uk/news/worldnews/africaandindianocean/nigeria/10570304/Nigeria-passes-law-banning-homosexuality.html

Appiah, Kwame Anthony. 1993. *In My Father's House: Africa in the Philosophy of Culture*. New York: Oxford University Press.

Appiah, Kwame Anthony. 2006. *Cosmopolitanism: Ethics in a World of Strangers*. New York. W. W. Norton & Company.

Aristotle, *Nicomachean Ethics*. Trans. Terence Irwin. (Indianapolis: Hackett Publishing Co, 1999): 1–8.

Bowden, Brett. 2003. "The Perils of Global Citizenship." *Citizenship Studies* 7: 349–362

Cullen, Countee "Heritage." https://www.poemhunter.com/poem/heritage/

Dabir, Emma i. 2016. "Why I am (still) not an Afropolitan," Journal of African Cultural Studies, 28:1, 104–108.

Ede, Amatoritsero. 2016. "The politics of Afropolitanism." *Journal of African Cultural Studies*, 28:1, 88–100).

Eze, Chielozona. 2005. "Cosmopolitan Solidarity: Negotiating Transculturality in Contemporary Nigerian Novels." *English in Africa*. 99–112.

Eze, Chielozona. 2014. "Rethinking African culture and identity: the Afropolitan model." *Journal of African Cultural Studies*. 26. 2: 234–247.

Eze, Chielozona. 2016a. "We Afropolitans" Journal of African Cultural Studies. Volume 28, 2016—Issue 1, 114–119.

Eze, Chielozona. 2016b. *Ethics and Human Rights in Contemporary Anglophone Women's Literature*. New York: Palgrave Macmillan.

Foucault, Michel. 1978. *The History of Sexuality*, 1, R. Hurley, trans. Penguin Books.

Gates, Jr., Henry Louis. 1988. "The Trope of a New Negro and the Reconstruction of the Image of the Black." *Representations*. 24:129–155.

Gikandi, Simon. 2005. "W.E.B. DuBois and the Identity of Africa." *Gefame: Journal of African Studies*. 2. 1, https://quod.lib.umich.edu/g/gefame/4761563.0002.101/--w-e-b-dubois-and-the-identity-of-africa?rgn=main;view=fulltext

Gikandi, Simon. "Foreword—on Afropolitanism." *Negotiating Afropolitanism*. Eds J. Wawrzinek and J.K.S. Makokha. Amsterdam: Rodopi. 9–11.

Heidegger, Martin. 1996. *Being and Time*. Joan Stambaugh trans. New York: State University of New York Press.

Human Rights Watch. 2016. "Nigeria: Harsh Law's Severe Impact on LGBT Community Encourages Widespread Extortion, Violence. Human Rights Watch." https://www.hrw.org/news/2016/10/20/nigeria-harsh-laws-severe-impact-lgbt-community

Kendhammer, Brandon. 2007. "DuBois the pan-Africanist and the development of African nationalism." *Ethnic and Racial Studies* 30.1: 51–71.

Laye, Camara. 1959. *The African Child*. Fontana Press.

Lynch, Hollis R. 1970. *Edward Wilmot Blyden: Pan-Negro Patriot, 1832–1912*. London: Oxford University Press.

Macquarrie, John. 1968. *Martin Heidegger*, Richmond, Virginia: John Knox Press.

Mandela, Nelson. 2010. *Conversations with Myself*. New York: Farrar, Straus and Giroux.

Mbembe, Achille. 1992. "The Banality of Power and the Aesthetics of Vulgarity in the Postcolony." *Public Culture*, 4 (2): 1–30.

Mbembe, Achille. 2001. *On the Postcolony*. Berkeley: University of California Press.

Mbembe, Achille. 2007. "Afropolitanism." In *Africa Remix: Contemporary Art of a Continent*, edited by Njami Simon and Lucy Durán, 26–30. Johannesburg: Johannesburg Art Gallery.

McKaiser, Eusebius. 2012. "Homosexuality un-African? The claim is an historical embarrassment." *The Guardian*. https://www.theguardian.com/world/2012/oct/02/homosexuality-unafrican-claim-historical-embarrassment

Mignolo, Walter. 2011. *The Darker Side of Western Modernity: Global Futures, Decolonial Options*. Durham, NC: Duke University Press.

Molesworth, Charles. 2012. "Countee Cullen's Reputation: the forms of desire." *Transition*. 107 ((2012):66–77).

Mudimbe, V. Y. 1988. *The Invention of Africa: Gnosis, Philosophy, and the Order of Knowledge*. Bloomington: Indiana University Press.

Musila, Grace. 2016. "Part-Time Africans, Europolitans and 'Africa lite'" Journal of African Cultural Studies. Volume 28,—Issue 1): 109–113.

Nyamnjoh, Francis B. "Incompleteness: Frontier Africa and the Currency of Conviviality." *Journal of Asian and African Studies*. 47(2): 129–154 (first published April 23, 2015) 1–18.

Oriogun, Romeo. 2017. Brunel International African Poetry Prize: Winning Poems. http://www.africanpoetryprize.org/winning-poems (October 23, 2017).

Ouologuem, Yambo. 1971. *Bound to Violence*. Heinemann Publishers.

Pahl, Miriam. "Afropolitanism as critical consciousness: Chimamanda Ngozi Adichie's and Teju Cole's internet presence" *Journal of African Cultural Studies*. Volume 28,—Issue 1 (2016): 73–87.

p'Bitek, Okot. 1966. *Song of Lawino and Song of Ocol*. Jordan Hill, Oxford, England: Heinemann.

Rabaka, Reiland. 2009. *Africana Critical Theory: Reconstructing the Black Radical Tradition, From W. E. B. Du Bois and C. L. R. James to Frantz Fanon and Amilcar Cabral*. Lanham, MD, Lexington Books.

Sassen, Saskia. 2000. "The Global City: Strategic Site/New Frontier." *American Studies* 41.2/3: 79–9.

Selasi, Taiye. 2005. "Bye-Bye Babar." *The LIP Magazine*. http://thelip.robertsharp.co.uk/?p=76

Simpson, J.A and Weiner, E.S.C. *Oxford English Dictionary*. Vol. XX. The Oxford English Dictionary. Vol. XVI. Oxford: Clarendon Press.

wa Thiong'o, Ngugi. 1965. *The River Between*. Jordan Hill, Oxford: Heinemann, 1965.

9

Fingering the Jagged Grain

Re-reading Afropolitanism (and Africa) in Taiye Selasi's *Ghana Must Go*

Aretha Phiri

Introduction: Afropolitanism Must Go!: Re-reading Africa(ns) in the World

Following her initial inquiry into how Afropolitanism "differs from traditional, elitist white pseudo-universalist cosmopolitanisms" (2015: 1), Anna-Leena Toivanen has more recently proposed its limits as an ethnic adjunct to cosmopolitanism. Conceding that while it is "certainly a well-intentioned, empowerment-driven gesture," she cautions that Afropolitanism's specific continental linkage "nevertheless risks promoting territorial and even racial biases that cosmopolitanism should ideally avoid" (2017: 190). Afropolitanism is finally, for Toivanen, "simply cosmopolitanism's new fashionable clothing: a lot of excitement surrounding little viable content" (2017: 202).

Notwithstanding debates around cosmopolitanism's limited idealist universalism (Gikandi 2002; Gilroy 2005), Afropolitanism's advancement of an African provenance of mobile and mutable, cosmopolitan subjectivities has been exposed to sustained criticism. Initiated by celebrated author, Taiye Selasi, in an essay entitled "Bye Bye, Babar" in 2005, Afropolitanism's initially popular mainstream and even critical acclaim has over the years been challenged.[1] Described as the worldly articulations of the "newest generation of African emigrants," Afropolitanism is ostensibly symptomatic of the hybrid diasporic trends of twenty-first century globalization. Yet despite the intent to put forward a progressive, 'African-oriented' cosmopolitanism that affirms Africa's place on the world stage, Afropolitanism has been resoundingly condemned for its veiled political conservatism. Including accusations that it is self-servingly elitist (Tveit 2013), culturally irresponsible (Ede 2016) and exploitative in its presentation of a "lite" version of the continent (Dabiri 2016; Musila 2016), Afropolitanism has more provocatively been described as a "fancy moniker" that, in masking the terror typically associated with Africa, actually evidences black African "self-hatred" (Aidoo 2016).

But although necessarily interrogating and problematizing its political efficacies, the discussions around Afropolitanism have become tedious primarily because they are so predictable. Stephanie Bosch Santana argues that Afropolitanism "remains a haunted and haunting term [that] makes a fitting spectre, for it is always in excess of itself" (2016:123). Indeed, reviews of Afropolitanism reveal how 'excessive' the readings of Africa from both without and within (its borders) continue to be, operating as they do on racially over-determined and potentially colonizing premises that envisage a timeless and authentic Africa and (its) Africans. Whether to keep black Africa in its historically imagined place (as 'Western' academics are wont to do) or to re-situate black Africa in the face of its historical and persistent marginalization and deligitimization in the global imagination (as 'Africanist' intellectuals tend to do), it appears that both positions elide what Simon Njami identifies as the historically "schizophrenic reality" of global processes of cultural and ideological mongrelization (2007: 13). In essence, they obscure the mechanisms of a consequently and an inevitably protean, shifting black Africanness that South African political analyst, Ebrahim Harvey (2006), describes as "more opaque, questionable, complex and potentially contradictory than ever before," despite the (pre)dominant narratives of social-economic and -political poverty and malaise. The increasingly incongruous picture and ever more contentious character of blackness in a postcolonial, post-apartheid milieu disrupts and will continue to destabilize arcane, quixotic notions of a quintessential, definitive African existence and identity.

In this regard, where attempts to analyze its conceptual validity (Mbembe 2011; Gikandi 2007) and moral capacity (Eze 2014, 2106) are warranted, well-intentioned counter attempts to further situate and normativize Afropolitanism are not unproblematic. Where Ashleigh Harris has argued that contemporary Afrodiasporic literature that is not sufficiently conversant with "African everyday life" hazards entrenching global hierarchies (2014) and Dan Ojwang and Michael Titlestad have maintained that the current trend of émigré writing unfortunately, "contorts the continent's past and present" and is "by definition, less specifically textured" (2014), a recent trend in pronouncing a burgeoning contemporary literature written in English by Africans in the diaspora, definitively "Afropolitan" literature, risks rehearsing ethnically the taxonomic imperatives of the global publishing industry. Described in Eva Knudsen and Ulla Rahbeck's recent publication, *In Search of the Afropolitan*, as the pursuit of a descriptive "'literary turn' in the study of Afropolitanism," the proposed "*space* of critical enquiry" engendered by Afropolitanism is here belaboured by the need to "think of it as a badge that may be attached to a contemporary prose narrative written by an African-descendent writer" (2016: 3, 10). That is, the proposition here of an Afropolitan literary aesthetics that provides a "new space of investigation into the effects of globalization on the African character—and the African place" (2017: 116) cannot help but be fraught discursively with the identitarian politics that has beleaguered postcolonial African literature and which is being increasingly resisted by contemporary black African writers in the diaspora.[2] Notwithstanding these diasporic writers' own anxieties around the commercial and political exigencies of the publishing industry's generic categorization of African literature, Africa's enduring dialectic—and now increasingly dialogic— internationalization has been repeatedly illustrated by canonical writers the likes of Chinua Achebe and Buchi Emecheta, to name but a few. As such the persistent inclination to locate through (pseudo-biological, cross-cultural) taxonomy the "African character—and the African place," does not just elide a sophisticated postcolonial global positionality and imagination; it unwittingly parallels an historical desire to anthropologize and pathologize black Africa(nness). To this end, an uncritical homogenization and racialization is rehearsed and Africa continues to signify in the imaginary an ethnic, cultural, and ontological particularity in ways that reinstate exclusionary, heteronormative hierarchies of blackness.

Although the appeal to an established category of literature that aspires to delineate salient aspects of African experience is merited, if unavoidable, literature's ability to complicate, elude, and surpass the intentions even of its author testifies to the inefficacy of ideological, prescriptive taxonomies. In this regard, it would perhaps be more efficacious to view "literature as a world" (Casanova 2005: 71–73) in its own right, complete with its own unquantifiable vagaries. This is not to endorse uncritically the anti-instrumentalist view of the (necessary) singularity of literature. It is to recognize, in evidencing the "irresolvable aporia of African writing," that this fiction needs also to be approached as a mediating space that writers and readers simultaneously navigate rather than attempt to triumphantly colonize; allowing for the suspension of the ethnographic imperative in favour of an ethical-ontological, fundamentally open, reading stance that facilitates infinite possibilities (Shabangu 2018: 348, 343).[3] Tellingly, where Chimamanda Ngozi Adichie has famously excoriated the "danger of a single story" (2009) and Chris

Abani has maintained that "story is fluid and belongs to nobody" (2007), Selasi has, in a retrospective discussion of her now contested essay, confessed that "Like all writers, I am obliged to let my writing live a life of its own—to enter discourses for which I did not intend it, to suffer interpretations I never imagined" (Knusden and Rahbeck, 2016: 290). In this way, through an aesthetic of less explicitly politicized, idiosyncratic versions of African diasporic culture, contemporary literature by Africans in the diaspora attempts to shift and broaden the discussion around blackness from an "African-centered approach" to one that interrogates the "globality of the diaspora-in-the-making" (Patterson and Kelley 2000: 26). Testament to and underwriting increasing technological and digital, modern innovations that both accentuate and undermine global interconnectedness, this contemporary literature affords a revision of Africa(ns) in the global imaginary and allows for the imagination of enduringly transitional and procedural existential states. That is, contemporary literature emanating from the diaspora necessarily and purposively fingers the "jagged grain" (Ellison 1995: 78) of existence—worrying the categorical identitarian spaces we unquestioningly occupy by illuminating, rather, "the strange corners of what it means to be human" (Okri 2014).

In this regard, Selasi's debut novel *Ghana Must Go* (2013) enacts a textual re-reading of diaspora in its exploration of the impulses of human existence that, in transgressing external, cultural borders, finally trespass the interior "boundaries of the self" (Selasi 2013c: 14). Demonstrating in her 2014 Ted Talk the need to privilege "human experience" over the "limiting trap" of Culture, Selasi enacts in her novel what Chielozona Eze describes as "transcultural affinity": a "moral investment in the being of others" that both acknowledges and transcends cultural particularities (2015: 223). More acutely, in re-imagining diaspora as an existential, rather than merely political, site that resonates with the lyrical aesthetics and malleable poetics of the blues musical genre, her revisionary cosmopolitan reading of the blues embeds the Afrodiasporic condition in an ethical frame in which respect for the diversity and specificity of all people renders him/her simultaneously responsive to the intrinsic otherness of the self, allowing thus for a more inclusive and expansive vision of (being in) the world.

'Fingering [the] jagged grain': Reading the blues in *Ghana Must Go*

Published in 2013 to critical acclaim, *Ghana Must Go* tells the story of the Sai's, an intergenerational family of overachievers residing in Boston, America. On the surface, the Sai's present an enviable story of transnational, diasporic success. The distinguished surgeon and accomplished African patriarch, Dr Kweku Sai, is married to the remarkably beautiful and eclectic Folasadé, with whom he has four variously accomplished children: Olu, the burgeoning surgeon following in his father's footsteps; Taiwo and Kehinde, the cultured and artistic twins; and Sadie, the blossoming Ivy-league student. But beneath the 'traditional' African diaspora success story lies a troubling narrative of chronic trauma not unlike that described in psychoanalytic criticism as characterized by permanently disruptive experiences that disarticulate "the self and creates holes in existence" (LaCapra 2001: 41).

Taking inspiration from the historical event of the expulsion and consequent mass-migration of an estimated two million Ghanaians from Nigeria in 1983, *Ghana Must Go*'s references to child rape and incest, forced and voluntary migrations and bloody civil wars experienced generationally by the family read overwhelmingly like an historical allegory of national and continental malaise. Yet underlined by relational infidelities and alienations, instances of self-harm and ideologies of (racial and physical) self-hatred that do not just mirror and render relatable a larger traumatic narrative, the novel's generic lament is concerned with domesticating the politically abstract at the familial, personal level.

Certainly the protracted focus at its opening on the interior workings of Kweku's death—his memories of his past life and his meditation on his imminent death—from the combined perspectives of his cinematographic, voyeuristic roving 'camera' and the omniscient narrator, suggest something more intricate and intimate—human—than mere national allegory. The emphasis on subjective interiority here—"when the challenge of the minute is the sole focus of the mind and the whole world slows down as to watch what will happen" (7)—and elsewhere in the novel echoes the African American blues modal expression of existential duress and not just at the level of political citizenship. Traditionally viewed as an expressive ontological idiom that articulated a "life of struggle" and functioned as an "antipsychotic" to help keep black people to "from losing their minds" in the navigation of a hostile mainstream, white American culture (Touré 2016), the blues are described existentially as an "autobiographical chronicle of personal catastrophe expressed lyrically"; as an expressive genre originating in "an impulse to keep the painful details and episodes of a brutal experience alive in one's aching consciousness, to finger its jagged grain, and to transcend it, not by the consolation of philosophy but by squeezing it from a near-tragic, near-comic lyricism" (Ellison 1995: 78-79). As such, while *Ghana Must Go*'s morbid opening and universally funereal tone—its painstaking and particular, lyrical exploration of the interiority of the experience of the threshold between death and life—employ and expand the simultaneously melancholic themes and elastic poetics of the blues to include and relay the communal *and* individuated psychical experiences of the African diaspora "beyond being 'citizen', beyond being 'poor'" (91), but at the "most gut level of human experience" (Neal 42).

Indeed, albeit a late nineteenth-century phenomenon signifying African American racial sensibility and authenticity, and notwithstanding its eventual commodification and appropriation by mainstream, white America, the blues' foundational embeddedness in the antiphonal call-and-response structure of African and slave oral cultures as well as subsequent integration of American spirituals rendered it a fundamentally hybrid mode; an expressive genre that simultaneously articulated and countered modernity's impositions in its reflection of a protean black spatiotemporal and material, cross- and trans-cultural diasporic experience. Cemented in the twentieth century and demonstrating thus a pliable, cosmopolitan ethos, the blues stylistically indicated "generations in the flux of change who desired and needed to meet the future without losing the past, who needed to stand alone and yet remain part of the group ... as they ventured into unfamiliar territories and ways" (Levine 1977: 238) through transgressive and potentially transcendent, non-prescriptive and non-restrictive, articulations of blackness.

Similarly, in deploying and expanding its originary migratory impulse *Ghana Must Go*'s revisionary expression of a blues mode is an attempt to articulate the intricacies, indeed tensions that characterize contemporary, twenty-first century, Afrodiasporic subjectivity and experience. Set predominantly in Boston but seguing between American and African states, the novel expresses the enduring postcolonial concerns of home and exile. Inscribed into its portrait of this spiritually unsettled family is an interstitial existential condition expressed in its perpetual navigation of the "shadowy gap between worlds" (221) in which, embedded in a space of non-belonging, the question of identity is always posed death-like—"in grayness, like shadows" (221), tentatively between subjective roots and routes. The Sai family is, in spite of its middle-class, urban(e) positionality and despite the novel's titular and sectional invocation of mobility and agency, not just culturally "'lost in transnation'" as Selasi herself has elsewhere explained (2005); they are, as is evident in the characters enduring sense of loss and demonstrated in the novel's fragmented and elliptical style, lost in subjective translation that implies their situatedness in a continuously transitional process of subjective (re-)interpretation.

The "Aching [Blues] Consciousness": Navigating Unfamiliar Territories

In this regard and notwithstanding the other children's existential duress, it is Sadie Sai who most embodies the blues mode.[4] Characterized by racial self-loathing and suffering from body dysmorphia that manifests in bulimia, her expression of anxiety at the material level of the body finally articulates "her whole being trembling with the effort to *be*" (36) existentially, *a priori* the exigencies of culture writ large. Describing the distressing process of purgation—"the vomit. How it emerges with *a logic*, in the *order received*. With a touch of the ceremonial, she thinks, in the action, the kneeling and performing the *same gruesome rite*, the repetition and the silence" (142; my emphasis), Sadie's 'rationalized' eating disorder, which enacts the disciplined Foucauldian body, both affirms and disrupts the whiteness within which she is embedded in its articulation of a collective, racialized "paralyzing absence and ineradicable desire" intoned in the blues. But in her performative abjection and simultaneous desire for existential otherness—in which "She doesn't want to be Caucasian . . . She wants to be [her best friend] Philae" (146)—is the expression finally "of an anonymous (nameless) voice issuing from the black (w)hole" (Baker 1984: 5). That is, echoing the blues expression of an individualized, personal pain and loss, and evidenced in her premature birth is an arrested existential development in which ultimately "She *doesn't* belong . . . isn't meant to" (158).[5]

It is indicative, then, of the psychical shift she experiences when she travels with her family from Boston to Accra upon news of her father's death. Ostensibly interpreted in the traditional postcolonial discourse of 'return' as a cultural homecoming in which the possibility for achieving subjective wholeness is premised on locating her patrilineal roots—that elusive "Man from the Story" (158), Sadie's transatlantic, transnational border-crossing here further enacts an existential transmigration that expresses the blues' modal yearning for (r)evolutionary transformation. Not only is she significantly moved by the presence of her paternal aunt, Naa, whose steadfast gaze reverses the (racial) imperial gaze by forcing her to look back in return and recognize the "striking resemblance" (264) of someone she has never known, Sadie is described when dancing the traditional Ghanaian Ga dance as accessing or being inhabited by "a stranger inside her that knows what to do, knows the music, these movements, this footwork, this rhythm" (270). Suggestively ethnocentric, this clichéd representation of diaspora infers the pervasive allure of both colonial and postcolonial identitarian, discursive politics in which African culture and subjects are exoticized and rendered prototypic.[6] But it is also the "manifestation of an intuitive connection to the transpersonal dimension" premised on "person-environment *interaction*" (Madison 2006: 247; emphasis in original). Building on her (mythological and mediated) heritage in order to enhance the embodied present, the experiential, interactional emphasis in this scene on "*these* movements, *this* footwork, *this* rhythm" (270) implies the temporality of geographical space and proposes culture as always vulnerable to the prospect of (re)translation and revision.[7] Her previously (self-) disciplined body, here affirmed through motion translates, in a cosmopolitan vein, "the body-as-habit to the body-as-event" and her being into the embodied "present of initiative" (Ricouer 2006: 40, 353). That is, in the translation of her physical movement(s) to an interior, spiritual mobility, Sadie's ability to access her "*surrogate heartbeat*" (267) does not just endorse an intuitive "transcultural affinity"; it simultaneously testifies to a cosmopolitan ethic which comprehends "humanity in all its guises" (Nussbaum1996: 9). Underwriting here a blues sensibility of black culture as that "thing [that] *circulates*" (Snead 1981: 149), she registers its inherent, existential instinct for "change, movement, action, continuance, unlimited and unending possibility" (Baker 1984: 8). This transmigration is indicative of a transcendent, mediated and malleable, blackness that advances a "definition of oneself through the world beyond one's own origins" and encourages "attentiveness to a range of modes of defining oneself and one's community in relation to the world" (Nwankwo 2005: 9, 11), and it is significant here that in reinterpreting the self-in-relation to the other into the self-in-relation to the self, Sadie finally "doesn't fall" (269). In embracing the other/stranger within the self she is able to re-read the normative world expansively to include the otherness/strangeness—the idiosyncrasies—of (her) being.

(Women) Singing the Blues: *Ghana Must Go* as a Feminist Praxis

Magnifying thus the promise of living through and transcending history in visionary anticipation of alternative futures, *Ghana Must Go* puts forward in a blues mode or aesthetic an agential transformative feminist praxis that orients diaspora "beyond strictly historical and national frameworks and instead through a textuality that can engender and embody" (Pinto 2013: 7) fundamental existential tensions. In line with its relative accent on women's spiritual, corporeal, and sexual experiences and presences, the novel reveals an absent(ed) female presence and desire that exists within a larger historical, patriarchal narrative of existential injury in the expression of a revised and renewed, that is, expansive and inclusive, social order.[8] Herein, the embodied experiences of the female characters signify a "world beyond themselves" (Butler 1990: ix), extending sociopolitical implications to include existential, materialist considerations of the Afrodiasporic condition in ways that consider further how "the intimate recesses of the domestic space become sites for history's most intricate invasions" (Bhabha 1992: 141). This is in order to better comprehend the ways in which the localized, domestic sphere is intricately linked to and inevitably invaded by, and so rendered a revisionary site for, history's broader societal permutations.

Tellingly, the translation generationally of the mother-daughter relationship from (the mother's) past experiences which arrest the development of the (female child's) present, reinterprets the Fanonian (1961) postcolonial narrative of the 'nausea of history' to include women's complex experiences of diaspora. Notwithstanding Sadie's sense of Fola's maternal neglect, Taiwo's sense of Fola's desertion, which echoes Fola's abandonment by her own mother, acknowledges contextual, existential vagaries (and vulgarities) that afford a necessary reconsideration of the limitations of a heteronormative, Afrodiasporic maternal project that fails to "protect" or "act as a shield" (290) to its progeny. Indeed, the novel's graphic delineation of the rape of a younger Taiwo by her twin brother Kehinde, a rape forcibly orchestrated by their deranged maternal uncle, Femi, who is a general in the national army, does not merely illuminate allegorically the patriarchal violence(s) of post-colonial, post-independent Nigeria; it allows us to imagine inclusively, in the despairing and awkward relations of and between the twins, the complex tonalities that attend sexual and other violations and the lingering subjective and relational effects therein.[9] Significantly, this affords a necessary reconceptualization of black experience not just as a collective cultural lament but as a signal means of rewriting a grand cultural narrative to accentuate, rather, "the notoriously and gloriously disorderly affair" that is human life (Selasi 2014).

Similarly and indicatively, where home traditionally functions as a (maternal) metaphor for belonging in (postcolonial) diaspora narratives, its elusive and fragile, fluid conception in the novel reconfigures the spatial to signify, as Selasi explains, not just "a place, but a way to be in and know the world" (2013b). Notwithstanding Fola's lack of intuitive affiliation with homes in the novel and Olu's realization finally that home for him is not external but resides in his wife, Ling's (soft, feminine) body, Kweku's own obsession with his designer house, which signals for him "a homeland reimagined" (5), affords a feminist, interactional reinterpretation of traditional African masculinity. Yearning for belonging and rootedness, it is finally the ambivalent symbolism of his slippers that are a significant legacy to his rootedless, scattered children. Signifying on the one hand the warmth, familiarity, and permanence typically associated with domicile, their strategic placement at the doorway of a dead Kweku's house conveys not just the sense of enduring physical migration that typifies the novel. Envisaged as residing *in situ* in the embodied self, this ontological revisionism of home as interactional is underlined in slippers weathered and worn and which symbolize existentially a transmigratory state of being affirmed in *Ghana Must Go*'s ambiguous conclusion and in which characters remain hauntingly and perpetually "unfinished, in rehearsal, a production in progress" (123) in a world without subjective resolution.[10]

Conclusion: Alter-native Narratives of Existence?

Selasi has upon reflection described writing her now infamous essay on Afropolitanism not from a position of power, but "from a position of pain," the "incredibly alienating" and "disorienting" experience of a stranded, "'de-territorialized' brown people" acutely aware "at all times of our non-belonging" (Bady and Selasi 2015: 158). Similarly articulating a "life of struggle," *Ghana Must Go* reads like a literary parallel to the blues' tonal articulation of the "most plaintive and melancholy music imaginable" (Baraka 2002: 78). But while about "some loss, some pain and some other things," the novel's characters, like the blues, is underpinned by a "sense of agency" (Morrison 2004: 18) that complicates the mournful tonality of a life lived under duress, expanding African diaspora's protracted, elegiac suffering into a conditionality or practice that both refracts and reflects the agential tenets of *a priori* existentialism.

Tellingly, Selasi has in a recent interview more assertively claimed her artistic "right to opacity. The right not to lay everything out. The right not to be transparent. The right not to always have to excuse, explain oneself, but to just be and to trust and know that as an artist, one must plumb the depths of one's own mysteries." Acknowledging African diasporic experience as located "both within and without borders," she extols the "difficult but sort of daily work of problematising the border in the first place" (Bowler 2017: 5), and so advances in her novel alter-native narratives of existence that resist at that same time that they re-examine enduring postcolonial nativist, cultural essentialisms—that attempt fundamentally to alter and transcend delimiting racialized discourses. In line with its extents and varieties of border-crossings, African diaspora in *Ghana Must Go* more aptly signifies an existential process of becoming; what Paul Zeleza describes as "a kind of voyage that encompasses the possibility of never arriving or returning, a navigation of multiple belongings, of networks of affiliation" (2009: 32).[11]

The novel simultaneously and similarly re-reads and revises (an abstract, idealist) Afropolitanism, creatively expressing "the aching, with longing" (251) for existential legitimation that characterizes the Afrodiasporic experience. Its descriptions of existential injury, at the familial and individual level and underlined by the intersectional interactions of race and culture, gender and sexuality, class and age, gesture at the fundamental, messy strangeness of the self—the inevitable idiosyncrasies that constitute and qualify the subjective experience; we encounter and are left in the novel with a portraiture "not of a People, the art history of Peoplehood, constant and strong, but the shorter, very messy, lesser history of people, small *p*" (166–7).

Comprised of an achronological, non-linear blues-like spatiotemporality, the novel's anachronistic rendering of (postcolonial) Africa and (contemporary) Afropolitanism puts forward an alter-native phenomenology of blackness predicated on the "now," that is, on "*when* and *where* it is being imagined, defined, and performed" (Wright 2015: 3). Underwriting thus a materialist reading of African diaspora it provides an inclusive and expansive vision that offers no redemptive or utopian vision of subjectivity but rather advances an existential condition premised on a continuously deferred *process* of self-actualization. In its reinterpretation and provocative expression thus of a transitional, protean black Africanness that both lives through and exceeds cultural particularity, *Ghana Must Go* pays a revisionary literary homage to the hybrid, fluid sensibility of the blues musical genre. Simultaneously encoded in and endeavouring to trespass and render transient culturally ritualistic borders, the novel does not just creatively advance an ontological revisionism of blackness; *Ghana Must Go* advocates a potentially transcendent blackness in its essential commitment to and vision finally of a transcendental, ethical humanism.

Notes

1 The term Afropolitanism has since been appropriated in the fashion industry as well as by lifestyle magazines and has been enhanced to include more philosophical, existential, and ethical interpretations.

2 Among others, Maaza Mengiste's cynical query in her article, "What makes a real African?" differently resonates with Binyavanga Wainaina's sardonic instructions on "How to Write about Africa." Helon Habila has similarly denounced in the global publishing industry, "literary pass-laws" that would seek to restrict where "African literature can go."

3 Not dissimilar to my and other critics' readings of the double bind of contemporary African diasporic writing, Mohammad Shabangu describes the "irresolvable aporia of contemporary African writing" as the manifestation of its "ambivalent position in the world literary arena that produces it and that, it appears, it produces in turn" (2018: 348).

4 Sadie is uncannily reminiscent of the character, Pecola Breedlove, in Toni Morrison's debut novel, *The Bluest Eye* (1979), who self-destructively yearns for blue eyes. Notwithstanding Selasi's confessed literary influence by and homage to Morrison, this further evidences the transatlantic and transnational—global—resonances and cross-currents of blackness across the diaspora.

5 It is interesting the extent to which Sadie's body dysmorphia and consequent eating disorder functions as an indictment on a universal Culture by extending the Foucauldian interpretation of the body as the politicized "object and target of power" that is pervasively Eurocentric and Anglo-Saxon to explore more intimately how the *self*-disciplined body becomes invasively both a "technique for the transformation of arrangements" and a symbol for "a network of relations" (1979: 136, 146) within black cultural structures.

6 Notwithstanding the dancing scene's apparent advocacy of an originary, arcane blackness which is reproduced and authenticated through and in the image of the performing body, Naa's initial description as a heavyset woman dressed in traditional attire and standing "with her elbow on the wall and her head on her fist and her hip pushing out, other hand on that hip, as if seeking to rest the full weight of her past on this crumbling brick wall' (263), problematically echoes

stereotypical pictures of traditional black African matriarchy and inversely recalls Olu's initial, complicit disdain for conventional articulations of Nigeria in particular and Africa in general.

7 Sadie's heritage is mythological because, notwithstanding the mythical reference to her father, she has never been to Africa and never known her African relations. Interestingly, the ability to do so is differently mediated—through absence and presence—by both her father and her aunt, testifying to the novel's expansive feminist praxis.

8 Various African American critics have noted the gendered inflections of the blues genre; in particular its feminine modalities of sexual/erotic desire, articulated by the likes of Bessie Smith and Billie Holiday, for example, are said to express "a camouflaged dream of a new [non-heteropatriarchal, non-sexist] social order" (Davis 1990:14).

9 Evidenced not least in Taiwo's illicit and ineffectual affair with her professor, the lingering effects of such violence and violation are demonstrated in Kehinde's apparent inability to connect emotionally—reflected in Kweku's comment that "Kehinde doesn't care about anything" (15)—and relative narrative absence/presence.

10 This is affirmed in Kweku's dying ruminations of "The slipper" as a symbolic, interactive 'practice' that protects "against the dangers of home" (39).

11 While the predominant mode of travel in the novel is flight, it is interesting how Zeleza's definition of diaspora as voyage draws on the image of the ship. Conjuring echoes of the black transatlantic slave trade and pointing to the current prominence of Black Transatlantic Studies, Ghana Must Go thus makes a significant modern and metaphysical contribution to and intervention in contemporary diasporic studies.

References

Abani, Chris (2007), "Telling Stories from Africa," June. Available online: https://www.ted.com/talks/chris_abani_on_the_stories_of_africa (accessed 7 November 2017)

Adichie, Chimamanda Ngozi (2009), "The Danger of a Single Story," July. Available online: http://www.ted.com/talks/chimamanda_adichie_the_danger_of_a_single_story.html (accessed 9 April 2015).

Aidoo, Ama Ata (2016). "Africa, Literature and the Cultural Renaissance: Keynote lecture," National English Literary Museum (NELM): Grahamstown, South Africa.

Bady, Aaron and Selasi, Taiye (2015), "From That Stranded Place," *Transition* 117: 148–65.

Baker, Houston A., Jr (1984). *Blues, Ideology, and Afro-American Literature: A Vernacular Theory*. Chicago and London: University of Chicago Press.

Baraka, Amiri (2002), *Blues People: Negro Music in White America*, New York: Perennial.

Bhabha, Homi K (1992), "The World and the Home," *Social Text* 31/32: 141–53.

Bowler, Danielle Alyssa (2017), "The Borders between Bodies and Belonging," *Mail and Guardian*, November: 3–9: 4–5.
Butler, Judith (1993), *Bodies that Matter: On the Discursive Limits of Sex*, New York: Routledge.
Casanova, Pascale (2005), "Literature as a World," *New Left Review* 31, 71–90.
Dabiri, Emma (2016), "Why I am (still) Not an Afropolitan," *Journal of Cultural Studies*, 28 (1): 104–8.
Davis, Angela Y (1990), "Black Women and Music: A Historical Struggle," in J. M. Braxton and A. N. McLaughlin (eds), *Wild Women in the Whirlwind: Afra-American Culture and Contemporary Literary Renaissance*, 3–21, New Brunswick: Rutgers University Press.
Ede, Amatoritsero (Davis, Angela Y (1990), "Black Women and Music: A Historical Struggle,"), "The Politics of Afropolitanism," *Journal of African Cultural Studies*, 28 (1): 88–100.
Ellison, Ralph (1995), *Shadow and Act*, New York: Vintage International.
Eze, Chielozona (2014), "Rethinking African Culture and Identity: The Afropolitan Model," *Journal of Cultural Studies* 26(2): 234–47.
Eze, Chielozona (2015), "Transcultural Affinity: Thoughts on the Emergent Cosmopolitan Imagination in South Africa," *Journal of African Cultural Studies* 27 (2): 216–28.
Eze, Chielozona (2016), "We, Afropolitans," *Journal of African Cultural Studies*, 28 (1): 114–19.
Fanon, Frantz (1990), *The Wretched of the Earth* [1961], Trans. Constance Farrington. London: Penguin.
Foucault, Michel (1979), *Discipline and Punish: The Birth of the Prison*. Trans. Alan Sheridan. New York: Vintage.
Gikandi, Simon (2002), "Race and Cosmopolitanism," *American Literary History*, 14 (3): 593–615.
Gikandi, Simon (2011), "Foreword: On Afropolitanism," in J. Wawrzinek and J.K.S. Makokha (eds), *Negotiating Afropolitanism: Essays on Borders and Spaces in Contemporary African Literature and Folklore*, 9–11, Amsterdam and New York: Rodopi.
Gilroy, Paul (2005), "A New Cosmopolitanism," *Interventions*, 7 (3): 287–92.
Habila, Helon (2014), "Tradition and the African Writer," *The Caine Prize for African Writing*, June 2014. Available online: http://caineprizeblogspot.com/2014/06/what-is african-literature-tradition.html (accessed 29 July 2015).
Harris, Ashleigh (2014), "Awkward Form and Writing the African Present," *The Johannesburg Salon: Volume 7*. Available online: http://jwtc.org.za/test/ashleigh_harris.htm (accessed 7 March 2015).
Harvey, Ebrahim (2016), "Blackness ain't what it used to be," *Mail & Guardian*, 3 March. Available online: http://mg.co.za/article/2016-03-03-blackness-aint-what-it-used-to-be (accessed 6 April 2016).
Knudsen, Eva and Ulla Rahbek eds (2016), *In Search of the Afropolitan: Encounters, Conversations, and Contemporary Diasporic African Literature*, London and New York: Rowman and Littlefield.
Knudsen, Eva and Ulla Rahbeck, eds. (2017), "An Afropolitan Literary Aesthetics: Afropolitan Style and Tropes in Recent Diasporic African Fiction," *European Journal of English Studies*, 21 (2): 115–28.

Levine, Lawrence (1977), *Black Culture and Black Consciousness: Afro American Folk Thought from Slavery to Freedom*, Oxford, London and New York: Oxford University Press.

Madison, Greg (2006), "Existential Migration: Conceptualising out of the Experiential Depths of Choosing to Leave 'Home'," *Existential Analysis*, 17 (2): 238–260.

Mbembe, Achille (2007), "Afropolitanism." *Africa Remix: Contemporary Art of a Continent*. Johannesburg: Jacana, 26–29.

Mengiste, Maaza (2013), "What makes a 'real African'?" *The Guardian*, 7 July. Available online: http://www.theguardian.com/commentisfree/2013/jul/07/african-writers-caine-prize (accessed 4 March 2014).

Morrison, Toni and Cornel West, eds. (2004), "Blues, Love and Politics," *The Nation* 6 May: 18–28. Available online: https://www.thenation.com/article/blues-love-and-politics/ (accessed 2 October 2016).

Musila, Grace (2016), "Part-Time Africans, Europolitans and 'Africa lite'," *Journal of African Cultural Studies*, 28 (1): 109–13.

Neal, Larry (1972), "The Ethos of the Blues," *The Black Scholar*, 3 (10): 42–48.

Njami, Simon (2007), "Chaos and Metamorphosis," *Africa Remix: Contemporary Art of a Continent*, Johannesburg: Jacana, 13–21.

Nussbaum, Martha C (1996), *For Love of Country?* Ed. Joshua Cohen. Boston, Massachusetts: Beacon Press.

Nwankwo, Ifeoma Kiddoe (2005), *Black Cosmopolitanisms: Racial Consciousness and Transnational Identity in the Nineteenth Century Americas*, Philadelphia: University of Pennsylvania Press.

Ojwang, Dan and Titlestad, Michael (2014). "African writing blurs into 'world' Literature," *Mail & Guardian,* April: 4–10.

Okri, Ben (2014), "A mental tyranny is keeping black writers for greatness," *The Guardian*, 27 December. Accessed online: http://theguardian.com/commentisfree/2014/dec/27/mental-tyranny-black-writers (accessed 18 October 2015).

Patterson, Tiffany Ruby and D. G. Kelley (2000), "Unfinished Migrations: Reflections on the African Diaspora and the Making of the Modern World," *African Studies Review*, 43 (1): 11–45.

Pinto, Samantha (2013), *Difficult Diasporas: The Transnational Feminist Aesthetic of the Black Atlantic*, New York and London: New York University Press.

Ricoeur, Paul (2006), *Memory, History, Forgetting*, Trans. Kathleen Blamey and David Pellauer, Chicago: University of Chicago Press.

Santana, Stephanie Bosch (2016), "Exorcizing the Future: Afropolitanism's Spectral Origins," *Journal of African Cultural Studies*, 28 (1): 120–26.

Selasi, Taiye (2005), "Bye-Bye Babar," 3 March. Available online: http://thelip.robertsharp.co.uk/?p=76 (accessed 10 January 2015).

Selasi, Taiye (2013a), *Ghana Must Go*, London: Penguin.

Selasi, Taiye (2013b), "Taiye Selasi on discovering her pride in her African roots," *The Guardian*, 22 March. Available online: http://theguardian.com/books/2013/mar/22/taiye-selasi-afropolitan-memoir (accessed 16 March 2015).

Selasi, Taiye (2013c), "African Literature Doesn't Exist," Available online: http://www.literaturfestival.com/archiv/eroeffnungsreden/die-festivalprogramme-der-letzten-jahre/Openingspeach2013_English.pdf (accessed 6 April 2015).

Selasi, Taiye (2014), "Don't Ask Where I'm from, Ask Where I'm Local," October. Available online: https://www.ted.com/talks/taiye_selasi_don_t_ask_where_i_m_from_ask_where_i_m_a_local (accessed 7 November 2014).

Selasi, Taiye (2015), "Taiye Selasi: Stop pigeonholing African writers," *The Guardian* 4 July. Available online: https://www.theguardian.com/books/2015/jul/04/taiye-selasi-stop-pigeonholing-african-writers (accessed 8 April 2016).

Shabangu, Mohammad (2018), "Refusing Interpellation: A Double Bind of African Migrant Fiction', *Safundi*, 19 (3), 338–356.

Snead, James (1981), "On Repetition in Black Culture," *Black American Literature Forum*, 15 (4): 146–54.

Toivanen, Anna-Leena (2015), "Not at Home in the World: Abject Mobilities in Marie NDiaye's *Trois femmes puissantes* and NoViolet Bulawayo's *We Need New Names*," *Postcolonial Text* 10 (1): 1–18.

Toivanen, Anna-Leena (2017), "Cosmopolitanism's New Clothes? The Limits of the Concept of Afropolitanism," *European Journal of English Studies*, 21 (2): 189–205.

Touré (2016), "Black and Blues," *Smithsonian Magazine*, September 2016. Available online: http://www.smithsonianmag.com/arts-culture/keeping-blues-alive-180960128/ (accessed 1 December 2016)

Tveit, Marta (2013). "The Afropolitan Must Go," November 2013. Available online: http://africasacountry.com/2013/11/the-afropolitan-must-go/ (accessed 2 December 214)

Wainaina, Binyavanga (2006), "How to Write about Africa," *Granta* 92. 19 January. Available online: http://granta.com/how-to-write-about-africa (accessed 10 January 2013)

Wright, Michelle M (2015), *Physics of Blackness: Beyond the Middle Passage Epistemology*, Minneapolis and London: University of Minnesota Press.

Zeleza, Paul Tiyambe (2009), "Diaspora Dialogues: Engagements between Africa and its Diasporas," *The New African Diaspora* in I. Okpewho and N Nzegwu eds, 31–58, Bloomington, Indiana: Indiana University Press.

10

"Part Returnee and Part-Tourist"

The Afropolitan Travelogue in Noo Saro-Wiwa's *Looking for Transwonderland: Travels in Nigeria**

M. Rocío Cobo-Piñero

> *There are no strangers. There are only versions of ourselves, many of which we have not embraced, most of which we wish to protect ourselves from.*
> MORRISON 2017: 38

This article aims to explore the role of travel writing as a tool for cultural critique, drawing on Taiye Selasi's Afropolitan willingness "to complicate Africa–namely, to engage with, critique, and celebrate the parts of Africa that mean most to [us]" (2009: 37). I approach Afropolitanism as an epistemological shift that can be political, seeking to confront and complicate hegemonic structures within and outside Africa. The first part of the article explores the resignification of travel writing by means of a critical reassignment of the genre, whose origins not only stem from European colonial accounts, but from non-Western travels. The analysis of the Afropolitan intervention in the following section is crucial to understand the relevance of mobility in pre-colonial African cultures and in the configuration of the contemporary world. The final part delves into Noo Saro-Wiwa's debut novel *Looking for Transwonderland: Travels in Nigeria* (2012) as an Afropolitan travelogue. In so doing, I seek to interrogate if the Afropolitan travelogue is truly emancipatory or underscored by the remnants of exoticism, colonialism, and empire. I also delve into the modes in which the Afropolitan gaze confronts the readers with the impact of globalization and modernization in Nigeria. Finally, I explore the innovative possibilities of writing Africa that Saro-Wiwa's travelogue offers.

Taking into account the challenges of travel writing as a genre and the venues it presents, I argue that the need to create a space for Afropolitan eyes within travel writing is crucial. Apart from the literary enrichment that such a perspective provides, it also challenges the asymmetrical dynamics of influence and agency traditionally established within the genre. My study is predicated on the premise that narrating images of the world is a form of power. Thus, I contend that "African Diaspora eyes" (Kelleher 2013) acts as a touchstone text for travel writing and they are absolutely fundamental for decolonizing knowledge.

1. Non-Western Gazes in Travel Writing

Noted Africanist historian Roy Bridges defines the genre of travel writing as "a discourse designed to describe and interpret for its readers a geographical area together with its natural attributes and its human society and culture" (2002: 53). To this wide-ranging description, Tabish Khair adds that travel writing also entails defining, consciously or unconsciously, the writer's relationship to a geographical area, its natural attributes and its society and culture; and just as significantly, the writer's relationship to his or her society and culture (2006: 4). Iderpal Grewal further underscores that travel historically has signified European and colonial modes of travel, erasing or conflating mobilities that are not part of this Eurocentric, imperialistic formation; for instance, migration, immigration, deportation, indenture, and slavery are often erased by the universalizing mode of European travel (1996: 2).

Achille Mbembe reminds us that the pre-colonial history of African societies was a history of people in perpetual movement throughout Africa, and "the history of the continent can hardly be understood outside the paradigm of itinerary, mobility and displacement" (2007: 27). In this sense, Khair's far-reaching and interventionist anthology, *Other Routes: 1500 years of African and Asian Travel Writing* (2006), demonstrates that there have been ancient alternative traditions to European travel writings in Africa and Asia; for the purpose of the present study, I will just focus on the first. Examples of these foundational travel accounts collected in the anthology are Maghriban al-Idrisi's pioneer cartographic studies in the eleventh century; ibn Battuta's pilgrimage through the lands of Islam in the fourteenth century; Olaudah Equiano's voyage from Nigeria to slavery and freedom, published in 1789; or the travel narrative-memoir princess Emily Said-Ruete (1881) wrote on her journey through Europe from her natal Zanzibar, contesting Western Orientalism from the point of view of a woman. Whereas discovery and expansion had fueled the writing of European travel literature since the fifteenth century and well into the Enlightenment, Amitav Ghosh sees "a sense of wonderment" in non-Western travel accounts, because "They do not assume a universal ordering of reality; nor do they arrange their narratives to correspond to teleologies of racial or civilizational progress" (2006: ix).

However, in the field of postcolonial studies, travel writing has often been demonized because of its "historical taintedness" (Clifford 1997: 39) and "moral arrogance" (Huggan 2009: 8), overlooking this other non-Western tradition of wonderers.[1] Critics have, at times, aligned travel narratives with other textual practices associated with colonial expansion such as mapping, botany, ethnography, or journalism. Travel writing, allowed Europeans to conceive of areas outside Europe as being under their control, as an extension of land through ownership, which constituted the so-called "rhetoric of Empire" (Spurr). Thus, travel writing became another discursive weapon in the arsenal of European imperialism that was particularly unkind to Africa in its representation; Henry Morton Stanley, David Livingston or Mungo Park are famous examples of this Eurocentric tradition. By contrast, David Spurr defines the postcolonial methodology in travel writing as an attempt both to analyze "the historical situation marked by the dismantling of traditional institutions of colonial power" and to "search for alternatives to the discourses of the colonial era" (1993: 6). María Lourdes López Ropero (2003) also contends that "the postcolonial travelogue" epitomizes the new developments that have taken place within travel writing from its limited Enlighted and Victorian biased representations of non-Western cultures and spaces to a political turn in the late twentieth century. For her, novels such as Caryl Philips's *The Atlantic Sound* (2000), a compelling revision of Europe's historical involvement in the slave trade through his trips across the Atlantic, prove this move to a more critical use of travel writing that deliberately challenges power and representation.

Travel writing can arguably be seen as having transgressive potential in allowing the writer to flout conventions that exist within his/her society, and that is evident in the foundational African travel accounts by Equiano and Said-Ruete mentioned before. In this sense, Debbie Lisle underlines the relevance of who does the writing, "especially when it comes to resisting the colonial heritage of the genre. Indeed, it is those who have been objectified most by travel writing who must be welcomed into the genre in order to resist its continuing colonial ethos" (2006: 87). However, Lisle is suspicious about the factual distance of the genre's implications in Empire, even when some contemporary best-selling travel writers, such as Bill Bryson or Michael Palin, embrace the celebration of the interdependence and common aims of culture in an interconnected global village, through what she calls a "cosmopolitan gaze" (2006: 68). This cosmopolitan vision, she claims, usually articulates universal standards of civilization by which to judge all cultures without questioning the logic of differentiation and the legitimization of exclusion, occupying a new hegemonic position of truth.[2] In addition, Lisle further contends that the cosmopolitan ethos reproduces a "discourse of modern cartography" by reinforcing the distinction between "here and there" and by underpinning familiar binary oppositions that contrast "a safe, civilized home and a dangerous, uncivilized elsewhere" (2006: 137).

On the contrary, the Afropolitan gaze challenges essential binarisms and is also informed by the postcolonial critical turn. Designated as "cosmopolitanism with African roots" (Gehrmann 2016, 61), the next section explores the Afropolitan stance as a political option that questions the legacies of Empire. The Afropolitan travelogue bears the seeds of multilayered narratives that stem from the African diaspora and from the willingness to resignify the place of Africa in the contemporary world.

2. Afropolitan Travelers: Unstable Belongings and the Culture of Mobility

Taiye Selasi underscored the "unhomely" belongings of Afropolitans in her now famous manifesto "Bye-Bye, Babar (Or: What is an Afropolitan?)."[3] She begins it by asserting the unstable meaning(s) of "Home" for Afropolitans, which is many things: "where their parents are from; where they spent their vacations; where they went to school; where they meet old friends; where they live (or live this year). Like so many African young people working and living in cities around the globe, they belong to no single geography, but feel at home in many" (2009: 36). This "multilocality" of experience (Selasi 2014) and the privilege of traveling of Afropolitans have been contested by some critics, like Emma Dabiri, who claims that we still do not hear the narratives of Africans who are not privileged. She aptly reminds us that most Africans have absolute immobility in a contemporary global world that works very hard to "keep Africans in their place on the African continent" (Dabiri 2015: 106). An argument that proves to be accurate when one looks into the immigration policies of Western countries and the legal obstructions to receive Africans, as well as the biased representation of African migration in the international media. In this same line of thought, African artist and scholar Okwunodu Ogbechi contends that "most African-based artists would find it difficult if not impossible to get a visa to visit Western museums or to show their works abroad" (qtd. in Dabiri 2017: 206).

The genius of Selasi's idea, according to Nigerian poet and philosopher Chielozona Eze, lies in contesting the largely uncritical application of Africa as a tag of identity to any person genetically linked with the continent, proposing instead a transgressive attitude that disrupts static and essentialist notions of belonging: "identity can no longer be explained in purist, essentialist, and oppositional terms or by reference only to Africa" (2014, 240). For Simon Gikandi, the term brings less pessimistic views about the representation of the continent as the Western "other" and away from victimhood (2011, 9). Achille Mbembe further argues that Afropolitanism refers to the many ways in which Africans, or people of African origin, "understand themselves as being part of the world rather than being apart" (Balakrishnan 2016, 29). Hence, the neologism propels a critical thinking of the place of Africa in the world, within a geography of circulation and mobility, and beyond Pan-Africanism.[4]

In addition, Africa has long served as a key site for journeying, more often conducted by outsiders to the continent and frequently by those who thought themselves to be traveling away from modernity. Afropolitan travels, in contrast, "are travels within African modernity; they represent efforts to make sense of Africa's current position in the world and of the world in Africa" (Moynagh 2015: 281).[5] If Africa has traditionally been written from the global North, contemporary travel writing by African writers departs from the more conventional trope of "Africa-as-primitive" or the "periphery to someone else's centre" in European travel writing (Moynagh 2015: 289, 291).

Mbembe accurately argues that "cultural blending" is typically African, rooted in its history from pre-colonial times: "It is this very culture of mobility that colonization once endeavoured to freeze through the modern institution of borders" (2007: 27). The transcultural anxieties and tensions in the cultural mixing are part of the Afropolitan experiences, old and new. Both the acknowledgment of difference and the transcendence of it are part of the "Afropolitan challenge" across spatial and experiential divides, resisting dual oppositions and clearly defined categories; thus, calling for a new cultural paradigm (Rask Knudsen and Rahbek 2016: 21). In this sense, Mbembe invokes the need to defamiliarize home and belonging, which allows for a better understanding of how different worlds interact in one locality:

> the interweaving of the here and there, the presence of the elsewhere in the here and vice versa, the relativisation of primary roots and

memberships and the way of embracing, with full knowledge of the facts, strangeness, foreignness, and remoteness, the ability to recognize one's face in that of a foreigner and make the most of the traces of remoteness in closeness, to domesticate the unfamiliar, to work with what it seems to be opposites—it is this cultural, historical, and aesthetic sensitivity that underlines the term 'Afropolitanism'.

(2007: 28)

The existential challenges posed by the experience of cultural blending and globalization in Nigeria are presented through Saro-Wiwa's Afropolitan travelogue, in which the author re-discovers her country of birth, journeying across ideas of belonging, otherness, and strangeness, while reflecting on its colonial past and its decolonial future.

Nigerian by birth and English by upbringing, the daughter of the popular Nigerian writer and environmental activist Ken Saro-Wiwa grapples with the complexities of her own identity as well as the more than three hundred ethnic groups that populate Nigeria, home to a hundred and eighty million people. *Looking for Transwonderland: Travels in Nigeria* is an Afropolitan travelogue, deeply invested in the personal, the social, and the political. The novel chronicles the four-month journey to Nigeria the author undertook out of her desire to see the country "under fresh eyes" (Derbyshire 2012: 47). After her father's execution in 1995 by the Nigerian military regime, Saro-Wiwa avoided visiting the African country for more than a decade. Hence, she is looking for what Simon Gikandi calls "a hermeneutics of redemption" (2011: 10), which is at the core of Afropolitanism. The fact that she also feels like a foreigner when she goes back to her native Nigeria, so a kind of defamilirization has been forced on her, is also part of the Afropolitan travelogue.

3. The Strangeness of Travel: Looking for the Self in Nigeria

Innovative travel writing, according to Edwards and Gaunlund (2012), explores the various levels of subjectivity, as well as the tensions between representing the traveling subject (in its privilege and wholeness) and challenging the unified sense of the self in motion. Moreover, conceptions of individuality are interrogated in relation to the unstable spaces of home and abroad, the familiar and the foreign. The traveling subject becomes "a possible site for active cultural and ideological struggle" (2012: 199). However, Saro-Wiwa's unique position as someone who travels back to the place where she was born provides fresh nuances to the "cultural and ideological struggle" this quotation is referring to. *Looking for*

Transwonderland opens with a Prologue that establishes the critical and ironical tone of the travelogue through a first-person narrative voice. Set in Gatwick airport, this space serves as the real and symbolic trigger of Saro-Wiwa's deep anxieties about her trip to Nigeria. After the airline announces an indefinite flight delay to Lagos, Saro-Wiwa observes the passengers' reactions, describing a group of irritated Nigerians who loudly demand more food vouchers; a couple of Italian men who identify the disgruntled crowd as insane and a group of English passengers, more contained in their response to the delay:

> Being Nigerian can be the most embarrassing of burdens. We're constantly wincing at the sight of some of our compatriots, who have committed themselves to presenting us as a nation of ruffians. Their efforts are richly rewarded at airports, where the very nature of such venues ensures that our rowdy reputation enjoys extensive, global reach ... I'm forced to watch the European and African mindsets collide in a way that equally splits my loyalty and disdain towards both.
>
> (2012: 2)

The airport is not only a site of cultural clash but the place that activates her traveling memories. She remembers when she was two years old and her family migrated from Lagos to Surrey (UK), but they would go back "home" every summer: "as a teenager, I virtually had to be escorted by my ankles onto a Nigeria Airways flight at the start of the summer holidays" (2012: 3). As a child, her perception of England was that of a bountiful land, whereas their summer returns to Nigeria frequently started with "brutal acculturation" at her father's village (2012: 4), where they spent a fortnight with no electricity or running water. By contrast, Nigeria was "home" for her parents, and England was the place where they owned a "house": "my parents believed that without their country they were nothing" (2012: 5). This generational gap is, according to Selasi, characteristic of Afropolitans: "While our parents can claim single countries as home, we must define our relationship to the places we live: how British or American we are (or act) is in part a matter of affect" (2009: 37).

The Prologue also discloses Saro-Wiwa's traumatic emotional entanglement to Nigeria after her father's execution. As a member of the Ogoni, a small, deeply aggrieved ethnic group that sits astride much of Nigeria's oil wealth in the South-East part of the country, Ken Saro-Wiwa had started a campaign in the 1990s against government corruption and environmental degradation. The traveling narrative informs us that oil was discovered in 1956 and primarily extracted by Shell Oil ever since. The information provided on the government's retaliations are brief: "His battle led to his being arrested and imprisoned several times ... My father's murder severed my personal links with Nigeria" (2012: 7). Saro-Wiwa avoided

Nigeria for more than a decade because the country signified for her "an unpiloted juggernaut of pain ... the repository of all my fears and disappointments" (2012: 8).

Looking for Transwonderland is an honest and fascinating account of the four-month travel to Nigeria the author undertook out of her desire to see the country "under fresh eyes" (Derbyshire 2012: 47). From the onset, she establishes her yearning to "travel freely around the country, as part returnee and part-tourist with the innocence of the outsider untarnished with personal associations. Then, hopefully, I could learn to be less scared of it, perhaps even like it, and consider it a potential 'home'" (2012: 9). The opening situates the travel as an existential journey that resignifies her affection towards Nigeria, together with her notions of belonging and modernity/development; these ideas as well as Saro-Wiwa's position as "part returnee and part-tourist" shape the Afropolitan travelogue.

Her expedition starts in hectic Lagos, the largest city in the South-West, where the car registration plates bear the motto "Centre of Excellence" (2012: 12), a message that Saro-Wiwa finds ironic due to the urban non-planning, dirt, unofficial wages and a political corruption that she describes with humorous touches on her arrival to the megalopolis. She had been warned before her trip to expect danger at any moment and "to treat everyone as a potential predator" (2012: 12). Consequently, her supposed "innocence" and neutrality are tainted by preconceptions and biases. She even acknowledges her alienation on her arrival to Lagos, where she feels a stranger, unable to understand the language of the Yoruba: "their melodic lingua franca sounded in the streets around me, as foreign to my ears as any language from Cameroon or Ghana ... It was the most alienating of homecomings" (2012: 13). These remarks anticipate her unfamiliarity with the surroundings, as well as the presentation of a "seeing I" that acknowledges the inability to translate difference, because she does not speak the language. As opposed to preceding travel writings that constructed visions of otherness through a seeming coherent subject position, capable of describing and organizing, Saro-Wiwa's narrative highlights the strangeness of the space, the instability of the traveling subject, and her own displacement.

Halfway through the first chapter, she briefly and aptly recounts the colonial background of Nigeria, ruled by the British until 1960, and how they exploited the southern ports and oil, leaving behind ethnic tensions and economic inequality that propelled the Biafra civil war in 1967 (28–29).[6] The military government that replaced former colonial control was sanctioned by the British and could not govern effectively; corruption and nepotism took root in the first stages of independence. Through these first snapshots of the country, Saro-Wiwa constructs her gaze as a partial outsider and, even though the picture is very much influenced by her Western upbringing, she draws on pre-colonial and colonial history to guide her through the journey.

In Badagry, a colonial slave port in the Lagos region, she visits a small Slave Relic Museum, where she imagines the slaves' sadistic treatment through some artifacts of the era. The narrator-traveler asks for permission to try one of the rusty metal rings on the neck, allowing the reader to feel the burden: "It bore down so heavily on my shoulders and collar bone that I had to hold it up with my hands to stop it from bruising my flesh" (2012: 52). She also mentions an ankle cuff, designed to be worn by two people; chains with piercing hooks; a lip hook to prevent disobedient slaves from speaking and eating; a cone-shaped drinking trough "designed for maximum humiliation" (2012: 53). It is through the description of these objects for torture and the agony they caused that Saro-Wiwa signifies on the strangeness of slavery, willing to retrace the steps of the slaves and walk the route they tracked before being shipped off: "The sadistic treatment of slavery is an eternal mystery to me ... My mind's eye pictured them chained to the deck on their backs for months on end, squirming in tides of faeces, urine, menses, vomit and brine as the boat rocked along the Atlantic waves" (2012: 54). She foregrounds the psychological wounds in Nigerian society, pointing to the involvement of some local families in the inhumane trade.

The chronicler returns to the theme of slavery during her visit to Benin, once the capital of the only kingdom on the Nigerian coastline that was not under British official control. However, the British provided guns, textiles, and other European goods in exchange for pepper, ivory, palm oil, and slaves: "the Europeans fomented war between African tribes in order to produce prisoners of war who could become slaves ... the presence of European firearms made it imperative for them to do so: if they didn't sell slaves, they wouldn't have firearms to defend against their armed enemies. It was a vicious circle" (2012: 248). Saro-Wiwa is careful not to produce uninformed comments, and thoroughly includes succinct historical data to support her explanations, which provide the narrative with certain objectivity.

The voyager later heads to the present capital of Nigeria, Abuja, where she comes across a newspaper in which young Nigerian men look openly for sugar mummies. Interested in this apparently new social interaction in the country, the narrator mentions seven of the classified ads. One of them brazenly announces: "Julius, 28, needs a rich, sexy single sugar mummy, aged between 30–45 for financial support in exchange for the fun of her life" (2012: 136). The so-called "Sugar Cares" section renders an unfamiliar perspective of Nigeria's social and gender roles to the returnee, who finds it somehow comforting that rigid social structures and behaviors are changing: "Peeping through this hole in our pious veil gave me a glimpse of the future, perhaps; the wobbling first steps towards gender equality, the end of polygamy, or some other kind of social change" (2012: 138). The use of the verb "peep through" confers a voyeuristic overtone to the account.

Like other Afropolitan narratives such as Chimamanda Ngozi Adichie's *Americanah* (2013) or NoViolet Bulawayo's *We Need New Names* (2013), the text unravels the trips with a sharp sense of humor, a strategy that assists Saro-Wiwa to disassociate Nigeria from her painful memories. The word "Transwonderland" on the title of the novel refers to the amusement park built in Ibadan in 1989. It epitomizes the longing the author once felt for Nigeria "to 'achieve' and be a place that people admire and want to visit, a credible tourist destination" (2012: 98). As a child, amusement parks symbolized everything that she fancied about the West, activating fantasies of a "Disney-esque promised land that was lustrous, modern, kitsch and fun" (2012: 98). Nevertheless, on her arrival to Transwonderland, she finds a decrepit, rusty, and desolated park that bears no resemblance with the "ultra-modern" pretension inscribed on the inauguration plaque (2012: 101).

The description of the park she had read on her tourist guide, "the closest thing Nigeria has to Disney World" (2012: 98), does not correspond with the recklessness she encounters. The touristic depiction of the park brings to mind Jean Baudrillad's (1994) theories of the simulacra, in which Disneyland is the perfect model of the American way of life, a social microcosm and a play of illusions. Saro-Wiwa realizes that transplanting this model to Nigeria proves fruitless, because it was never real: "Creating these fake textures and colours—transcending nature—seemed the ultimate achievement" (Saro-Wiwa 2012: 98). Hence, her childhood dream of a modern, artificial Nigeria is confronted by the reality of a decaying park, a conflict that metaphorically problematizes modernity and its meanings.

Transwonderland, as an imitation or double of Disneyland, can also be connected to Homi Bhabha's ([1994] 2004) ideas on mimicry, which becomes a strategy to challenge colonial discourses of modernity:

> It is from this area between mimicry and mockery, where the reforming, civilizing mission is threatened by the displacing gaze of its disciplinary double . . . the excess or slippage produced by the ambivalence of mimicry (almost the same, but not quite) does not merely rupture the discourse, but becomes transformed into an uncertainty which fixes the colonial subject as a partial presence.
>
> (2004: 123)

The representation of Transwonderland ironically blurs the lines between mimicry and mockery, where modernity is identified with a fake, deteriorating park. Another apparent instance of mimicry in Nigeria is Nollywood, the third largest film industry in the world in terms of output. Nevertheless, as Saro-Wiwa pertinently explains, Nigerian cinema has no international sponsorship, being purely indigenous and financed by local producers and marketers, who "demand a strong 'Nigeriannes' to the storylines ... Nigerians will watch Nollywood films, no matter how bad, because everyone likes to see their own culture played back to them" (2012: 78). Nollywood and the urban setting of the movies, primarily filmed in Lagos, signify on the postcolony, which becomes a "dramatic stage" (Mbembe 2001: 102). Mbembe's designation of the postcolony serves to describe how subaltern performers must confront the contradictions of modern life, including the manifold failures of the state and private corporations, new technologies and religious conflicts.[7]

Africanist film scholar Carmela Garritano approaches Nollywood as a prolific and extraordinarily heterogeneous archive of Africa's engagement with the world and as a worldly cultural practice of self-creation "through which Africans manage to recognize and maintain with the world an unprecedented familiarity" (2014: 44).[8] This Afropolitan notion of worldly interaction and self-creation associated to Nollywood contrasts with the stereotyped representations of Africa in the Hollywood film industry. In line with this idea, the title of Taiye Selasi's Afropolitan manifesto, "Bye-Bye, Babar," encompasses a cinematographic reference to John Landis's Hollywood production *Coming to America* (1988), in which Eddie Murphy represents a naïve prince from Zamunda, who travels to New York and "conjures the images of African immigrants" and "cultural condescension" (Selasi 2009: 37). For Saro-Wiwa, the movie *Coming to America* belongs to her childhood memories during their Port Harbour summer retreat, where they watched the movie in their VCR at least once a day, "to the point that we knew the dialogues inside out. By summer's end we learnt to swear like Eddie Murphy" (2012: 273). This memory proves the far-reaching influence of the US film industry in the 1980s Nigeria, which contrasts to the current popularity of Nollywood.

Babar in the title of Selasi's essay is also the name of the notorious elephant in Jean de Brunhoff's traditional children tale *L'histoire de Babar* (1931), translated into English as *The Story of Babar*. The fables are allegories of French colonization, as seen by the complacent colonizers: the naked African natives, represented by the "good" elephants, are brought to the imperial capital, acculturated, and then sent back to their homeland on a civilizing mission. Brunhoff's son continued the series and wrote *Babar Comes to America* (1965), a large display of all the artifacts of civilization. Assimilating Western customs and returning to their native Africa on a civilizing mission is part of these cultural references, which contrast with Saro-Wiwa's present comments on the self-representation of Africans through Nollywood, an industry that "represents a certain independence of mind and spirit ... Watching ourselves on screen makes for a pleasant change after being bombarded with foreign stories and images" (2012: 80–1). Her initial conception of Nollywood as "amateur" eventually changes when she interviews the movie director Teco Benson, who informs her about the artistic potential of the industry. In addition, she has a chance to watch a wide variety of Nollywood movies along her journey, including shrewd comments on their plots, cast, and artistic evolution.

Saro-Wiwa is also insightful in her observations about the degradation of nature in Nigeria, which stems from the unsustainable and ruthless capitalistic project of modernity. Under her father's memory, she describes the deforestation of Bane; the extinction of animals at Yankari's reserve; the desertification in Maiduguri—once holding one of the world's most voluminous bodies of fresh water, now sucked for dry irrigation— the oil spills in the Niger Delta; the ceaseless blaring of gas that depletes the rivers of their fish stocks and poisons the soil, disrupting ancient farming practices and "swelling the number of frustrated unemployed men" (2012: 280). Being the twelfth-largest oil producer in the world, oil shortages are a regular part of Nigerian life, whose government imports "billions of dollars worth of refined fuel" (2012: 194). These accounts of devastation narrate the aftermaths of the Eurocentric model of progress, and confront her own initial ideas of advancement, presented earlier in the Prologue and based on her annual summer trips to Nigeria: "a country where the only 'development' I witnessed was the advance of new wall cracks and cobwebs, and where 'growth' simply meant larger damp stains on the ceiling" (2012: 3).

One of the last visits leads her to the village of Esie, close to the city of Benin, where hundreds of mysterious ancient stone sculptures were excavated in the 1930s: "intriguingly, the sculptures appeared to be images of people from ethnic backgrounds from all over Nigeria ... I was fascinated by the idea that a *cosmopolitan civilization* once existed" (2012: 266, emphasis added). She informs us that researchers had carbon-dated these figures to 11 AD, but who and why made them is still a mystery. This discovery connects with Mbembe's aforementioned claims of cosmopolitanism being an integral part of the precolonial experience of African nomads. When describing the sculptures, she notices that some of them had the facial complexion of the Jos region; a female figure held a bottle of alligator pepper connected to the Yoruba spiritual medicine; the numerous bead necklaces on one of the figurines were reminiscent of Ibiblio culture from the South-East; one of the largest sculptures depicted female Nupe warrior wielding a dagger and other female heads' coiffures suggested Fulani and Nok links. This account shows the precolonial cosmopolitan influences of the manifold African cultures and the integral role of mobility.

Debbie Lisle suggests that contemporary travel writing engages in the wider debates of global politics "through its structuring tension between *colonial* and *cosmopolitan* visions" (2006: 5, emphasis in the original). In examining this complex relationship, Lisle questions whether the cosmopolitan gaze is merely "a blander mutation of colonial vision" (2006: 5) or if it really allows for difference, heterogeneity, and contingency in the global realm. In this fashion, Saro-Wiwa's traveling narrative displaces her preliminary ideas of the self and the other, ultimately embracing a cosmopolitan ideal that finds its roots in pre-colonial times.

4. Final Considerations: Afropolitan Travels in a Globalized World

Looking for Transwonderland opened with Saro-Wiwa's anxieties about her travel to Nigeria, informed by her father's murder and her preconceptions of the country, which had become a monolithic "other" in her imagination. Her trip develops as an existential journey towards the self and her own foreignness. Halfway through the trip she acknowledges that "Uncertainty seemed to be the most persistent traveling companion in Nigeria" (2012: 163). This uncertainty contrasts with classic European travel writings that interpreted a geographical area for its readers, frequently imposing essentialist values during the process of cultural and social translation (Pratt 1992; Spurr 1993; Khair 2006; Lisle 2006). Since childhood, Saro-Wiwa is convinced that modernity and development are absent in Nigeria, but she does so under the parameters of her Western upbringing. Her visit to the amusement park in Ibadan, Transwonderland, acquires symbolic connotations, laying bare the artificial foundations of Western modernity and the environmental damage it has caused in Nigeria. Eventually, she acknowledges a different kind of modernity: her Afropolitan consciousness leads her to embrace the idea that there are no strangers and to relativize fixed notions of home and belonging, beyond nation-states (Selasi 2009; Mbembe 2007).

Her situated narrative account illustrates the relevance of history and the production of knowledge, reevaluating the impact of slavery and colonization. At the end of her travel, she is critical with an extended homogenization of Nigeria that erases their ethnic differences and cultures under the umbrella of corruption, an over-simplified designation that she had internalized before her travel to Nigeria: "[the] ethnic disparities were significant at a national level. But in a global context, what were the differences between us now? From a foreigner's point of view, the Bini, Yoruba, Ogoni, Igbo and Hausa are all the same; we're all Nigerians, demoted by modern-day corruption—that great equalizer" (2012: 256). This reflection pinpoints the complexities and tensions that globalization brings about; the interesting view of this particular Afropolitan travelogue is that it acknowledges Nigerian social and cultural diversity, situating history and its aftermaths in a globalized world.

Saro-Wiwas's final reconciliation with Nigeria is portrayed in the Epilogue, a full-circle account of her return to Lagos, where she started the trip. The urban setting functions as the scenario for the performance of cultural blending. There, she goes to a Femi Kuti's concert, the son of the emblematic musician Fela Kuti, who was "the unanointed king of Nigeria, our highest-quality export, a near-deity who invented Afrobeat, a combination of jazz, funk and highlife rhythms" (2012: 307). His son Femi, "took the best elements of Nigerian music and mixed them with foreign genres to create something so fresh and superior, it gives listeners a swaggering pride in being Nigerian" (2012: 309). Musical blending acquires symbolic echoes that bring to mind the opening of Taiye Selasi's Afropolitan manifesto in a London Bar, where a DJ spins a Fela Kuti remix, "fusing hip-hop dance moves with a funky sort of *djembe*" (2009: 36).[9] This musical connection also underlines the manifold representations of the Afropolitan ethos, both within Africa and abroad.

Notes

* The research for this article was supported by the VPPI-US postdoctoral contract from the University of Seville and the project FFI2017-84555-C2-1-P Bodies in Transit 2, from the Spanish Ministry of Science, Innovation and Universities.

1 Most of the postcolonial approaches to travel writing assume the European origin of the genre and tackle it as a discursive tool that aided in the construction of Empire. See Pratt 1992; Holland and Huggan 2000 or Justin Edwards and Rune Graulund 2011.

2 New theories of cosmopolitanism acknowledge the need to situate the concept and include in the discussion the problematic notions of gender and race, among other categories that have been suppressed from the Euro-centered narrative. See Mignolo 2000; Appiah 2006; Vieten 2012; Braidotti 2013; Glick Schiller and Irving 2015.

3 Homi Bhabha, in his seminal article "The World and the Home," coined the term "unhomely," which refers to the effects of enforced social accommodation, historical migrations, and cultural relocations: "The home does not remain the domain of domestic life, nor does the world simply become its social or historical counterpart. The unhomely is the shock of recognition of the world-in-the home, the home-in-the-world" (1992: 141).

4 Mbembe clarifies that Marcus Garvey's Pan-Africanism was rooted on an idea of belonging to a particular racial grouping, whereas his reading of Afropolitanism goes beyond race and emerges out of the recognition of the multiple origins of those who designate themselves as "African" or as "African descent" (Balakrishnan 2016: 30).

5 Maureen Moynagh refers to the current body of travel writings by Africans through Teju Cole, Ivan Vladislavic, Binyavanga Wainaina, and Noo Saro-Wiwa, as well as "The Pilgrimages Project." This transnational endeavor, sponsored by Chinua Achebe Center for African Writers and Artists, sent fourteen writers to thirteen different African cities and one city in Brazil, Salvador da Bahia, for a two-week period in 2010, with the endeavor to write non-fiction travel books for publication in a series of joint efforts by publishers in Lagos, Nairobi, and Cape Town.

6 According to Lasse and Moses (2014), after the independence of Nigeria, two British legacies prevented the evolution of a stable political system and social

relations: colonial rule divided the population along ethnic lines, but incorporated the groups thus defined in a centrally governed federal state. Established as a federal state, postcolonial Nigeria was split into three main regions, each dominated by one or two ethnic groups: Hausa-Fulani in the north, Yoruba in the west, and Igbos in the east. Hundreds of other ethnic minorities of different size made up the rest of the population. On 30 May 1967, the east's political leadership declared its independence as the Republic of Biafra. The estimated deaths as a result of the conflict amount to three million and the civil war was widely regarded as a watershed in the postcolonial global order.

7 See Tsika (2015) for a compelling analysis of the highly profitable Nollywood film industry and its international impact. Although the original languages of production were Yoruba and Igbo in the 1960s, the unprecedented national success of the Nollywood film *Glamour Girls* (1994) led to a gradual and generalized switch to English.

8 Garritano's introductory article is part of the special issue *Close-Up: Nollywood—A Worldly Creative Practice*, published by the international journal *Black Camera*, in which their contributors seek to track and theorize the "gestures" and "solicitations" Nollywood makes to the world, its articulation of what Edward Said calls a "will to worldliness" (2014: 46).

9 A *djembe* is a rope-tuned skin-covered goblet drum, usually played standing up with bare hands, and originally from West Africa.

Works cited

Adichie, Chimamanda Ngozi. (2013), *Americanah*, London: Fourth Estate.
Appiah, Kwame Anthony. (2006), *Cosmopolitanism: Ethics in a World of Strangers*, New York: Norton.
Balakrishnan, Sarah. (2016), "Pan-African Legacies, Afropolitan Futures. A Conversation with Achille Mbembe," *Transition*, 120 (Feb): 28–37.
Baudrillard, Jean. ([1981]1994), *Simulacra and Simulation*, Ann Arbor: University of Michigan Press.
Bhabha, Homi. (1992), "The World and the Home," *Social Text* 31/32: 141–153.
Bhabha, Homi. ([1994] 2004), *The Location of Culture*, New York: Routledge.
Braidotti, Rosi. (2013), "Becoming-World," in Rosi Braidotti and Patrick Hanafin (eds), *After Cosmopolitanism*, 8–28. New York: Routledge.
Bridges, Roy. (2006), "Exploration and Travel Outside Europe (1720–1914)," in Peter Hulme (ed), *The Cambridge Companion to Travel Writing*. Cambridge: Cambridge University Press.
Bulawayo, NoViolet. (2013), *We Need New Names*, London: Vintage.
Clifford, James. (1997), *Routes: Travels and Translation in the Late Twentieth Century*, Cambridge: Harvard University Press.
Dabiri, Emma. (2014), "Why I'm not an Afropolitan," January 21. Available online: http://africasacountry.com/2014/01/why-im-not-an-afropolitan/ (accessed July 15, 2017).

Dabiri, Emma (2017), "The Pitfalls and Promises of Afropolitanism," in Paulo Lemos Horta (ed.), *Cosmopolitanisms*, 201–212, New York: New York University Press.
Derbyshire, Jonathan. (2012), "The Book's Interview," *New Statesman*, January 2.
Edwards, Justin and Rune Graulund, eds. (2011), *Postcolonial Travel Writing: Critical Explorations*, London: Palgrave.
Edwards, Justin and Rune Graulund, eds. (2012), *Mobility at Large: Globalization, Textuality and Innovative Travel Writing*, Liverpool: Liverpool University Press.
Eze, Chieloza. (2014), "Rethinking African Culture and Identity: The Afropolitan Model," *Journal of African Cultural Studies*, 26 (2): 234–247.
Garritano, Carmela. (2014), "Introduction: Nollywood—An Archive of African Worldliness," *Black Camera* 5 (2): 44–52.
Gehrmann, Susanne. (2016), "Cosmopolitanism with African Roots. Afropolitanism's Ambivalent Mobilities," *Journal of African Cultural Studies*, 28 (1): 61–72.
Gikandi, Simon. (2011), "Foreword: On Afropolitanism," in Jennifer Wawrzinek and J. K. S. Makokha (eds), *Negotiating Afropolitanism: Essays on Borders and Spaces in Contemporary African Literature and Folklore*, 9–13, New York: Rodopi.
Ghosh, Amitav. (2006), "Foreword," in Tabish Khair et al (eds), *Other Routes. 1500 Years of African and Asian Travel Writing*. Oxford: Signal Books.
Glick Schiller, Nina and Andrew Irving, eds. (2015), *Whose Cosmopolitanism? Critical Perspectives, Relationalities and Discontent*, New York: Berghahn.
Grewal, Inderpal. (1996), *Home and Harem: Nation, Gender, Empire, and the Cultures of Travel*, Durham: Duke University Press.
Holland, Patrick and Graham Huggan, eds. (2000), *Tourists with Typewriters: Critical Reflections on Contemporary Travel Writings*, Ann Arbor: University of Michigan Press.
Huggan, Graham. (2009), *Extreme Pursuits: Travel/Writing in an Age of Globalization*, Ann Arbor: University of Michigan Press.
Kelleher, Fatimah. (2013), "What Space for African Eyes? Travel Writing and Africa in the 21st Century," *African Arguments*, 21 February. Available online: http://africanarguments.org/2013/02/21/what-space-for-african-eyes-travel-writing-and-africa-in-the-21st-century-%E2%80%93-by-fatimah-kelleher/ (accessed October 30, 2016).
Khair, Tabish. (2006), *Other Routes: 1500 Years of African and Asian Travel Writing*, Bloomington: Indiana University Press.
Lasse, Heerten and Dirk Moses. (2014), "The Nigeria-Biafra War: Postcolonial Conflict and the Question of Genocide," *Journal of Genocide Research* 16 (2–3): 169–203.
Lisle, Debbie. (2006), *The Global Politics of Contemporary Travel Writing*, Cambridge: Cambridge University Press.
López Ropero, María Lourdes. (2003), "Travel Writing and Postcoloniality: Caryl Phillips's *The Atlantic Sound*," *Atlantis* 25 (1): 51–62.
Mbembe, Achille. (2007), "Afropolitanism", in Njami Simon (ed), *Africa Remix. Contemporary Art of a Continent*, 26–30, Johannesburg: Johannesburg Art Gallery.
Mbembe, Achille. (2001), *On the Postcolony*, Los Angeles: University of California Press.

Mignolo, Walter. "The Many Faces of Cosmo-polis: Border Thinking and Critical Cosmopolitanism," *Public Culture* 12 (Fall): 721–748.

Morrison, Toni. (2017), *The Origin of Others*, Cambridge: Harvard University Press.

Moynagh, Maureen. (2015), "Afropolitan Travels: 'Discovering Home' and the World in Africa," in Paul Smethurst and Julia Kuehn (eds), *New Directions in Travel Writing Studies*, 281–296, London: Palgrave McMillan.

Ngozi Adichie, Chimamanda. (2013), *Americanah*, New York: Fourth Estate.

Pratt, Mary Louise. (1992), *Imperial Eyes: Travel Writing and Transculturation*, New York: Routledge.

Rask Knudsen, Eva and Ulla Rahbek. (2016), *In Search of the Afropolitan: Encounters, Conversations, and Contemporary Diasporic African Literature*, London: Rowman & Littlefield.

Saro-Wiwa, Noo. (2012), *Looking for Transwonderland: Travels in Nigeria*, London: Granta Publications.

Selasi, Taiye. (2009), "By-Bye, Babar (or: What is an Afropolitan?)," *The International Review of African American Art*, 22 (3): 36–38.

Selasi, Taiye. (2014), "Don't Ask Me Where I'm from, Ask Me Where I'm a Local," *TED Global*. Available online: https://www.ted.com/talks/taiye_selasi_don_t_ask_where_i_m_from_ask_where_i_m_a_local?language=en#t-949872 (accessed May 20, 2017)

Spurr, David. (1993), *The Rhetoric of Empire: Colonial Discourse in Journalism, Travel Writing, and Imperial Administration*, Durham: Duke University Press.

Tsika, Noah A. (2015), *Nollywood Stars: Media and Migration in West Africa and the Diaspora*, Bloomington: Indiana University Press.

Vieten, Ulrike. (2012), *Gender and Cosmopolitanism in Europe: A Feminist Perspective*, Farmhand: Ashgate.

11

"Something Covered But Not Hidden"

Obscurity in Teju Cole's Oeuvre as an Afropolitan Way of Worlding

Julian Wacker

"What does Afropolitanism even mean in Gikuyu?" was renowned Kenyan author Ngugi wa Thiong'o's sole response when I asked him about his view on *Afropolitanism* during his keynote lecture at the 2015 Annual German Association for Postcolonial Anglophone Studies (GAPS) Conference. Ngugi's answer not only reveals his own well-known view on the decolonization of English languages but speaks to more general problems surrounding the term Afropolitanism: scholars from various fields, generations, geographic locations, and ideological positions are caught in a contest to charge the term with meaning. This quest for meaning-making has entrenched an academic feud between advocates and opponents that effectively often holds productive analyses in a chokehold. On the part of creative writers and scholars, the attitudes towards the term Afropolitanism greatly differ. Some, like Taiye Selasi, Achille Mbembe, and Simon Gikandi, openly embrace the term to describe their variant conceptualizations while others, most notably Biyavanga Wainaina, Emma Dabiri, and Chimamanda Ngozi Adichie refuse it and have tried to overcome it. Amatoritsero Ede, for instance, criticizes a supposed Afropolitan stance—that he ties back to Taiye Selasi—towards the label "African writer":

> *The* Afropolitan, I argue in comparison [to Francophone writers who identify as Afropolitan], can be typified as rather apologetic and often excuses his/her rejection of *the* African writer label on its being typically Western interpellation that is essentialising, reductionist and professionally limiting or a pigeonholing
>
> (2016: 92; own emphasis added)

Although Selasi, Mbembe, and Gikandi offer multifarious theorizations of what "Afropolitan" can come to mean, i.e., complicating what it means to relate to African localities, its critique tends to focalize certain aspects while crucially neglecting others. As Susanne Gehrmann has aptly pointed out, "three major reproaches are now regularly being addressed as regards Afropolitanism, namely: (1) its elitism/class bias, (2) it's a-politicalness and (3) its commodification" (Gehrmann 2016: 62). Drawing on Wainaina's 2012 critique of Afropolitanism in his unrecorded lecture "I'm a Pan-Africanist, not an Afropolitan," Stephanie Bosch Santana has pointed out Wainaina's suggestion that "Afropolitanism extends its commodity-driven mentality to literature by treating texts as 'singular products'." (Bosch Santana 2016: 121). Read against Ede's observation, Teju Cole, however, feels comfortable in an ambivalent space towards the label—and any label, really—as in his view none of them are able to accurately cover his artistic pallet on their own. As he states in an interview with Taiye Selasi: "I'm a bit of a problem for the categorisers, partly because I don't fight the categories. I'm comfortable being described as Afropolitan, or African, or American, or pan-African. Or Yoruba, or Brooklynite, or black, or Nigerian. Whatever. As long as the labels are numerous" (Selasi 2016: n.pag.).

Taking this self-prescribed fluctuation between categories as a first observation, this essay examines the theme of obscurity in Teju Cole's oeuvre. As I argue, Cole's different texts, if set in relation, reveal a striking investment in the obscure, with the individual texts answering to and obscuring one another. In mapping relations between *Blind Spot* (2017), *Known and Strange Things* (2016), *Every Day is for the Thief* (2007), and *Open City* (2011), I will show how Cole's work is continuously envisioning worlds only to estrange them time and again. This creates a deliberate search for meaning in the reader, who is placed in a position of continuous unease and insecurity towards the texts' assertions. Reminiscent of Edouard Glissant's notion of opacity, Teju Cole's work thus questions dominant ways of interpreting and understanding world, which consequently hark back to Enlightenment thought. As such, it is through Cole's work that we might be able to frame one possible understanding of Afropolitan writing as a deliberate form of worlding which obscures and contests the categories, boundaries, and identity politics that affect contemporary writers with ties to the African continent. Before elaborating on Cole's obscure poetics, this essay establishes a connection between Afropolitan writing and world literature, highlighting some of the current debates in both fields.

Throughout this piece, I take the following observation as a vantage point into my inquiries: For one, the debate surrounding Afropolitanism largely benefits from a renewed focus on actual literary texts. While the various takes on Afropolitanism described above most clearly display a stark insecurity towards how to approach the phenomena it is associated with, the debate has largely shied away from and yet moved beyond genuine engagements with literary texts. All too often a critique of Afropolitanism, or Afropolitan writing, is based not on analyses of writing produced by contemporary authors but instead on ideological discussions that are largely detached from it and have created their very own discursive dimensions. Moreover, such a possible, favorable "literary turn" in the study of Afropolitanism (Rask Knudsen/Rahbek 2016: 3) needs to be accompanied by a different *approach* to these texts. Although Rask Knudsen and Rahbek's *In Search of the Afropolitan* (2016) marks a crucial and important turning point in the analysis of what they refer to as "Afropolitan literature",[1] the inquiry to trace the figure of "the" Afropolitan reproduces the very same essentializing ideas that, as this chapter's reading of Cole's work shows, some Afropolitan texts set out to challenge. As Teju Cole's texts propose an understanding of his work as an assemblage of texts, this bears repercussions on Afropolitan writing as well, which can possibly be described through temporary constellations that come into being through their relations.

Contesting Poles: Afropolitan Writing, World Literature, and the Pitfalls of Categorization

In making contact between Afropolitan writing—or, to stick with this chapter's focus, more precisely Teju Cole's writing—and the concept of anglophone African world literature, we run risk of assigning it a status as belonging to the exclusive category of world literature while barring other texts more strongly tied to African localities from this capacity. Although (African) world literary studies has commonly used David Damrosch's take that the migratory capacity of literary texts to "circulate beyond their culture of origin, either in translation or in their original language" (Damrosch 2003: 4) defines their belonging to the category of world literature, or as Phengh Cheah has recently distinguished it as a *global literature* detached from world literature's once normative context (Cheah 2018: 89), an evolving strand has started to diversify this thinking. Cheah's work on *worlding literature* brings to the fore a re-evaluation of the concept "world" by questioning its normative frame, which, in the study of world literature, is often an "unexamined conception of the world as market exchange across the globe [that] defines the world in terms of spatio-geographical extension." (Cheah 2018: 92). This strong affiliation between world literature and an understanding of "world" in the vein of late capitalism can be counteracted by the idea of *worlding*, which "opens up productive avenues of thought for the study of world literature because it suggests a stance of sheer being-with other modes of life that is prior to the emergence of the rational subject." (Cheah 2018: 98) It is "world literature's world-making capacities" (Neumann and Rippl 2017: 162), according to Birgit Neumann and Gabriele Rippl, which account for the various ways in which texts from different geographical and cultural contexts imagine world. This edited volume, as does the series, sounds this very notion when it interrogates different national and transnational literatures, or genre fictions, anew in reading them as world literature. As for the case of anglophone African world literatures, Rippl and Neumann argue that

> *the* Afropolitan model stresses their multifaceted interplay and foregrounds spaces of entanglement without ignoring the importance of locally embedded practices and situated knowledge. According to this logic, African spaces form a discontinuous network, bringing together plural African geographies as well as the various diasporic spaces in the Americas, Europe and elsewhere.
>
> (2017: 164; own emphasis added)

While I situate my own view of how Afropolitan texts imagine world in close proximity to these observations, understanding Afropolitan writing and world literature as assemblages in contact—which I will elaborate on later in my analysis of Cole's work—can further help avoid playing into the hands of what Rippl and Neumann have identified as "the current regime of world literature" (Rippl and Neumann 2017: 182), which confines literary text to a newly-fashioned hierarchy.

Tendencies to compare texts from different contexts in the study of world literature remain problematic—especially when it comes to texts written by authors with any relation to the African continent. As Alexander G. Weheliye argues in his fascinating piece *Habeas Viscus*,

> as long as numerous individuals and populations around the globe continue to be rendered disposable by the pernicious logics of racilization, and thus exposed to different forms of political [and epistemological] violence on a daily basis, it seems futile to tabulate, measure, or calculate their/our suffering in the jargon of comparison.
>
> (2014: 14)

Drawing on the black feminist theories of Hortense Spillers and Sylvia Wynter, Weheliye challenges the very concept of comparativity in the same breath:

> Comparativity frequently serves as a shibboleth that allows minoritized groups to gain recognition (and privileges, rights, etc.) from hegemonic powers (through the law, for instance) who, as a general rule, only grant a certain number of exceptions access to the spheres of full humanity, sentience, citizenship, and so on. This, in turn, feeds into a discourse of putative scarcity in which already subjugated groups compete for limited resources, leading to a strengthening of the very mechanisms that deem certain groups more disposable or not-quite-human than others.
>
> (2014: 13f.)

While Weheliye's work delicately excavates the racializing qualities of bare life and biopolitics discourses, his interrogation of comparative approaches holds value for framing literary criticism and the study of world literature as well. If we perceive world literature and its capacity to circulate globally on its way to become a twenty-first-century equivalent to (capital "L") Literature, we can very well read it in relation to the conceptualization of "Man", which Weheliye uses to describe the hegemonic positionality in the hierarchy between humans, not-quite-humans, and non-humans. In world literature discourse, under the badge of comparativity, certain types of marginalized writings may gain recognition, privileges, and circulation through, for instance, academic recognition and literary prizes which assign access to "full worldliness" only to a scare number of written texts. Competing for limited resources, some texts are rendered more disposable or not-quite-Literature/worldly than others. One might be ready to jump forth and argue that in literary studies we have long overcome outdated ideas such as "canonization," "true literary merit," and indeed "Literature"—and yet, we continuously create racializing assemblage of writing.

The comparative elevation of Afropolitan texts on the grounds of their belonging to a highly commodified global literature reverberates in the—at times no less problematic—Afro-centrist critique of Afropolitanism. Siyanda Mohutsiwa, for instance, describes her reaction to being named on *Ventures Africa*'s "15 African creatives to watch out for in 2016" list in her controversial piece "I'm Done With African Immigrant Literature" as follows:

> I was proud to be one of the only people on that list who was not London-based or Brooklyn-born. The act of being an African living in Africa seemed to me at that point to be almost revolutionary. I cannot hide the small and perhaps arrogant joy that comes to me when I know that all I create is 100% inspired by my uninterrupted African life.
>
> MOHUTSIWA 2016: n.pag.

While she definitely proves a point in criticizing the tendency to overlook writers actually based on the African continent in the international book market, she yet constructs her own biography as completely—that is to say 100 percent—uninterrupted African life. One almost feels tempted to read "real" or "authentic" as additions to that statement. This uninterrupted, "real" African life, according Mohutsiwa, only takes place in localities on the African continent and is contrasted by a generation of writers who establish their life center primarily outside of Africa—she might call this "interrupted" African life. In this narrative, which appears rooted in Afro-centrist, and perhaps even nativist ideologies, Mohutsiwa uses location as a hallmark to essentialize and demarcate Africa as an exclusive, corralled space that focuses inward. These are exactly those nativist tendencies, against which Mbeme has long since spoken out (cf. Mbembe 29). This argument is neither new nor innovative but all the while it is influential: Not much has changed in the Afro-centrist critique of migration from the continent since its ascension in the 1950s. And still, Mohutsiwa's short essay—despite all its intended polemic—epitomizes a rift between authors writing from the African continent and those who locate themselves in diasporic contexts: This discourse fashions the prerogative of interpretation with regard to the essentialist question of what Africa actually *is* as strictly tied to location.

In his direct response to Mohutsiwa's article, "I Am Not Done with African Immigrant Literature," Malawian author Shadreck Chikoti utters his discontent with her views:

> I get afraid, very afraid, when somebody, anybody, prescribes to me which books to read and not to read. When somebody gives me a template of what African literature ought to look like. And boy! You can imagine the shock I got when I read an article on okayafrica.com written by the gifted Siyanda Mohutsiwa, in which she gave a prescription for African literature, authenticating some forms and denouncing another.
>
> CHIKOTI 2016: n.pag.

If we, in a very first step, understand Afropolitan potentialities as challenges to essentialisms instead of indicating a certain kind of worldliness, Chikoti's essays certainly evoke these ideas. Where Mohutsiwa seeks to solidify, Chikoti dissolves. He adds: "Who says that African authors should only be inspired by Africa and only set their stories in Africa and only talk about Africa? I think we are missing it." (Chikoti 2016: n.pag.) Chikoti contests location as the defining factor in categorizing and validating literary texts. Thus, a writer born in an African locality and still living on the continent does not necessarily qualify as an African writer; to him the whole idea of labeling these texts proves to be irrelevant. Rather, the unique, the singular text should be seen as an individual piece of art which forges relations to a variety of other texts bridging locations and labels alike.

This online conversation between Mohutsiwa's article and Chikoti's response is one of the latest in a series of disagreements over contemporary politics of categorization and identity politics. An earlier attempt to deconstruct a possible category of "African literature" stems from Taiye Selasi who, after allegedly coining the term "Afropolitan," once again triggered a wave of criticism when she declared that "African literature doesn't exist" in her opening speech at Literatur Festival 2013. As she notes:

> My very basic assertion is that the practice of categorizing literature by the continent from which its creators come is past its prime at best. Our dogged insistence upon doing so, in the case of the African continent foremost, betrays a disregard both for the complexities of African cultures and the creativity of African authors. If literature is, as its finest practitioners argue, universal —then it deserves a taxonomy neither based on nor supportive of racial distinction, but reflective of the workings of the race-less human heart.
>
> SELASI 2013a: 1f.

Selasi speaks here to another trend which can be mapped as an Afropolitan tendency: the centralization of the individual self over collective associations. A central question remains: why is the backlash against writers so fierce if they address the importance of individual emancipation, the fluidity of identities as well as cultures, and problems of categories? The answer might be as simple as it is telling: It is exactly because they are doing so. We can approach Afropolitan texts through their ambiguous affiliations which oscillate between evoking and transgressing taboos: in affairing with lifestyles, identity politics, and literary forms that have predominantly been associated with Western societies and cultural production against the binary opposite of what has been constructed as "quintessentially" African, they provocatively challenge the dominant modes of representing African experiences we have been confronted with for decades.

The critique of Afropolitan texts largely mirrors Afro-centrist ideologies, which tend to tie African writing and African experiences strictly back to specific African localities. However, all too often these perspectives nourish dangerous totalities: Typically, only those experiences and texts are validated as focusing on "real" African concerns which are directly linked to the African continent in terms of writing, production, and circulation. While I completely acknowledge that these perspectives stem from a great and justified dissatisfaction with how texts written by writers based in African countries are received and distributed globally—and thus at times prove to be an important, often polemic intervention—they nonetheless largely discredit diasporic experiences. Those writers who find meaning in multiple Africas elsewhere, i.e., in diasporic lives and cultures, are denied claims of authenticity, knowledge, and lastly "Africanness" in speaking about issues and localities on the African continent. Through its self-referential logic, the afro-centrist critique of Afropolitanism renders itself political while imposing a veil of a-politicalness on Afropolitan theorists and texts. While speaking of (or for) an in such a way territorialized representation of Africa, these afro-centrist and nativist concerns are constructed as a political absolute.

Many of those texts labeled Afropolitan, however, create translocal imaginaries instead of fostering national African or pan-African identifications. As Neumann and Rippl put it, "[w]ith its emphasis on both rootedness and mobility, the concept of Afropolitanism must be understood as an attempt to bring together two distinct frameworks for understanding African identity, namely the frameworks offered by Pan-Africanism and the black Atlantic respectively" (2017: 182). They describe authors Taiye Selasi, Teju Cole, and NoViolet Bulawayo as "intermediaries or translators who negotiate between the conflicting, but entangled values, histories and economies of the Global South and the Global North" (2017: 182). While I do not seek to characterize Afropolitan texts as distinctively and exclusively adjoining the oppositional models of pan-Africanism and the Black Atlantic, I agree that these writers complicate our common understanding of geographical, historical, economical, and moral concerns. In its affairing with collectivities, forms, media, and markets, Afropolitan writing offers trajectories to question essentialist outlooks on (African) identity formation and politics of representation.

In the following, I will sketch how Teju Cole's oeuvre further strains the debate surrounding the contested term Afropolitanism. His texts reveal an obscure poetics, which can—and at times wants to—be read in the tradition of Édouard Glissant's concept of opacity. Cole's texts, as my analysis establishes, comment on one another and propose to be read in relation. The resulting challenging of concepts such as, amongst others, perception, interpretation, and categorization provides fruitful insights into the discussions of Afropolitan writing and its potential to imagine world(s).

Obscure Relations: Reading Teju Cole's Writing as an Assemblage

The photography volume *Blind Spot* actively engages the idea of thinking about Cole's texts as an assemblage, as a constellation of texts that interact with one another. As one of the small pieces of text in the volume reads, "Assemblages inhabit their own complexity and color" (Cole 2017: 274). This resonates with the theory of assemblages by Deleuze and Guattari— and later theorists like Manuel DeLanda—who have framed assemblages to produce their own, ever-emerging meanings through specific, temporary relations between their parts. Assemblage theory thus seeks to counter essentialisms and totalities, which create seamless wholes whose "parts cannot subsist independently of the relations they have with each other"

(DeLanda 2006: 10). With regard to the categorization of Afropolitan writing, this manifests itself in a tendency to either praise the new sensibilities these "Africans of the world" tend to raise or, on its flipside, overgeneralize certain traits such as a global, commodified, selfish black "urban" elite who is supposedly at the center of their own narratives as well as overemphasize a product-driven mentality. These categories, as seamless wholes (as in the case of Rahbek and Rask Knudsen's "the" Afropolitan), then come to represent the qualities of their different parts, while these different parts can supposedly stand in for the whole. We can grasp this *ex negativo* with Édouard Glissant, whose poetics of relation was influenced by and speaks to Deleuzian assemblage theory: "Opacities can coexist and converge, weaving fabrics. To understand these truly one must focus on the texture of the weave and not on the nature of its components." (1997: 190) Theories of assemblages neither propose that each part represents the whole nor do they assume that the whole represents the sum of its parts. Instead, DeLanda, who extends Deleuze's and Guattari's fragmented assemblage theory, sketches a whole which is described by "emergence and exteriority" (2006: 10). Such an assemblage consists of emergent properties, i.e., "the properties of a whole caused by the interactions between its parts" (2006: 9). The various parts in turn must be conceived as retaining their autonomy, "so that they can be detached from one whole and plugged into another one, entering into new interactions" (2006: 10). Cole's writing, if read as an assemblage which can be understood through the interactions between its different texts, enunciates a certain obscurity; it obscures meaning through relations, so to speak. Take the following segment from *Blind Spot*:

> Aren't all the photographs and texts, the fragments and experiments, even the things you say into a microphone, even the things you don't say, aren't they all installments toward a unified project? She said, though these are not her exact words: I have always felt that *Open City* was one way you approached the problem. You're still circling the problem now, she said, obsessed, she said, and approaching it in other ways. You will probably always be returning to it, she said, making herself comfortable in the folds of my brain. But it is the same problem, she said, though she didn't directly say what the problem was, or with what degree of success or failure I had approached it so far.
> COLE 2017: 126

There is much to gain from this passage. For one, on a meta-level, the (fictional) interviewer poses the question if all four of his texts are working towards one unified project. *Open City*, according to the nameless interviewer, might be one angle to approach the said problem, a problem that the texts will return to time and again. But what is the problem? The text does not provide an answer, it remains obscure here what exactly the problem is. Its presence is there and lingers but it is covered, obscured. The narrator further complicates the passage's reliability, stating that "these are not her exact words" (Cole 2017: 126). It is not important here to solve the problem; rather, the text argues that we should accept that it remains obscure. Another passage caters to a similar idea:

> I have always been haunted by this sense of the migratory properties of works, so that at times I feel as though the photographs and captions in *Blind Spot* have escaped from a novel named *Open City*, or that there are things said here, and which belong here, that first belonged in *Known and Strange Things*. This is not an avenue of thought I wish to foreclose under the dismissive term self-referential. The continuities involved are interesting for their own sake.
>
> COLE 2017: 240

Are there relations between *Blind Spot*, *Open City*, *Every Day is for the Thief*, and *Known and Strange Things*, or are there not? The lyrical I— as unreliable as it always is in Cole's fiction—here at least does not wish to exile the relations by labeling them "self-referential,"; the text allegedly dismisses the idea of metafiction. However, the continuities between the texts "are interesting for their own sake" (Cole 2017: 240), create their own meaning through their very interaction. The relations are not hidden they are covered. It takes time to find them but even if we do, they remain obscure.

The notion of reading Cole's writing as interacting texts, as a textual assemblage, bears repercussions on the way we, as humans, categorize. One common, if not the predominant form of classification, still appears to be grouping texts together according to similar characteristics. Texts which are said to significantly differ are then subsumed under another umbrella term. Multiple sub-categories branch out, typologies emerge. Those texts located in the liminal spaces between certain already established categories are allowed to be read as, for instance, "migrant writing," "transnational literature," and "Afropolitan literature." Although Trinh Minh-ha reminds us that "[c]ategories always leak" (1989: 94), the categories we create—despite their proclaimed permeability—are, to borrow Manual DeLanda's term, frequently constructed as *seamless wholes*. In its general sense, this speaks to the postmodern turn in literary studies, which has for the last fifty years relentlessly chipped away at the notions of stable knowledges. It has stressed the fluidity and fictionality of categorizations and the constant interplay of emerging and abating characteristics as the core of genre theory. Assemblage theory can be thought of as working with rhizomatic constellations. It comes to describe a specific constellation, which is brought about through the relations of its different parts, and branches out endlessly. This is what Glissant alludes to when he urges us to focalize the texture of the weave. The assemblage then emerges in an event, which only ever comes into being in its particular constellation. The rhizome, as Umberto Eco argues, can of course be structured, can become an assemblage. It is nevertheless "a fiction that we indulge in for the sake of our temporary convenience" (2014: 54). Under these premises, Afropolitan writing describes temporary constellations and their potential that is brought about through relating different texts to one another. Or, to put it differently: Afropolitan writing as a category then comes to designate ever-changing fields of tension and relation, assemblages, rather than an aggregated, yet supposedly permeable whole. In thinking about Afropolitan writing as an assemblage, we can find ways to complicate the essentialisms and binarisms that lie beneath common approaches to Afropolitan as well as world literature.

Envisioning and Estranging Worlds: Obscurity in *Blind Spot*

In debating (and claiming) obscurity, Teju Cole's *Blind Spot* strains our urge to categorize. Take the following condensed elaboration on the etymology of the word "obscure":

> Obscure is an adjective first attested in English around 1400. It means dark, or, figuratively, either morally unenlightened or gloomy. It comes from the Old French obscure or oscur, which means dark, clouded, gloomy, dim, or not clear, and is attested in the twelfth century. The French term is directly from the Latin obscurus, which means dark, dusky, shady, or, figuratively, unknown, unintelligible, hard to discern, or from insignificant ancestors. The word's roots are from ob, over, and -scurus, covered.
>
> COLE 2017: 162

This etymological maneuver, which transposes the desire to enlighten hidden meanings through its very form, brings to the fore the potential in obscurity, which speaks to us, as readers, on multiple levels: its unintelligible, unknown nature makes us wonder what there is to discern. Its cloudiness, its gloominess makes us focalize to see more clearly. Its dark, dusky, shady character probably makes us feel a slight unease when we engage with it, something that estranges us, something that might haunt us like imagery from a horror movie. These aspects are true, for the photograph that accompanies the description. It shows a horse, which one can typically find in a merry-go-round, covered in a thick, milky plastic foil. The cover is ripped in half to the horse's right, partially stitched together by pieces of adhesive tape. Like a scar that is about to be torn open again, its semi-opening simultaneously creates a crevasse into a world unknown to the lens and the eye, to what lies beneath the cover. We might be able to discern a few things through the gloomy façade: another inanimate horse's leg seems to stick out through the crack and yet another carousel wagon might be hidden on the far right of the photograph. Most of what lies beneath the awning, however, remains unclear. It is the contextual clues we bring to the photograph which tell us that it might be a provisional showman's storage. This at the very least reassures our own guesses. It is "something covered but not hidden" (Cole 2017: 108), as the text states at a different point, that this obscurity evokes. It is present in the moment the aperture shuts the light out to take a photograph, it is present in the moment our pupil absorbs the reflected light even before our optic nerve and brain construct what we come to see. And yet, it remains obscure. These musings on both text and photograph help us to grasp Afropolitan writing, at the very least in Cole's case, as invested in questioning dominant ways of categorization. Allegorically, this obscurity stands as a counterpoint to the ways we order, for instance, literary texts, people, and, in a last consequence, world.

Blind Spot triggers affective reactions and seduces the reader to illuminate and enlighten its obscurity. As such, the volume performs its eponymous theme: The text opens so many junctions, crossings, and connections that whenever one has found one, one is already missing another, creating another blind spot. This is further emphasized, as Saul Austerlitz has noted in his article on *Blind Spot*, through its very form, reversing the inclusion of photographs in his two novels and his essay collection "with hundreds of Cole's photographs illuminated, explained, or mystified by brief snippets of text" (Austerlitz 2017: n.pag.). I wish to readjust these observations slightly: While the photography volume only pretends to illuminate or explain, it certainly mystifies. *Blind Spot* uses its manifold, possible relations as a mode to obscure. Obscurity through relations—this notion undoubtedly speaks to Edouard Glissant's *Poetics of Relation* and his concept of opacity. Glissant describes opacity as a means to counteract the hegemonic structures of transparency as a barb of Western thought. As Glissant clamors "for the right to opacity for everyone" (1997: 194), he centers on this opacity as the individual experience, which, in turn, relates to other experiences and takes as its foundation a theory of difference. He writes: "I thus am able to conceive of the opacity of the other for me, without reproach for my opacity for him. To feel solidarity with him or to build with him or to like what he does, it is not necessary for me to grasp him" (1997: 193). The right to opacity, according to Glissant, counters the transmutations in the process of trying to become the other; rather, opacity is a means of becoming-other, of making contact with the other without attempting to read and understand it. Claiming one's own opacity, one's own unreadability and un-enlightenment, then requires accepting another person's opacity: "Opacities coexist" (1997: 190). Glissant distinguishes between opacity and obscurity, while the latter can be an expression of the former: "The opaque is not the obscure, though it is possible for it to be so and be accepted as such" (1997: 191). The obscure in Glissant's sense is closely related to the unintelligible, to something which lies out of reach. For him, obscurity is escorted by exclusion; the attempt to understand and make it transparent is what he calls "grasping." Opacity then prefers the idea of "giving-on-and-with" (1997: 192) as a means to avoid grasping and enlighten the obscure. This reverberates with Cheah's understanding of worlding literature,

> that returns to the openness of world enjoins us to consider the limits of the normative account of world literature as literary exchange among cultural subjects [and] leads to a re-envisioning of relations with others beyond the humanistic values of tolerance, respect, and mutual understanding that inevitably lead to hierarchical subordination under (Western) reason.
>
> CHEAH 2018: 107

Although Cole's texts do not imagine world as marked, in Cheah's understanding, by a fundamental condition of togetherness prior to reason, his work performs worlding in such a way that it challenges and critiques the very proceedings of Western thought. In reworking Glissant for the twenty-first century, the texts challenge the hegemonic positionality of Western reasonings of world. His work does not, in an overtly postmodern sense, fundamentally erase any universality behind the concepts of truth or knowledge. In other words: It is not the case that there lies nothing behind the curtain, cracks, and rifts. Through ways of covering, of obscuring, Cole's texts engage with dominant views of world and point towards alternative ways of seeing that lie in the obscure itself. His visual and textual philosophy of the obscure thus does not make him an obscurantist scholar, i.e., someone who is deliberately withholding knowledge from the public. Rather, it aims to show that alternative forms of knowledge can lie in the shadows, in the obscure, in the covered.

It is this relation between the opaque, on the one hand, and the obscure as one form of expressing opacity on the other that Teju Cole's *Blind Spot* takes as a vantage point to create its own concept of obscurity. While the aforementioned etymological excursion in the text acknowledges, similar to Glissant, the obscure as something "unknown" and "unintelligible," the passage ends, however, in the word "covered." Cole's photography in *Blind Spot* is concerned with things covered, shielded from direct perception by the gaze. Much like the empty plastic bottles in another photograph are surrounded and thus covered by a large plastic bag in what appears to be a metal container (Cole 2017: 109). The description that accompanies this picture largely remains on a descriptive level and in so doing, pays careful attention to every detail in the picture. I argue, however, that the last sentence "something covered, but not hidden" (Cole 2017: 108) draws attention to a larger pattern one can map out in *Blind Spot* and Cole's oeuvre. If we relate this to the passage that gives out to trace the etymology of the word obscure, one cannot but notice that both end with a note on something covered. Read in relation to one another, obscurity then assumes the potential of something covered but not hidden. Something that is there but obscured, covered, indiscernible.

The trope of the blind spot appears at multiple different points in Cole's oeuvre. In the following passage from *Open City*, narrator Julius debates his own profession and compares his work to a large blind spot, with Glissant sounding in his very words:

> [T]he mind is opaque to itself, and it's hard to tell where, precisely, these areas of opacity are. Opththalmic science describes an area at the back of the bulb of the eye, the optic disk, where the million or so ganglia of the optic nerve exit the eye. It is precisely there, where too many of the neurons associated with vision are clustered, that the vision goes dead. For so long, I recall explaining to my friend that day, I have felt that most of the work of psychiatrists in particular, and mental health professionals in general, was a blind spot so broad that it had taken over most of the eye. What we knew, I said to him, was so much less than what remained in darkness, and in this great limitation lay the appeal and frustration of the profession.
>
> COLE 2011: 238f.

The very same passage is quoted in the epilogue to Cole's essay collection *Known and Strange Things*, titled "Blind Spot." In the lines before the passage is quoted, the narrator—given the collection's largely non-fictional genre often taken to be Cole himself—elaborates on the relation between fiction and reality, between *Open City* and its uncanny connection to the narrator's own experiences as he is suddenly suffering from papillophlebitis:

> When we write fiction, we write within what we know. But we also write in the hope that what we have written will somehow outdistance us. We hope, through the spooky art of writing, to trick ourselves into divulging truths that we do not know we know. Open City, published two months before my eye troubles began, is in part an examination of the limits of sensitivity and of knowledge.
>
> COLE 2016: 383

The narrator's illness allegorically overemphasizes the many blind spots that are inherent in any form of perception, interpretation, and representation. It directs our attention to those things that are present in the moment we perceive but are shunned from further processing.

The photographs in *Blind Spot* are greatly concerned with things obscure. Covers, rifts, shadows, cracks—the photography plays with the notion that something is contained in the picture but not entirely possible to discern. A crack opens up to something—but to what? A cover shields something from our view—but what does it cover? We do not know but we know that possibility lies in this obscurity—the possibility of interpretation, of individual meaning-making in the process of our own perception, and in envisioning the worlds that lie beneath the crack and behind the curtain. But this is not what *Blind Spot* and Cole's oeuvre do, it is not about interpreting what lies beyond but accepting that we do not know what is covered. There lies power in something covered that is not hidden. This mapping of obscurity, of course, is only one of the countless ways to read the text as a temporary assemblage. Coming back to the previous discussion of Afropolitan writing and worlding literature, Cole's texts bring to the fore a desire to challenge established categories, one of which certainly is the imagination of a single, totalized Africa, by enunciating an obscure mode.

Open City and *Every Day is for the Thief*: The Case of the Unnamed Narrator

One of the most interesting relations between Cole's texts is the question if the narrator of *Open City*, Julius, is also the protagonist of his first and subsequently republished novel *Every Day is for the Thief*. Yvonne Kappel has previously pointed out the latter's potential in destabilizing demarcations of genre:

> Constantly blurring the generic conventions of the traditional and postcolonial travelogue, it goes beyond the colonial/postcolonial divide and thus exceeds a priori established categorizations; instead, it foregrounds transcultural engagements that cut across time and space, highlighting the ambivalent tensions inherent in Western concepts.
>
> KAPPEL 2017: 68

She thus concludes that "Teju Cole's travelogue inhabits an in-between state that disrupts pre-established genre formations and clear-cut divisions between a colonial and postcolonial world" (Kappel 2017: 71). I would like to add to her brilliant findings on how the novel formally challenges neatly ordered categories that leaving its narrator unnamed is a crucial choice which further emphasizes this investment in challenging the ways we perceive the world and the texts' notion of obscurity. The novels tempt readers to think that they share one narrator. *Open City*'s narrator Julius, a psychiatrist practicing in New York, finds both meaning and estrangement in his nightly walks through the city and has familial ties to both Germany and Nigeria. Visiting Nigeria again after fifteen years of absence, the narrator in *Every Day is for the Thief*, now resides in New York and is "training in psychiatry" (Cole 2007: 90). As narrators, both of them also foreground their preoccupation with telling—and fabricating—their own story. The unnamed narrator unmistakably makes clear that "this is my story now, not his" (Cole 2016: 23) after a lengthy elaboration on the relation between one of his favorite novels and his own experiences. Similarly, Julius reminds readers that "we are not the villains of our own stories" and that we "play, and only play, the hero" (Cole 2011: 243). The fact that the narrator in *Every Day is for the Thief* is unnamed, however, stands out. The texts lure us in to think that two narrators with ancestral ties to Nigeria, who now live in New York and work as psychiatrists must be one and the same person. This deliberate unnaming thus excavates the urge to equate and homogenize black experiences on the mere grounds of a few similarities.

Conclusion: Obscurity as an Afropolitan Way of Worlding

Undoubtedly, Afropolitan writing and world literature will remain contested categories. This essay has demonstrated, however, how a renewed focus on literary texts can contribute to and revitalize current debates. Through approaching Teju Cole's work as an assemblage of texts, we can learn to understand Afropolitan writing as marked by dynamic tensions, deliberately refuting clear-cut generic and political affiliations. These relations certainly create frictions; frictions that we need to embrace creatively without relying on essentialisms and totalities. In the case of Teju Cole's *Blind Spot*, I have mapped how the volume itself foregrounds a thinking of it as an assemblage that reaches out to Cole's other texts. These relations, however, claim obscurity in their attempt to estrange the ways in which we perceive, interpret, and categorize both text and world. As such, the photography volume interrogates our common ways to represent. Through its refusal to define clear, tangible categories, this stance is vulnerable to criticism which argues that such an approach drifts into arbitrariness, ambiguity, and obscurity. As my analysis of Teju Cole's *Blind Spot* shows, that is exactly the point. Our preconceived notion of categorization, which is crucially influenced by (post-) Enlightenment thinking, does not account for ambiguity, does not do well in tolerating obscurity. The unnaming of the narrator in *Every Day is for the Thief* thus works as a counterpoint to Julius in *Open City*, bringing to the fore problematic homogenizations of black lives in today's world. In this reading, the texts claim obscurity and remind us of the many blind spots our categorization of literary texts, humans, and world always entails. The obscure poetics in Cole's oeuvre is one exemplary Afropolitan way of worlding, deliberately challenging dominant representations of black life in the twenty-first century through a structural and thematic philosophy of what lies in the dark.

Note

1 In my understanding, "writing" covers the artistic pallet of Afropolitan texts more accurately than "literature" as it stretches across various genres and media.

Works cited

Austerlitz, S. (2017), "Book Review: The Seen and Unseen in Teju Cole's *Blind Spot*," *The National*, June 15. Available online: https://www.thenational.ae/arts-culture/book-review-the-seen-and-unseen-in-teju-cole-s-blind-spot-1.38794 (accessed September 15, 2018).
Bosch Santana, S. (2016), "Exorcizing the Future: Afropolitanism's Spectral Origins," *Journal of African Cultural Studies* 28 (1): 120–126.
Cheah, P. (2016), *What is a World? On Postcolonial Literatures as World Literatures*. Durham: Duke University Press.
Cheah, P. (2018), "Worlding Literature: Living with Tiger Spirits," *Diacritics* 45 (2): 86–114.
Chikoti, S. (2016), "I Am Not Done with African Immigrant Literature," *Africa in Words*, February 18. Available online: https://africainwords.com/2016/02/18/i-am-not-done-with-african-immigrant-literature/ (accessed December 30, 2017).
Cole, T. (2011), *Open City*, New York: Random House.
Cole, T. [2007] (2014), *Every Day is for the Thief*, New York: Random House.
Cole, T. (2016), *Known and Strange Things*, New York: Random House.
Cole, T. (2017), *Blind Spot*. New York: Faber.
Damrosch, D. (2003), *What is World Literature?* Princeton: Princeton University Press.
DeLanda, M. (2006), *A New Philosophy of Society: Assemblage Theory and Social Complexity*, London and New York: Continuum.
Eco, U. [2007] (2014), *From the Tree to the Labyrinth: Historical Studies on the Sign and Interpretation*, Cambridge and London: Harvard University Press.
Ede, A. (2016), "The Politics of Afropolitanism," *Journal of African Cultural Studies* 28 (1): 88–100.
Gehrmann, S. (2016), "Cosmopolitanism with African Roots: Afropolitanism's Ambivalent Mobilities," *Journal of African Cultural Studies* 28 (1): 61–72.
Glissant, É. (1997), *Poetics of Relation*, Ann Arbor: The University of Michigan Press.
Kappel, Yvonne (2017), "Re-membering the Travelogue: Generic Intertextuality as a Memory Practice in Teju Cole's Every Day is for the Thief," *ZAA* 65 (1): 67–83.

Mbembe, A. (2005), "Afropolitanism," in S. Njami and L. Durán (eds), *Africa Remix: Contemporary Art of a Continent*, 26–30, Ostfildern-Ruit: Hatje Cantz.

Minh-ha, T. (1989), *Woman, Native, Other: Writing Postcoloniality and Feminism*, Bloomington: Indiana University Press.

Mohutsiwa, S. (2016), "I'm Done With African Immigrant Literature," *OkayAfrica*, February 8. Available online: http://www.okayafrica.com/im-done-with-african-immigrant-literature/ (accessed December 30, 2017).

Neumann, B. and G. Rippl (2017), "Celebrating Afropolitan Identities? Contemporary African World Literatures in English," *Anglia* 135 (1): 159–185.

Rask Knudsen, E. and U. Rahbek (2016), *In Search of the Afropolitan: Encounters, Conversations, and Contemporary Diasporic African Literature*, London: Rowman & Littlefield International.

Selasi, T. (2014), "African Literature Doesn't Exist," *Opening Address, 13th International Literature Festival Berlin*, September 4. Available online: http://www.literaturfestival.com/archiv/eroeffnungsreden/die-festivalprogramme-der-letzten-jahre/AfricanLiteratureDoesntExist.pdf (accessed July 20, 2019).

Selasi, T. (2016), "Teju Cole talks to Taiye Selasi: 'Afropolitan, American, African. Whatever'," *The Guardian*, August 5. Available online: https://www.theguardian.com/books/2016/aug/05/teju-cole-taiye-selasi-interview-known-strange-things (accessed December 30, 2017).

Weheliye, A. (2014), *Habeas Viscus: Racializing Assemblages, Biopolitics, and Black Feminist Theories of the Human*, Durham: Duke University Press.

12

The Hesitant Local

The Global Citizens of *Open City* and *Americanah*

Lara El Mekkawi

In defining contemporary African identities over the past 15 years, Afropolitanism has been a popular term associated with those living in several locales; it is a merging of African and cosmopolitan, that creates a new category for African writers, one that deviates from a single story narrative and from a forced political background. Afropolitanism has been associated with mobility, movement from one locale to another and broadening one's circles of affiliation; thus, becoming Africans of the world. However, with a term such as Afropolitanism that connects being African to being worldly, one wonders, where the line is drawn between being cosmopolitan and being African? In merging the two terms, what is omitted and what is gained? This paper looks at the mobility imbedded within Afropolitan writings, specifically Chimamanda Ngozi Adichie's *Americanah* and Teju Cole's *Open City,* and how it obstructs the identification of localities and globalities, creating another hybrid in the mix, the hesitant local.

Before exploring Afropolitanism, it is important to note the variable nature of cosmopolitanism itself. The use of "cosmopolitanism" as a method of understanding the world has been wide. In numerous instances, it has been affixed, where philosophers, writers, sociologists, etc. have explored the term based on their personal identification with it. It is vernacular (Bhabha 1996), it is partial (Appiah 2006), it is empathic (Weik von Mossner 2014), and the list goes on. Pheng Cheah defines cosmopolitanism in "What is a world? On world literature as world-making activity," as an optic of the imagination and not one of perceptual experience that allows us to imagine the universe that we can actually see. Through the optic of cosmopolitan imagination, it is possible to see oneself as "part of the world, a circle of belonging that transcends the limited ties of kinship and country to embrace the whole of humanity" (26). This transcendental imagination does not discard or overcome the ties of kinship and country—it allows individuals to engage with the world through negotiating local issues in relation to the globe, by opening up the spaces of locality that are often overlooked or ignored in universal endeavors, as shall be presented through analyzing the hesitancy factor found in cosmopolitanism specifically when affiliations have to be made. Whether one commits to it fully, partially, or with hesitation, with diasporas expanding and borders fading, cosmopolitanism remains pertinent. In this work, the hesitant factor in cosmopolitanism is believed to be an intrinsic element that has enabled it to be a critical concept used in comprehending contemporary affiliations, as observed in the novels that are perceived as Afropolitan; here, Afropolitanism is understood as a form of cosmopolitanism, an expansion and a narrowing, where the notion of being a citizen of the world is limited to being an African of the world.

A common criticism of cosmopolitanism is that it is out of date, elitist, and irrelevant; that it is incapable of addressing the problems of today's shared world because it does not describe it; what it does instead is represent a covering up of global and local struggles through universalism. One of such critics is scholar Craig Calhoun, who finds cosmopolitanism as an accessory to globalization—that not only is a tool for capitalism, but is also elitist and aids "high culture" as opposed to culture. For Calhoun, thinking of cosmopolitanism as an interconnectedness in the world and a propagator of equality is false; it rather establishes "inequality" and "uprooting." Moreover, Calhoun acknowledges a Western center in terms of cosmopolitan relations. In "*The Class Consciousness of Frequent Travelers: Toward a Critique of Actually Existing Cosmopolitanism,*" he criticizes contemporary cosmopolitanism as a concept that is not universal or global at all, but is instead narrow and exclusive:

> Contemporary cosmopolitanism commonly reflects the experience and perspective of elites and obscures the social foundations on which that experience and perspective rests. Thinking about cosmopolitanism as ethical universalism reinforces the lack of attention to the social foundations on which it rests—even when ethical universalism might be a basis for egalitarian critique.
>
> (440)

However, critics like Calhoun do not recognize the dispersed and unprivileged as cosmopolitan, leaving them as outcasts within the global. Similar attestations are found against Afropolitanism.

In contrast to this eurocentric notion of cosmopolitanism, scholars like Bruce Robbins observe that cosmopolitanism has shifted toward an individual view of the global, a multiple entity formed of small scales. It is not a distant entity, separate from nationalism, from hegemony, but instead it is affiliated with different cultures and locales, each forming a relationship with the world based on their own experiences. Such associations complicate cosmopolitanism's own components, making it unable to stand on its own. As such cosmopolitanism can be defined as the state of in-betweeness, a collision of the transnational, the global, the international, and the local. Cosmopolitanism registers hesitancy in picking a side between whether cosmopolitanism is part of a locality or a globality.

Merging African with cosmopolitan, alters the components of this worldly outlook even more, by limiting its reach on one side by specifying an affiliate, while broadening its reach from the other by connecting cosmopolitanism to the world at large. In simpler terms, the implications of "citizen of the world" change when ascribing it to an African link. Similar to cosmopolitanism, Afropolitanism has also been difficult to define and has been utilized in different spheres, both in popular intellectual cultures and in academic ones. Many have attempted to define the spaces that encompass Afropolitanism, from Selasi to Mbembe, with many basing their own understandings of the term on one or the other.

Taiye Selasi adopts a global position and refutes border constraints where identity becomes personal, based on one's locality more than on historical background; narratives become multiple and overlapping, allowing African writers to be treated as "artists" first, and "citizens" second. In "Bye-Bye Babar," Selasi declares: "We are Afropolitans: not citizens, but Africans of the world" (2005); the substitution of "citizens" with "Africans" is not merely a clever wording, but it carries hefty implications with it, for with being a citizen comes a notion of belonging that is not easily applicable to all. To be familiar with the world does not necessarily imply citizenship, therefore in representing Afropolitans as Africans of the world as opposed to citizens; does Selasi alleviate the need for complete integration?

To be an African of the world can be easy, if said African is a citizen of a G8 country; however, for Africans coming from the continent, possessing only African passports, to be of the world is much more difficult, and it involves a painful amount of paperwork. In being an African of the world, one is aware of her centers, that either allow or impede world travel, if travel is to be a definitive factor in defining Afropolitanism. If it is not, then to be an African of the world becomes much less problematic, as it goes hand in hand with being a global citizen, for with globalization, world culture becomes part of one's culture and knowledge. The struggle in being an African of the world would be in distinguishing what is local and what is global when all is familiar, for the privilege of mobility is not always available to those who perceive themselves as worldly. The global African's familiarity with both African and non-African cultures and spaces, may point to a kind of ease of Africanness in the world that it is easy for the Adichies, Selasis, and Coles of the world to move as Africans. However, Afropolitanism has had to defend itself from this notion because it is an oversimplification to think that the African is seamlessly "at home in the world" to borrow a phrase from Timothy Brennan even for these well-heeled Afropolitans. Instead, they inhabit a space of hesitancy, making them as I call, "hesitant locals," unsure of how to function within the world as Africans.

Achille Mbembe reasserts Afropolitanism as a critical movement that opposes nationalism and nativism in order to get out of a reliance on victimhood, and embraces a cosmopolitan perspective in relation to African identity. As opposed to Selasi, Mbembe does not limit Afropolitanism to a new and utopian sense of the world traveler, but he rather merges the historical and cultural aspects of those with roots in the continent. For Mbembe, the question of who is an Afropolitan, transcends race, encompassing anyone and everyone who has a relationship with the African continent; white South Africans, Asian diasporic Africans all fit into the category as they all relate to Africa. Moreover, to be Afropolitan does not involve merely leaving Africa, but also coming to the continent, therefore opening up boundaries of cultural exchange; migrants to Africa are as Afropolitan as immigrants from Africa. Mbembe gives Afropolitanism the same sense of power that Selasi does but in a more inclusive manner, alleviating the need for victimization found in the discourse attached to Africa and the Black Diaspora: "It is a way of being in the world, refusing any form of victim identity—which does not mean that it is not aware of the injustices and violence inflicted on the continent and its people by the law of the World" (Mbembe 30). Mbembe's definition realistically takes into consideration who is an African of the world, and more specifically what it means to be African. In looking at mobility and border limitations, it is important to look at who exactly is moving within the world, and what are the constraints that impede her.

As Mbembe grounds Selasi's Afropolitanism and gives it the depth and relatability that it lacks for academic interpretation, other scholars such as Eze, Salami, Gehrmann, and Harris base their own research on Mbembe's and expand on the idea of being an African of the world. In "We, Afropolitans," Chielozona Eze explores the different spatial connotations linked to being an Afropolitan. He emphasizes not only international travel but also inner mobility in the composure of an Afropolitan identity; it is related to exceeding not geographical boundaries, but rather mental barriers associated to nationalism through openness, which is evident in Chimamanda Ngozi Adichie's *Americanah*. In "Cosmopolitanism with African roots. Afropolitanism's ambivalent mobilities," Susanne Gehrmann studies the rise of Afropolitanism and the controversies surrounding the term; as she acknowledged the class bias behind Afropolitanism, Gehrmann considers the term to be salvageable, exploring diasporic identities in a decentered manner as in Teju Cole's *Open City*. In her blog, *MsAfropolitan*, Minna Salami writes "Afropolitanism and Identity Politics" with an intention to show the necessity of an Afropolitan viewpoint in identity politics. She highlights that Afropolitanism is not a misleading concept that aims to reimagine Africa in Western eyes, but instead it is a "glocal, analytical interaction of cross-cultural, philosophical, psycho-social and spiritual textures informed by past, present and future Africa" (*MsAfroloptanism*) that is not necessarily based on interactions with the West, or any physical place for that matter, as it is with Africans globally, be it intercontinentally or beyond the continent. Indeed, geographical spaces do not concern Afropolitanism, according to Salami, it is "a social, cultural, political, philosophical, psychological, spiritual one." Ashleigh Harris sheds light on a grittier sense of Afropolitanism that does not reflect a stance of elitism in "Afropolitan Style and Unusable Global Spaces" (2017). Harris argues that being put in the world, does not translate to being at home in the world, as usually implied with cosmopolitanism. Instead, even those in the "unusable global space," those "compressed" into public space and not "in-between" them, are Africans of the world. Again, the global movement found in cosmopolitanism, does not necessarily have to be outside the continent; intercontinentally, major differences can be found, as an African identity is not a shared singular one. Even though the narratives found in *Open City* and *Americanah* show mainly the interaction of Nigerian individuals with the United States, the UK, and Europe, their interaction with Africans around the world showcases the difference in national African identities, which shows that even within the continent, familiarity is not a given.

Afropolitanism as a field of analysis grows, and what remains interesting about the different understandings of it is that it steers away from the risk of forming its own single story; narratives that fall into the category of Afropolitan allow a multiple and overlapping reading that in the cases of *Americanah* and *Open City* re-center and decenter locals respectively.

In analyzing the works of Chimamanda Ngozi Adichie and Teju Cole, the spaces of the local and global are explored in various forms and are represented by issues of race, ethnicity, and education. Both authors themselves fit into the category of Afropolitan due to their active presence on social media and within global spaces; Miriam Pahl analyzes the critical cosmopolitanism in their Afropolitanism in order to assess global culture and challenge contemporary notions on African identity. Both Adichie and Cole's internet presence typify the diversity found in Afropolitanism. Through the use of cyberspace, they transcend issues of national borders. As Adichie takes Ifemelu's blog from *Americanah* and continues posting in it outside the confines of the novel, and Teju Cole delves into worldwide critical experimentations on Twitter and Instagram, they merge issues of locality and globality by making both accessible to everyone. This essay argues that their works bring forth an interesting commentary on the Afropolitan in relation to cosmopolitanism, which in turn looks at issues of comfort within local and global spheres: does an Afropolitan identification, fit into the notion of being a hesitant local? Which is to say, does such an individual ever fully fit in?

Award-winning author Chimamanda Ngozi Adichie's sixth publication *Americanah* is a widely acclaimed work that is licensed for publication in twenty-nine languages. It is a narrative that studies race and identity in a global context; Ifemelu and Obinze leave military-ruled Nigeria, and settle on completely different lives in the West; where Ifemelu goes to the US to continue her studies, Obinze is bound to pursue illegitimate methods of global travel. As Ifemelu attempts to assimilate within the global setting, Obinze is rejected and remains localized within the borders of his nation, unable to find home elsewhere. *Americanah* explores issues of familiarity in different contexts, shifting centers instead of distancing from them. Adichie delves into the intricacies that characterize a local as hesitant; specifically when localities shift, thus making it difficult to assume familiarity and comfort within one's setting. As we shall see with Ifemelu and Obinze, forming new localities remains an apprehensive act and the characters remain hesitant in engulfing themselves in them; they stand at a fault between the two sides, unsure of their allegiance.

The novel can be divided into three stages: before, during, and after living in the West; for both Ifemelu and Obinze, these three stages shake up their lives and the formation of their identities. However, their cosmopolitan stances in life do not begin with their departure from Nigeria, but instead they have been encountering Western, or specifically American culture, their whole lives for Nigeria itself is a cosmopolitan country that transcends boundaries through cultural and ethnic openness. As Wesley Macheso notes, even during their school days, multicultural awareness is prevalent in Ifemelu, Ginika, Kayode, Emenike, and Obinze's everyday lives; the music they listen to, the books they read, the TV shows they watch are mainly of a cosmopolitan nature. Obinze is complemented for his attentive interest in American culture:

> Everybody watched American shows, but he knew about Lisa Bonet leaving *The Cosby Show* to go and do *Angel Heart* and Will Smith's huge debts before he was signed to do *The Fresh Prince of Bel Air*.
>
> (53)

Obinze's interest in American culture made it impertinent for him to leave Nigeria in pursuit of America; it had been his dream. The globalization of television, allows Obinze to connect to America; it gives him a sense of familiarity, that he could be "at home" there. This knowledge of American culture perhaps makes him an African of the world, and in turn Afropolitan, before ever even endeavoring to leave.

Truly, these students are to be seen as "Africans of the world" for their interests. Therefore, from the onset, to be Afropolitan entails a sense of familiarity with global culture, which transcends national boundaries.

Matters of travel become important when one thinks of the future, especially travel to America and Europe is representative of success. By making it to these countries, one's status is immediately elevated, not because of the homeland's inferiority, but because of the idealistic conception third worlders have of these paces. Adichie deals with middle- and upper-class citizens of Nigeria, specifically in Lagos and Nsukka, presenting characters that have the ability to travel, while others are bound to one place; Kayode who is able to vacation in England is representative of Selasi's Afropolitan globetrotter, whereas Ifemelu and Obinze have to wait for the opportunity to be provided in order to travel, which is when the socio-political situation in Nigeria becomes threatening and their visa applications to America and Britain have been approved. As naïve students, the West represents a better alternative; however, the characters are quickly disillusioned with the idea of making it in the West, through their separate struggles of assimilating. It is through the engagement with America and England, that Adichie pinpoints the challenges with Afropolitanism that African travelers face. She does so by portraying the reality of middle-class African travelers or immigrants, and not that of the elite Nigerian travelers depicted in magazines such as can "identifiable: by expensive clothing, jewelry and luxury vehicles," whether they are in Paris or Harare (Afropolitan 2014).

Even the title, *Americanah*, signals to an engagement with America; which is where the novel mainly centers, around Ifemelu's experience in the USA, an experience that is far from dreamlike. Dealing with issues of racism, unemployment, and general second-class treatment, she constantly faces alienation, frustration, rejection which ultimately leads to depression. As her situation gradually improves, finding a stable job and forming a serious relationship with Curt, she is able to see America from the other side of the spectrum, that of privilege. Slowly but surely, she assimilates; no longer treated with hostility, which is due more to her foreignness and poverty than her race. It is only when Ifemelu is stable, treated more or less like a citizen, that she is able to look at issues that are American, such as race, which greatly impact her day-to-day life there.

> The only reason you say that race was not an issue is because you wish it was not. We all wish it was not. But it's a lie. I came from a country where race was not an issue; I did not think of myself as black and I only became black when I came to America.
>
> (359)

Specifically, when she dates Curt, she realizes the differences in how she is treated or how she goes about in comparison to her white lover. Also, the inability to explain the nuances of racism to Curt who only has the best intentions and in a sense is incapable of seeing the prejudice Ifemelu faces, just make these issues more and more evident for Ifemelu.

Her return to Nigeria is not without its struggles either; as she becomes an "Americanah," as Ranyinudo teases her, "looking at things with American eyes." (476) Though home is familiar after all these years, it also becomes strange.

Ifemelu is rendered a hesitant local, unable to fully assimilate anywhere. Her experience represents the distinction between a cosmopolitan and an Afropolitan, for to be an African of the world is quite different from being a citizen of the world. What does it mean to be a citizen of the world? To be a citizen, is to have access, to be able to work, to vote, to have similar rights to others. As an immigrant or visitor, that is not the case, with constant limitations set up, to be of the world does not necessarily mean to belong in it. Ifemelu is indeed an African of the world, connecting with some, while remaining distant from others; sharing experiences while continuing to be alienated from full interaction.

Obinze's experience in England sheds light on issues of alienation and apprehension. He perhaps occupies the "unusable global space" that Harris describes. As soon as his visa expires, he becomes an illegal, unwelcome in the world and forced to turn to unlawful acts in order to remain there. As his dreams of making something of himself in the States or in England fall short, he is quickly disillusioned. Only back in Nigeria is he able to succeed, through means he had always hoped to stay away from. In the global context, Obinze is not Afropolitan in a comforting sense. He is rejected from the world, and quickly sent back to his home country. In his narrative, questions of who is to be welcomed within the world, who is the West expected to open its doors to, are highlighted: When one is brought up to consider the latter a liberation from the limitations of the local, why is it wrong to want to leave? When at Emenike and Georgina's dinner party the topic of immigration comes up, it becomes an almost unanimous consensus that only those who have suffered, those who have lived in great poverty, been raped, and blatantly oppressed, should have the right to become citizens of the world. But in the case of people like Obinze, who hope for a better life, who hope to have a choice to leave and explore the world, immigration becomes a selfish desire, one that ought to be rejected:

> [. . .] all understood the fleeing from war, from the kind of poverty that crushed human souls, but they would not understand the need to escape from the oppressive lethargy of choicelessness. They would not understand why people like him, who were raised well fed and watered but mired in dissatisfaction, conditioned from birth to look towards somewhere else, eternally convinced that real lives happened in that somewhere else, were now resolved to do dangerous things, illegal things, so as to leave, none

of them starving, or raped, or from burned villages, but merely hungry for choice and certainty.

(202)

In Obinze's case, being Afropolitan is not as clear cut as Selasi would have it; for to be African within the world implies being invited into it; thus being African and worldly remain quite separate. As his mentality is one that is cosmopolitan, his nationality prevents him from actualizing it through mobility. He is only welcome in specific parts of the world and is limited in others. The hesitancy in Obinze's case is related to his return and settling in Nigeria. In Nigeria, he makes something of himself, thus joining the ranks of the elite that through financial means have more accessibility within the world. As mentioned earlier, even without the factor of mobility and travel, Obinze can be seen as an Afropolitan because of his interests. As an experienced adult, he is forced to accept a reality and a future that a younger and naiver Obinze rejected. Yet, as the world rejected him in return, he secures himself in the Nigeria that he was so hesitant and unwilling to stay in. As he encounters Ifemelu years later, he is faced with the reality of change; both experienced the world differently, yet both are worldly.

Within the specific locale of Nigeria, both Obinze and Ifemelu fall into the categorization of an Afropolitan, specifically Obinze who had an early on curiosity about the West, that Ifemelu only adopted later on. Even though their experiences disillusioned them, they remain Afropolitan because they become aware of the multifaceted factors that relate and distinguish them within the world, which according to Chielozona Eze, makes one an Afropolitan.

In "We, Afropolitans," Eze defines an Afropolitan identity as one that is open, aware of the multiple influences of its composition. Afropolitans become universal people due to their own openness to the world; to be Afroplitan is to recognize the sameness one shares with others while embracing the differences. He writes:

> The first question Afropolitans ask when they encounter other people is: what do I (or can I) have in common with this person? The next question is: what is beautiful or admirable in this other? The third is: what can I learn from this person? By the time they have answered all these questions, the issue of how they are different from that person would have taken care of itself. Difference becomes merely a reference point of individuality and respect rather than a point of exclusion of the other.
>
> (118)

Eze's Afropolitan is not defined by his travel experiences but by the openness in attitude of the individual in question. However, this attitude is not to be seen as naïve and idealistic; *Americanah* exposes the true struggle of being an

Afropolitan and the demand for a worldly openness and acceptance. Ifemelu spends years in America taking on numerous layers of difference as she assimilates: she becomes black for the first time in her life, with this new category she identifies with a whole new group: "I did not think of myself as black and I only became black when I came to America" (212). With each familiarity comes a distinction. She is black, but she is not African American, she identifies with some issues of race, but she is to never grasp the full length of their struggle. Ifemelu encompasses this idea of Afropolitan as someone welcoming the familiar while trying to understand and engage the differences.

As for the significance of travel in Afropolitanism, Susanne Gehrmann recognizes the importance of mobility in the formation of an Afropolitan identity; this mobility does not necessarily have to be of a physical nature but can take on a digital form, "which encompasses a quick circulation of ideas and images via the cyberspace that characterizes both the construction and contestation of Afropolitan lifestyles and cultural production" (Gehrmann, 61). Ifemelu's blogs are an affirmation of such an outlet for the Afropolitan identity, as are Adichie's. Such an implementation of Afropolitanism as a form of critical cosmopolitanism validates its politically transformative potential (Pahl 74). Even Obinze, who is very much aware of cosmopolitan culture through the media, is part of it. Therefore, to be Afropolitan in a sense that is compliant to Eze, is to continuously re-center and take on new layers of identity in order to truly become a person of the world, which can be aided through digital consumption of information as presented by Gehrmann.

Americanah shows the complications in being an African of the world, and that in fact, to be Afropolitan does not guarantee an ease in mobility, but instead carries varying complications for those who are open to the world, as we see in Ifemelu and Obinze's varying experiences. Both characters are exemplary of hesitant locals, who do not fully fit in anywhere they go; who are not to be seen as fully excluded but as worldly; who are forced to deal with limitations yet still choose to engage on a global scale.

This openness in mobility and observation of the other is prevalent in Teju Cole's *Open City* as well. Unlike *Americanah*, it is not easy to divide *Open City* into sections, for the protagonist Julius does not go through any transformation internally, but instead remains as a distant commentator of all that is happening in whatever situation he is in. The novel follows in the footsteps of the nineteenth-century *flâneur*, in the artistic style of W.G. Sebald, and J.M. Coetzee. With the main protagonist Julius, roaming the streets of New York, interchangeably referring to literature, art, history, as well as personal memories, it becomes easy to label this intellectual and well-traveled individual as cosmopolitan. As Pieter Vermeulen notes, such a manner of being depicts that of the *flâneur*, which "anticipates a cosmopolitan ethos that thrives on intercultural curiosity and the virtues of the aesthetic" (41). Through his walks, he interacts with several people; however, he remains distant, preferring to connect to people abstractly and ideologically rather than through up-close communication:

> The just risen sun came at the Hudson at such an acute angle that the river gleamed like aluminum roofing. At that moment—and I remember this as exactly as though it were being replayed in front of me right now —I thought of how, in his journals, Camus tells a double story concerning Nietzsche and Gaius Mucius Cordus Scaevola[. . .]. Scaevola had been captured while trying to kill the Etruscan king Porsenna and, rather than give away his accomplices, he showed his fearlessness by putting his right hand in a fire and letting it burn. [. .]Nietzsche, according to Camus, became angry when his schoolmates would not believe the Scaevola story. And so, the fifteen-year old Nietzsche plucked a hot coal from the grate and held it. Of course, it burned him. He carried the resulting scar with him for the rest of his life.
>
> (*Open City* 246)

Julius goes into this memory right after Moji confronts him about him raping her eighteen years before. Instead of responding to her, he remains silent and rather recalls a story that though not his own, relates to the situation. Such an outlook on the world, that is disaffected yet engaged, is exemplary of the signature cosmopolitan dynamic of "(re)attachment, multiple attachment, or attachment at a distance" (Robbins, "Actually Existing") (Vermeulen 41).

As the novel easily falls into the tradition of *flâneurism*, embracing cosmopolitan perspectives, one wonders whether it's affect stops there, or does it fit into the category of Afropolitanism, due to both its author's and protagonist's links to Africa? Teju Cole was born in the United States and raised in Nigeria; professionally, his writing and photography take him all around the world. Cole is undoubtedly Afropolitan, in a Selasian manner. As for Julius, he fits into Mbembe as well as Eze's philosophical Afropolitanism. Julius is half-Nigerian and half-German, and associates to several locales such as New York, Brussels, and Lagos. Through his observations he also encounters many different Africans of the world, who based on Mbembe's definition and Eze's can be seen as Afropolitan; Julius encounters Ghanaians, Nigerians, Rwandans, Congolese, and many other Afropolitans in New York and in Brussels. All of them, by simply having a connection to Africa are therefore Afropolitan, to Julien's dismay:

> When my address filtered its way back to me, I gave it to the cabdriver and said to him: So, how are you doing, my brother? The driver stiffened and looked at me in the mirror.

> Not good, not good at all, you know, the way you came into my car without saying hello, that was bad. Hey, I'm African just like you, why you do this? He kept me in his sights in the mirror. I was confused. I said, I'm sorry about it, my mind was elsewhere, don't be offended, ehn, my brother, how are you doing? He said nothing, and faced the road. I wasn't sorry at all. I was not in the mood for people who tried to lay claims on me.
>
> COLE 40

The above quotation shows Julius's constant struggle with "people laying claims" on his identity. Even though he established a link by referring to the driver as brother, thus acknowledging a link, he was annoyed by the driver's insistence on what behavior this connection required, a proper greeting instead of simply stating his address. This shows how Julius does not adhere to the same sort of warm-hearted connectedness that the driver feels towards other Africans. Moreover, this sort of mannerism of detachment and strained connectedness is evident in his encounters with others throughout the narrative; meeting and engaging with many but resisting any intimate sense of connectedness based on geography.

Still, despite the cosmopolitan narrative that *Open City* confines to, without an African locality, Julius finds himself a middleman between cosmopolitan reality and local memory; with a distant regard to his surroundings, he is a remote observer of the city, embracing it without completely engulfing himself within it. Mobility and spatiality are key concepts within the novel, and though confined to New York, and later on Brussels, as "open cities," they take on numerous identities, giving the voyeur a lot to consider. New York specifically is representative of the title *Open City*. It acts as a hub for overlapping cultural borders, "speedy transport and aesthetic sensations ranging from the cityscape's interplay with natural phenomena such as cloud formations to arts and music from all over the world" (Gehrmann 68).

As he walks through the streets of New York, Julius encounters people from diverse races and various classes, and recalls the different experiences they have in these open cities. Though Julius is able to freely move around between places, he is very conscious of the limitations many have in terms of mobility. As Susanne Gehrmann notes: "Far from being apolitical, Cole's protagonist negotiates his place in New York City and the world along ambivalent boundaries of race and class while keeping up with his compelling transcultural lifestyle. The spatial and cultural mobilities expressed in the literature of 'the Afropolitan generation' indeed confirm Mbembe's repositioning of Africa as a philosophical locus of passage and mobility" (69).

Moreover, in accordance with Eze, and the openness of the Afropolitan individual, Julius is presented as just that, an open individual, yet in a manner that is much different from that of Ifemelu and Obinze. Julius's openness and interest in the world is manifested through a detached façade. Through his literary knowledge and narrations, Julius is definitely worldly and not biased; his passion for aesthetics carry the Afropolitan attitude of openness: "He never dismisses Western music or architecture as Eurocentric. Nor do these Western cultural products replace his appreciation of those of Africa. His love for Gustav Mahler never displaced his enjoyment of Fela Kuti" (Eze 115). As Julius encounters and converses with people from different walks of life, he deals with them in an open manner, acknowledging their differences without prejudice but rather allowing himself to learn from them.

However, with such an openness to culture and acceptance to difference, comes a certain detachment in Julius's character that brings with it a closed attitude towards the world around him, where even though he is aware and open of what is happening around him, he does not really engage. This closeness is what marks him as an African of the world, forever aware of his ethnicity and the history of his people. Being extremely conscious of race and class, he is not always able to transcend contemporary issues that disrupt the continuity of life and is forced to reflect on what has happened in the past. Be it through personal experience or in relation to his African roots, he is at times unsettled:

> We experience life as a continuity, and only after it falls away, after it becomes the past, do we see its discontinuities. The past, if there is such a thing, is mostly empty spaces, great expanses of nothing, in which significant persons and events float. Nigeria was like that for me: mostly forgotten, except for those few things that I remembered with an outsize intensity. These were the things that had been solidified in my mind by reiteration, the recurred in dreams and daily thoughts certain faces, certain conversations, which, taken as a group, represented a secure version of the past that I had been constructing since 1992.
>
> (155–156)

As much as Julius would like to keep walking and looking forward, encompassing what is around him and taking in experiences in an existential and de-centered manner, he cannot shed his history, which at times stares him right in the face, be it indirectly through racist occurrences, as with the children asking him if he were a gangster, or directly as Moji does when she accuses him of rape. His insistence on life as a continuity, alleviates a need for a center and rather de-centers individuals by allowing them to be open and not to carry strong attachments to experience but rather progressing intellectually. With the quotation above, the narrator admits to the difficulty of such a complete de-centering. As Minna Salami points out, "Afropolitanism and Identity Politics," cosmopolitanism is perceived as having no grounding within reality, *Open City* cannot be seen as such, for it is grounded within issues that are very much grounded, such as racism, immigration, and oppression. With this distinction we see the difference between Afropolitanism and Cosmopolitanism. Afropolitanism is not merely a subcategory of cosmopolitanism but it is quite distinct due to the different implications of being an African in the world. Though it does relate it to Africa, as the protagonist is half-Nigerian, it also centers tensions in an open, global sense: "The country was in the grip of uncertainties—the sense of anomie was apparent even to a visitor" (100). Through this description of Brussels, the non-idealistic reality of open spaces is explored.

Open City is a global narrative par excellence, as the narrator tells stories from both the West and African histories and literatures. As Julius attempts to remain unattached and de-centered, he fails, for life experiences are not just continuous, but are building blocks that shape one's identity. It is this struggle to remain detached, taking no responsibility for what has occurred, that puts Julius in the category of a hesitant local, denying the influence of the local in the global context of open cities. He and we the readers do not consider him an African of the world, as much as an objective observer. It is when his past creeps up on him, be it through his memories betraying him or through encounters on the street, that he is forced to face who he is, where he comes from, and his connection to all that he comments on. In contrast to *Americanah* where the characters clearly have centers and their hesitancy comes in the attachments that they form in the different locales that they engage in, *Open City*'s protagonist's hesitation comes from his inability to fully de-center and disengage.

In conclusion, the portrayal of the global citizen varies, as do the forms of identifying with the world. Feelings of identity become difficult, and one is left disconnected in the local and global context. Both Cole and Adichie's novels trouble claims of locality, analyzing different notions of belonging and assimilation within the nation and the globe in order to find familiarity. The question remains, in expanding the dimensions of the local, one wonders what sorts of localities and globalities are being constructed in writing specifically from the African continent? What does the globe look like from an African perspective? And what do we gain from an African point of view on cosmopolitanism? Trying to think within the framework of these questions and through different interpretations of what constitutes an Afropolitan identity as well as a cosmopolitan identity, exposes the field for its multiplicity as well as its complications. To be of the world, means to face the problems and prejudices of the world. While familiarizing in different places, does one lose the centers they had formerly attained? Or is it possible to encompass several spaces simultaneously? To be hesitant in forming new locals, is to be critically aware of what's at stake within the global. Both *Americanah* and *Open City* allow a critical Afropolitan analysis that lays out quite differently in both cases. By understanding what it means to be an African of the world, it becomes possible to understand the significance of an Afropolitan point of view in looking at global literature.

Works cited

Adichie, Chimamanda Ngozi. *Americanah*. Anchor, 2013.
Calhoun, C. "The Class Consciousness of Frequent Travelers: Towards a Critique of Actually Existing Cosmopolitanism." *Debating Cosmopolitics*. Ed. Daniele Archibugi. N.p.: Verso, 2003. 87–112.
Cheah, P. "What Is a World? On World Literature as World-making Activity." Daedalus 137.3 (2008): 26–38. Available online: https://www.jstor.org/stable/40543795 (Accessed May 1, 2016).
Cheah, P, and Robbins, B. *Cosmopolitics: Thinking and Feeling beyond the Nation*. Minneapolis: U of Minnesota, 1998.
Cole, Teju. *Open City*. New York: Random House, 2011.
Derrida, J. *On Cosmopolitanism and Forgiveness*. London: Routledge, 2001.
Eze, Chielozona. "We, Afropolitans," *Journal of African Cultural Studies*. 28.1 (2016): 114–119. April 16, 2016.
Gehrmann, Susanne. "Cosmopolitanism with African roots. Afropolitanism's ambivalent mobilities," *Journal of African Cultural Studies* 28.1 (2016): 61–72. Available online: https://doi.org/10.1080/13696815.2015.1112770 (accessed April 15, 2016).
Harris, Ashleigh. "Afropolitan Style and Unusable Global Spaces." *Cosmopolitanisms*, 2017, doi:10.18574/nyu/9781479829682.003.0019. August 20, 2018
Macheso, Wesley. "The 21st Century African as a Cosmopolitan Individual in Chimamanda Ngozi Adichie's Americanah—AfricanWriter.com." *AfricanWritercom*. January 20, 2015. Available online: https://www.africanwriter.com/the-21st-century-african-as-a-cosmopolitan-individual-in-chimamanda-ngozi-adichies-americanah/ (accessed May 10, 2016).
Mbembe, A. (2007). "Afropolitanism." In S. Njami & L. Durán (Eds.), *Africa Remix: Contemporary art of a continent* (p. 26–30). Johannesburg: Johannesburg Art Gallery.
Pahl, Miriam. "Afropolitanism as critical consciousness: Chimamanda Ngozi Adichie's and Teju Cole's internet presence." *Journal of African Cultural Studies*. 28.1 (2016): 114–119. April 16, 2016.
Salami, Minna. "Afropolitanism and Identity Politics." *MsAfropolitan*. April 14, 2015. Available online: https://www.msafropolitan.com/2015/04/afropolitanism-identity-politics.html (accessed April 10, 2016).
Selasi, Taiye. "Bye-Bye Babar." The LIP. The LIP Magazine, March 23, 2005. Available online: http://thelip.robertsharp.co.uk/?p=76 (accessed April 14, 2016).
Vermeulen, Pieter. "Flights of Memory: Teju Cole's Open City and the Limits of Aesthetic Cosmopolitanism." *Journal of Modern Literature* 37.1 (2013): 40–57. Available online: https://www.jstor.org/stable/10.2979/jmodelite.37.1.40 (accessed July 22, 2019)

NOTES ON CONTRIBUTORS

Shilpa Daithota Bhat is Assistant Professor in Ahmedabad University, Gujarat, India. She is the recipient of the *Bensley-Osler Library Research Travel Grant*, McGill University, Canada (2017), and the first recipient of *Lorna Marsden International Visitor Fellowship* to York University, Canada (2015). A *Commonwealth Fellow* to the University of Toronto, she was also a recipient of the *Pacific Asia Network of Canadian Studies* to Korea University. Her areas of interest are South Asian Narratives, Diaspora and Postcolonial theories, Canadian Studies, and Children's Literature. She is the author of *Indians in Victorian Children's Narratives: Animalizing the "Native", 1830–1930* (Lexington, Rowman and Littlefield, 2017).

M. Rocío Cobo-Piñero is a postdoctoral fellow and lecturer at the University of Seville, Spain. She completed part of her PhD in Universidade do Espírito Santo, Brazil. Her international education also includes an MA in African American Studies at the University of Pennsylvania, USA. She has been a visiting scholar at the School of Oriental and African Studies (SOAS, University of London), and the Institute for Black Atlantic Research (IBAR, University of Central Lancashire). Her research focuses on African and African American women writers, migration, gender, and cultural studies. She has published, among others, in the *Journal of Postcolonial Writing; Atlantis; Ilha do Desterro: A Journal of English Language, Literatures in English, and Cultural Studies; Revista Co-herencia* and in the volume *Women on the Move: Body, Memory and Femininity in Present-Day Transnational Diasporic Writing* (Routledge, 2018). Dr. Cobo-Piñero is a member of the collective project FFI2017-84555-C2-1-P Bodies in Transit 2, funded by the Spanish Ministry of Science, Innovation and Universities.

Amatoritsero Ede is an Assistant Professor of English at the University of The Bahamas' English Studies Department. His research encompasses new African literary aesthetics, translation, world literature and African language writing, Afro-futurism, globalization and diaspora. His essay, "The Politics of Afropolitanism" has been well-received. He is also a poet, and publisher of the Maple Tree Literary Supplement (MTLS) at www.mtls.ca

Lara El Mekkawi is a PhD student in English at the University of Waterloo. Her research interests are in Cosmopolitanism and World Literature; Lara studies the complicated connotations behind being a part of the world. She also freelances as a book editor. She has edited Nadia Tabbara's debut book *Harness Your Creativity* (2018) and co-edited a poetry collection titled *And We Chose Everything* (2018), and is currently editing Nour Abou Fayad's debut novel *The Complete Opposite of Everything* (2019).

Chielozona Eze graduated from Purdue University's Philosophy and literature program in 2003. He is a professor of African and African American literatures at Northeastern Illinois University and Extraordinary Professor of English at Stellenbosch University, South Africa. His most recent book is *Race, Decolonization, and Global Citizenship in South Africa,* University of Rochester Press, 2018.

James Hodapp is Assistant Professor of English in Residence at Northwestern University in Qatar. His primary fields of research and teaching are African literature, World Literature, and postcolonial studies. He has published articles in *The Journal of Postcolonial Writing, Critical Arts: A Journal of South-North Cultural Studies, African Literature Today, Research in African Literatures, ARIEL, The Global South, The Chronicle of Higher Education, English in Africa, The Journal of Graphic Novels and Comics, Short Fiction in Theory & Practice, African Studies Review, Wasafiri, The Blackwell Encyclopedia of Postcolonial Studies,* and in several anthologies on world cinema and literature. Previously, he was an assistant professor in the department of English at the American University of Beirut.

Julie Iromuanya is the author of *Mr. and Mrs. Doctor* (Coffee House Press), a finalist for the PEN/Faulkner Award, the PEN/Robert W. Bingham Prize for Debut Fiction, the Etisalat Prize for Literature (now 9 Mobile Prize for Literature), and the National Book Critics Circle John Leonard Prize for Debut Fiction. Her scholarly-critical work most recently appears in *Meridians: Feminism, Race, Transnationalism* and *Callaloo: A Journal of African American Arts and Letters*. She was the inaugural Herbert W. Martin Fellow in Creative Writing at the University of Dayton. Iromuanya earned her B.A. at the University of Central Florida and her M.A. and Ph.D. at the University of Nebraska-Lincoln where she was a Presidential Fellow, Richard H. Larson Fellow, and award-winning teacher. She is an assistant professor in the creative writing program at the University of Chicago.

Juan Meneses is an assistant professor in the Department of English at the University of North Carolina, Charlotte, where he teaches courses on global literature and visual studies, and a translator. He has published work in venues such as *Journal of Modern Literature, Modern Fiction Studies,* and *Journal of Graphic Novels and Comics* and translations in *The Massachusetts Review of Books* and *West Branch*. His book, *Resisting Dialogue: Modern Fiction and the Future of Dissent,* is forthcoming with the University of Minnesota Press.

Birgit Neumann is Professor of English Literature and Anglophone Studies at Heinrich-Heine-University Düsseldorf (Germany). Her research focuses on world literatures, postcolonial studies, memory studies, and intermediality. She has published monographs on memory in Canadian novels (2005) and on xenophobia in eighteenth-century British literature (2009). A monograph (co-authored with Gabriele Rippl) on ekphrasis in postcolonial literatures is forthcoming in 2019 from Routledge. She has co-edited special issues and volumes on *Anglophone World Literatures* (with Gabriele Rippl, 2017), *Ecocriticism in Anglophone Literatures* (with Sonja Frenzel, 2017), *Global Perspectives on European Literary Histories* (with César Dominguez, 2018), and on *New Approaches to the Anglophone Novel* (with Sibylle Baumbach, 2019). A handbook on *Anglophone World Literatures* (co-edited with Stefan Helgesson and Gabriele Rippl) is currently in preparation.

Aretha Phiri, PhD from Edinburgh University, is a senior lecturer in the Department of Literary Studies in English (DLSE) at Rhodes University and a research fellow at the Stellenbosch Institute for Advanced Study (STIAS) in South Africa. Her research examines the intersectional interactions of race, ethnicity, culture, gender, and sexualities in comparative, transnational, and transatlantic considerations of identity and subjectivity, with a focus on African, African American, and American literature. She has published in various accredited journals including *English Studies in Africa*, *Safundi*, *Agenda*, *Cultural Studies*, *European Journal of English Studies*, and the *Journal of American Studies*.

Anna von Rath studied at the University of Potsdam (Germany), the English and Foreign Languages University in Hyderabad (India), and Westminster University, London (UK). She has worked at the Department of English and American Studies at the University of Potsdam and is currently a fellow of the Research Training Group Minor Cosmopolitanisms. Her primary research interests encompass anglophone literatures and cultures, postcolonial theories and practices, critical race, and whiteness studies.

Julian Wacker teaches English, Postcolonial and Media Studies at the University of Muenster/Germany, where he is also a PhD candidate. His thesis focuses on representations of space and identity politics in grime culture and examines its remediation in contemporary British inner-city fiction. His research areas also include black and Asian British film in the twenty-first century, black neo-Victorian/neo-Edwardian imaginaries, and Afropolitan writing. A historical survey of black and Asian British popular texts (Cambridge University Press) as well as articles on grime poetry and queer re-tellings of Yoruba folklore are forthcoming.

INDEX

Abani, Chris 139, 141–2, 153–4
  "New Religion, The" 145–6
  Virgin of Flames, The 142–3
abolitionism 113
Abyssinian Chronicles (Isegawa, Moses) 117
Acharya, Gunvantrai
  Dariyalal 58
Achebe, Chinua 105, 121
  Things Fall Apart 76, 119, 134
Achmed (servant to Carl, Prince of Prussia) 47
Adichie, Chimamanda Ngozi 4, 13, 76, 112, 153, 207
  Americanah 4, 42–3, 76, 175, 206–12, 216
  Purple Hibiscus 117
aesthetics 139–43, 144
Afer, Publius Terentius 136
Africa 46, 59, 71, 106
  apartheid policy 62
  archaeology 178
  black 152, 153, 154, 160–1, 161 n.6
  geography 86
  history 108
  identity. *See* African identity
  Nollywood 177
  publishing industry 2
  "real" African life 190
  religion 108
  Selasi, Taiye 167
  stereotypes 177
  travel 170–1
  Western focus 117
  Western media representation 116–17
"Africa" (Diope, David) 134, 140

African 107
African-Americans 73
African body, the 143–7
African Child, The (Laye, Camara) 134
African identity 14, 88–9, 131–40, 142–8, 152–3
  eco-Afropolitanism 90
  Eze, Chielozona 171
  Gilroy, Paul 16
  Mbembe, Achille 16, 88–9, 206
  Neumann, Birgit and Gabriele Rippl 192
  Open City (Cole, Teju) 213–14, 216
African letters 119
African literature 4, 103–4, 116, 152–4
  Chikoti, Shadreck 190
  diaspora 191
  Francophone African literature 117–18
  location 189–90, 191
  Mohutsiwa, Siyanda 189–90
  Selasi, Taiye 191
  in the West 120–2, 133–4
  Western focus 117
  as world literature 119–23, 186–9
African personality 133
African village, the 132
African worldliness 7–8 (*see also* global recognition)
African Writers' Series 119
Africanity 133
Afro-centrism 190, 191–2
Afro-cosmopolitanism 147
Afro-pessimism 4, 60
Afrodiasporic literature 152–3
Afropeans 117–18, 121
Afropolitan aesthetics 139–43, 144

INDEX

Afropolitan gaze 170
Afropolitan literature 2–6, 17–18, 153
  Afropolitan novels 118–22
  commodification 51, 116–18, 120, 121
  Germany 51–2, 53 n. 1
  New World 110, 112–13
  travel writing 168
"Afropolitan Must Go, The" (Tveit, Marta) 61–2
Afropolitan novels 118–22
"Afropolitan Style and Unusable Global Spaces" (Harris, Ashleigh) 207
Afropolitanism 3–11, 50, 53, 85–6, 135–9, 216 (see also Afropolitans)
  academic study of 8
  centrality 14
  commodification 73–4, 186
  critique of 2–3, 4–5, 14, 91, 139, 151–3, 185
  Dabiri, Emma 73, 139
  dystopian 73
  eco-Afropolitanism 87–92, 99–100
  Ede, Amatoritsero 139, 185–6
  Eze, Chielozona 60–1, 71, 206
  Gehrmann, Susanne 186, 206–7, 212
  genealogy 7
  Germany 48–9
  Gikandi, Simon 87, 90, 110, 138
  Harris, Ashleigh 207
  Indian Ocean Afropolitanism 64, 66–7
  intra-African 14
  Makokha, J. K. S. 63
  Mbembe, Achille 4, 15–17, 39, 71, 86, 138–9, 206
  Mbembe, Achille and Sarah Nuttall 86
  meaning 185–6
  migration. See migration
  mobility. See mobility
  Musila, Grace 139
  Neumann, Birgit and Gabriele Rippl 192

  New World 110, 112–13
  philosophical basis 148
  political agenda 5–6
  Salami, Minna 207
  SchwarzRund 37, 38–48, 49–50, 51, 52, 53
  Selasi, Taiye 13–14, 44–5, 86, 135–6, 138, 147
  Toivanen, Anna-Leena 151
  travel 171, 205–6, 209, 212
  Vassanji, M. G. 67
  wa Thiong'o, Ngugi 185
  Western focus 7–8
"Afropolitanism" (Mbembe, Achille) 15–16, 111
"Afropolitanism and Identity Politics" (Salami, Minna) 207, 215
Afropolitans 73–4, 76, 206 (see also Afropolitanism)
  Adichie, Chimamanda Ngozi 211–12
  Ede, Amatoritsero 185–6, 211
  Mbembe, Achille 206
  SchwarzRund 49–50
  Selasi, Taiye 40, 60, 61, 73, 137–8, 205
  Sterling, Cheryl 73
Agary, Kaine 1–2
agency 114-15
America 133
  "racial passing" 79–80
  racism 81, 209–10
Americanah (Adichie, Chimamanda Ngozi) 4, 42–3, 76, 175, 207–12, 216
Amin, Idi 65, 68
amusement parks 176
And Home Was Kariakoo (Vassanji, M. G.) 59, 63, 64, 65, 66–7, 68–9
animist cosmology 26
apartheid policy 62
Appiah, Kwaime Anthony 50, 91, 136
Apter, Emily 17
Arendt, Hannah 137
Aristotle 144
Asians 57–8, 63–9
assemblages 192–3, 194–5

*Atlantic Sound, The (*Philips, Caryl) 169
Atlantic studies 15–16
Austerlitz, Saul 196
Ayling, Pere 77, 78

Babar Comes to America (Brunhoff, Laurent de) 177
Bady, Aaron 74
Balanchandran, P. K. 68
Bandele-Thomas, Biyi
  Man Who Came in from the Back of Beyond, The 122
  Sympathetic Undertaker and Other dreams, The 122
Barnard, Rita 92
Barrett, A. Igoni
  Blackass 71–2, 74–5, 76–7, 78, 79, 80–2
Baudrillad, Jean 176
Beer in the Snooker Club (Ghali. Waguih) 8–9
being 78
Beti, Mongo
  Mission to Karla 119
Bhabha, Homi 176, 180 n.3
Biskaya (SchwarzRund) 37, 38–48, 49, 51, 52, 53
Black 107
Black Atlantic Letters 105, 107
Black Atlantic model 15–16, 192
Black Atlantic writers/writing 109, 113
Black Atlantic: Modernity and Double Consciousness, The (Gilroy, Paul) 15–16, 21
Black Diaspora 110
Black human agency 109, 114, 115
Black Internationalism 109
Black Lives Matter Movement 105
Black Panther (film) 109
Black Paris 110
Black Skin, White Masks (Fanon, Frantz) 75, 78, 82
"Black Woman" (Senghor, Léopold Sédar) 134, 140
"Black Woman, The" (Garvey, Marcus) 133–4, 140

Blackass (Barrett, A. Igoni) 71–2, 74–5, 76–7, 78, 79, 80–2
blackness 152, 153, 154, 160–1, 161 n.6
Blind Spot (Cole, Teju) 186, 192–4, 195–9, 200
blues, the 155–8, 160, 161
Blyden, Edward Wilmot 133
body, the 143–7, 157
Bratman, Michael E. 114–15
Brennan, Timothy
  "national longing of form, The" 23–4
Bridges, Roy 168
Britain 174, 175
Brunhoff, Jean de
  L'histoire de Babar (*The Story of Babar*) 177
Brunhoff, Laurent de
  Babar Comes to America 177
Buell, Lawrence 90
Bulawayo, NoViolet 4, 13
  "Hitting Budapest" 117
  We Need New Names 99, 104, 117, 175
Bwesigye, Brian 2–3
"Bye Bye Barbar" (Selasi, Taiye) 13, 110, 120, 151, 159, 177
citizenship 205
contemporary Afropolitans 40, 60
home 170
opacity 160

Calhoun, Craig 90, 204
  "*Class Consciousness of Frequent Travelers: Toward a Critique of Actually Existing Cosmopolitanism, The*" 204
Caminero-Santangelo, Byron 94
Campt, Tina 47
capitalism 96, 97–9
  slavery 106–7
Casanova, Pascale 87–8
Cazenave, Odile and Patricia Célérier 117–18
Cheah, Pheng 18, 25, 49, 52, 87
  temporality 122

"What is a world? On world literature as world-making activity" 203–4
worlding literature 187–8, 197
Chikoti, Shadreck 190
Christianity 107, 108, 141, 146–7
cities 142
citizenship 137–8, 205
"*Class Consciousness of Frequent Travelers: Toward a Critique of Actually Existing Cosmopolitanism, The*" (Calhoun, Craig) 204
classification 194
Coetzee, J.M. 212
Cole, Teju 4, 13, 186–7, 207, 213
　Blind Spot 186, 192–4, 195–9, 200
　Every Day is for the Thief 186, 194, 199–200
　Known and Strange Things 186, 194, 198
　obscurity 186, 193–4
　Open City. See *Open City*
colonialism 25, 65, 76–7, 105
　African literature 103, 104–5
　Bhabha, Homi 176
　body, the 143
　L'histoire de Babar (*The Story of Babar*) 177
　Nigeria 77, 174, 175
　slavery 107
　travel writing 178
Comaroff, Jean 91
Coming to Hollywood (film) 177
Commerce with the Universe: Africa, India, and the Afrasian imagination (Desai, Gaurav) 58
community 20, 24, 27, 44–5
　Black German 47, 48
　Ismaili 68
　wellbeing 144
comparative approaches 188–9
consciousness 138
conviviality 137
cosmopolitan contamination 136–7
cosmopolitan gaze 170
cosmopolitanism 26, 49, 60–1, 85–7, 89–91, 136–7, 203

Afro-cosmopolitanism 147
Calhoun, Craig 204
Cheah, Pheng 203–4
Harris, Ashleigh 207
Mandela, Nelson 132
Robbins, Bruce 205
Salami, Minna 215–16
Saro-Wiwa, Noor 177
Selasi, Taiye 134–5
slavery 111
Toivanen, Anna-Leena 151
travel writing 178
"Cosmopolitanism with African roots. Afropolitanism's ambivalent mobilities" (Gehrmann, Susanne) 206–7
counter-cultural movements 110
Cullen, Countee 131, 135
　"Heritage" 131
culture 108
cultural blending 171–2
cultural plurality, Kenya 20, 21–3

Dabiri, Emma 4–5, 139, 170
　"Why I'm Not an Afropolitan" 73
Damrosch, David 6, 187
dance 40
Dar-es-Salaam 65
Dariyalal (Acharya, Gunvantrai) 58
decolonization 113, 119
DeLanda, Manuel 192, 193
Deleuze, Gilles and Félix Guattari 192–3
deracialization 42, 44
deracination 107, 111
Derrida, Jacques 19
Desai, Gaurav
　Commerce with the Universe: Africa, India, and the Afrasian imagination 58
diaspora 13, 14, 17, 61, 62, 152–4 (*see also* migration *and* movement)
　African literature 191
　Afrodiasporic literature 152–3
　Black Diaspora 110
　Dust (Owuor, Yvonee Adhiambo) 21

Ghana Must Go (Selasi, Taiye) 158, 160
Mbembe, Achille 39
SchwarzRund 47
Selasi, Taiye 73
slavery 111
Diope, David
  "Africa" 134, 140
"Discovering Home" (Wainaina, Binyavanga) 117
Disneyland 176
Dostoyevsky, Fyodor
  Notes from Underground 140
Du Bois, W.E.B. 115, 131, 133
Dunbar, Paul Laurence 141
  "Sympathy" 140
dust 25–6
Dust (Owuor, Yvonee Adhiambo) 14–15, 18–27

Eco, Umberto 195
eco-Afropolitanism 87–92, 99–100
eco-cosmopolitanism 90
Ede, Amatoritsero 51, 139, 185–6
  "Politics of Afropolitanism, The" 60
Edwards, Justin and Rune Graulund 172
Ekwensi, Cyprian
  People of the City 119
"Elegy for a Burnt Friend" (Oriogun, Romeo) 141
Ellison, Ralph 141
  "Invisible Man" 140
environment, the 178 (*see also* eco-Afropolitanism)
Equaino, Oluadah 169
  Interesting Narrative of the Life of Oluadah Equaino, or Gustavus Vassa, the African, The 111
Esie stone sculptures 178
Essed, Philomena 41
ethnic cleansing 65, 68
Europe 46–7, 120–1
Every Day is for the Thief (Cole, Teju) 186, 194, 199–200
exoticism 112

Eze, Chielozona 60–1, 71, 89, 171, 211
  "We, Afropolitans" 206, 211

Faber, Geoffrey 119
Faber and Faber 119–20
Fanon, Frantz 72, 158
  Black Skin, White Masks 75, 78, 82
Farred, Grant 95
Fela Kuti 136
feminism 147, 158–9
flâneurism 212–13
Foucault, Michel
  History of Sexuality, The 143
Francophone African literature 117–18, 119
freedom 140–1, 147
Freitas, Lançarote de 106
Friedman, Susan Stanford 18

Gandhi, Mahatma 66
Garritano, Carmela 177
Garuba, Harry 120
Garvey, Marcus
  "Black Woman, The" 133–4, 140
Gate, Henry Louis, Jr., 114
Gaye, Marvin 140
Gaye, Marvin, Sr., 140
Gehrmann, Susanne 38, 51, 186, 212, 214
  "Cosmopolitanism with African roots. Afropolitanism's ambivalent mobilities" 206–7
gender 45–6 (*see also* feminism)
George, Olakunle 119
Germany 39, 43, 47, 48–9, 51–2
Ghali. Waguih
  Beer in the Snooker Club 8–9
  Ghana Must Go (Selasi, Taiye) 4, 46, 60, 104, 154–61
Ghanaians 155
Ghosh, Amitav 169
Gikandi, Simon 60, 87, 90, 110, 138, 171
Gilroy, Paul
  Black Atlantic: Modernity and Double Consciousness, The 15–16, 21

Glissant, Edouard 186, 193, 194, 196–7
Poetics of Relation 196
global citizenship 137–8 (*see also* cosmopolitanism)
global issues 89, 216
global mobility 3, 4, 207
global recognition 1–3, 6
Global South 89
globe, constructedness 122
Gonçalves, Antão 106
Graham, James 95, 97
Great Britain 174, 175
Grewal, Iderpal 168
Gujarat 65–7 (*see also* Asians)
Gupta, Anirudha 68

Habeas Viscus (Weheliye, Alexander G.) 188–9
Habila, Helon 5
hair 42–3, 44
Hamburger Schule 43
Hamitic principle 107
Harris, Ashleigh 152, 207
 "Afropolitan Style and Unusable Global Spaces" 207
Harvey, Ebrahim 152
Heart of Redness, The (Mda, Zakes) 91–9
"Heritage" (Cullen, Countee) 131
hesitant local 206, 208, 210, 212, 216
L'histoire de Babar (*The Story of Babar*) (Brunhoff, Jean de) 177
historical fiction 19–20
History of Sexuality, The (Foucault, Michel) 143
"Hitting Budapest" (Bulawayo, NoViolet) 117
Hodapp, James 58
Hofmeyr, Isabel 66
Hollywood 177
home/homeland, concept of 59, 64, 94, 159 (*see also* place)
 Saro-Wiwa, Noor 170, 173
homosexuality 139–40
Houseboy (Oyono, Ferdinand) 119

"How to Survive the Fire" (Oriogun, Romeo) 141
Huggan, Graham 112
Hughes, Langston 131
human flourishing. *See* wellbeing
human-land relations 94, 95, 97, 98

I Do Not Come to You by Chance (Nwaubani, Adaobi Tricia) 117
ibn Battuta 169
identity
 African. *See* African identity
 Asian migrants 64–5, 68–9
 Blackass (Barrett, A. Igoni) 80–1
 Nigeria 78
 SchwarzRund 45–6, 49
 Selasi, Taiye 73
 Vassanji, M. G. 59
Idrisi, Maghriban al- 169
"I'm a Pan-Africanist, not an Afropolitan" (Wainaina, Binyavanga) 186
"I'm Done With African Immigrant Literature" (Mohutsiwa, Siyanda) 189–90
immigration 170–1, 210–11 (*see also* migration)
imperialism 169, 170
In Search of the Afropolitan (Rask Knudsen, Eva and Ulla Rahbeck) 153, 187
incompleteness 137
India 66, 68
Indian Ocean Afropolitanism 64, 66–7
Ingold, Tim 21
Interesting Narrative of the Life of Oluadah Equaino, or Gustavus Vassa, the African, The (Equaino, Oluadah) 111
internet, the 207
"Invisible Man" (Ellison, Ralph) 140
"Invisible Man" (Oriogun, Romeo) 140
Isegawa, Moses
 Abyssinian Chronicles 117
Islam 108
Ismailis, the 68

Journal of African Cultural Studies 110
July, Robert 115

Kafka, Franz
  Metamorphosis 71–2, 83
Kanneh, Kadiatu 116
Kappel, Yvonne 199
Kelly, Natasha A. 48, 49
Kenya 19–20, 21–4
Khair, Tabish 168
  Other Routes: 1500 years of African and Asian Travel Writing 168–9
Kiguru, Doseline Wanjiru 122
Kilomba, Grada
  Plantation Memories. Episodes of Everyday Racism 42
Kissack, Mike and Michael Titlestad 94–5
Known and Strange Things (Cole, Teju) 186, 194, 198
Krishnan, Madhu 69
Kuti, Fela 136, 179
Kuti, Femi 179–80

Lacan, Jacques 81
Lagos 74, 174
Landis, John 177
landscape 25
Laye, Camara
  African Child, The 134
Letters of the Late Ignatius Sancho: An African, to which are Prefixed, Memoirs of his Life (Sancho, Ignatius) 111
life, fragility of 141
Lisle, Debbie 169–70, 178
literacy 103, 113–15
literary market 121–2
literary prizes 121–2
literary production 121
literary texts 187
  classifying 194
literary turn 153, 187
literature 18 (*see also* African literature)
Livingstone, David 169
local, the 216 (*see also* hesitant local)

Locke, Alain 131
Looking for Transwonderland: Travels in Nigeria (Saro-Wiwa, Noor) 1–2, 172–80
López Ropero, María Lourdes 169
Los Angeles 142

Macheso, Wesley 208
Madhvani, Manubhai
  Tide of Fortune: A Family Tale 69 n.3
Makokha, J. K. S. 63
Man Who Came in from the Back of Beyond, The (Bandele-Thomas, Biyi) 122
Mandela, Nelson 132
maps 122
Mbembe, Achille 4, 15–17, 39, 71, 86, 138–9, 206
  "Afropolitanism" 15–16, 111
  cultural blending 171–2
  movement 110–11, 168
  postcolony, the 177
  travel 171–2
Mbembe, Achille and Sarah Nuttall 86
Mbue, Imbolo 4
Mda, Zakes
  Heart of Redness, The 91–9
memory 19–20
Mengestu. Dinaw 4, 13
meshworks 21
Metamorphosis (Kafka, Franz) 71–2, 83
metropolitan market 120–2
Mignolo, Walter 135
migration 20, 57, 58, 60, 61, 62–3, 67–8 (*see also* diaspora *and* movement)
  Afro-centrism 189–90
  Asians 63–9
  Ghanaians 155
  Western policies 170–1
mimicry 176
Minh-ha, Trinh 194
Mission to Karla (Beti, Mongo) 119
mobility 3, 203, 205–6 (*see also* diaspora *and* movement)
  Africa 171

Gehrmann, Susanne 212
Selasi, Taiye 138, 147
Sterling, Cheryl 73
modernity 62, 106, 116
   Dust (Owuor, Yvonee Adhiambo) 26–7
   Nigeria 176, 178
   Saro-Wiwa, Noor 176, 178
   Selasi, Taiye 138
Mohutsiwa, Siyanda 189–90
   "I'm Done With African Immigrant Literature" 189–90
Molesworth, Charles 131
movement 47, 49, 59, 81 (*see also* diaspora *and* migration)
   Mbembe, Achille 110–11, 168
   publishing 120
   slavery 107
   travel writing 168-9
MsAfropolitan (blog) 207
Mudimbe, V.Y. 133
Mufti, Aamir 17
multiculturalism
   Kenya 20, 21–3
Murphy, Laura 74
music 40
Musila, Grace 1, 2, 3, 139
Mysorekar, Sheila 48

nation, the 23–4, 49, 146
"national longing of form, The" Brennan, Timothy 23–4
nationalism 49, 133
Negotiating Afropolitanism (Wawrzinek, Jennifer and J.K.S. Makokha) 110
neoliberalism 91
Neumann, Birgit and Gabriele Rippl 188, 192
"New Religion, The" (Abani, Chris) 145–6
New World Afropolitanism 110, 112–13
New World writers 109, 115
Nicholas V (pope) 106, 107
Nigeria 74, 76–7, 80, 172
   homosexuality 139
   migration 155

Nollywood 176–7
Saro-Wiwa, Noor 173–80
social mobility 77–8
Transwonderland 176
Nimis, John 118
Njami, Simon 152
Nollywood 176–7
Notes from Underground (Dostoyevsky, Fyodor) 140
novels
   Afropolitan 118–22
   eighteenth-century 23–4
   "passing" 72
   "racial passing" 79–80
Nuttall, Sarah and Achille Mbembe 62
Nwaubani, Adaobi Tricia 17
   I Do Not Come to You by Chance 117
Nyamnjoh, Francis 137

obscure/obscurity 186, 193–4, 195–200
Ogbechi, Okwunodu 171
Ojwang, Dan and Michael Titlestad 152–3
Okri, Ben 121
Omotosho, Yewande 112
"one drop policy" 80
Oonk, Gijsbert 58
opaque/opacity 186, 193, 196–8
Open City (Cole, Teju) 4, 104, 115–16, 199–200, 207, 212–16
   eco-Afropolitanism 99
   obscurity 186, 193–4, 198
openness 132, 135, 139–43, 148, 215
"Origin of Butterflies, The" (Oriogun, Romeo) 144–5
Oriogun, Romeo 139–40
   "Elegy for a Burnt Friend" 141
   "How to Survive the Fire" 141
   "Invisible Man" 140–1
   "Origin of Butterflies, The" 144–5
Other/Self dichotomy 116–17, 157–8
Other Routes: 1500 years of African and Asian Travel Writing (Khair, Tabish) 168–9

"Out of Africa" theory 107
Owuor, Yvonee Adhiambo
  Dust 14–15, 18–27
Oyono, Ferdinand
  Houseboy 119

p'Bitek, Okot
  Song of Lawino 134
  Song of Ocol 134
Pahl, Miriam 207
Palwine Drinkard, The (Tutuola, Amos) 119
Pan-Africanism 73–4, 111, 112–13, 133, 180 n.4, 192
Paris 109, 110
Park, Mungo 168
Parry, Benita 122–3
People of the City (Ekwensi, Cyprian) 119
Peterson, Richard 121
Philips, Caryl
  Atlantic Sound, The 169
Pile, Steve 78–9
place 90
Place Within: Rediscovering India, A (Vassanji, M. G.) 69 n.2
Plantation Memories. Episodes of Everyday Racism (Kilomba, Grada) 42
Plessy v. Ferguson (1896) 79–80
pluriversality 135, 140
Poems on Various Subjects, Religious and Moral (Wheatley, Phyllis) 114
Poetics of Relation (Glissant, Edouard) 196
politics 91–2, 94–9
"Politics of Afropolitanism, The" (Ede, Amatoritsero) 60
politics of refusal 5
Portugal 106–7
postcolonialism 52–3, 104, 169
postcolony, the 177
Pratt, Mary Louise 25
publishing industry 1–2, 103, 119–22, 153

Purple Hisbiscus (Adichie, Chimamanda Ngozi) 117

queer theory 46

race 40–1, 50, 142 (*see also* "racial passing")
  Blackass (Barrett, A. Igoni) 74–5, 80–2
  Dubois, WEB 115
  Nigeria 76–8
  social mobility 73, 75–8, 81, 82
"racial passing" 79–80, 83
racialization 188–9
racism 41–4, 46–7, 50, 209–10 (*see also* "racial passing")
  Blackass (Barrett, A. Igoni) 72, 74–5, 80–2
  Nigeria 76–8
  "one drop policy" 80
  social mobility 73, 75–8, 81, 82
Rahimanana, Jean Luc 118
Rask Knudsen, Eva and Rahbek, Ulla 92, 187
  In Search of the Afropolitan 153, 187
reason 114
River Between, The (wa Thiong'o, Ngugi) 134
Robbins, Bruce 205
rural/urban tensions 89, 92–4

Said-Ruete, Emily 169
Salami, Minna
  "Afropolitanism and Identity Politics" 207, 215
  MsAfropolitan 207
Santana, Stephanie Bosch 152, 186
Saro-Wiwa, Ken 173
Saro-Wiwa, Noor 172
  Looking for Transwonderland: Travels in Nigeria 1–2, 168, 172–80
Sassen, Saskia 142
SchwarzRund 37, 52
  Biskaya 37, 38–48, 49, 51, 52, 53
Sebald, W.G. 212

Selasi, Taiye 13–14, 44–5, 86, 135–6, 138, 147
   Africa 167
   African literature 191
   "Bye Bye Barbar". *See* "Bye Bye Barbar"
   consciousness 138
   feminism 147
   Ghana Must Go 4, 46, 60, 104, 154–61
   mobility 138, 147
   opacity 160
Self/Other dichotomy 116–17, 157–8
Senghor, Léopold Sédar 133
   "Black Woman" 134, 140
sexuality 140, 143
simulacra theory 176
skin 78–9, 81–2
skin-whitening 82
slave narratives 107, 109, 111–12
slave trade 106–7, 110
slavery 61, 79, 106–7
   education 113–15
   Nigeria 175
   rebellions 109, 113
   Saro-Wiwa, Noor 175
   slave narratives 107, 109, 111–12
   slave trade 106–7, 110
   violence 111
smelling 146
social mobility 73, 75–6, 108–9
   Nigeria 77
Song of Lawino (p'Bitek, Okot) 134
Song of Ocol (p'Bitek, Okot) 134
South Africa 92–3
Soyinka, Wole 5, 119, 121
space 25–6, 78, 86, 87–8 (*see also* place)
Spurr, David 169
Stanley, Henry Morton 169
state control 143
Sterling, Cheryl 73
suffering 111, 155 (*see also* victimhood)
sugar mummies 175
Sympathetic Undertaker and Other dreams, The (Bandele-Thomas, Biyi) 122

"Sympathy" (Dunbar, Paul Laurence) 140

temporality 24–6, 78, 87, 122
Terence (Publius Terentius Afer) 136
"The Pilgrimages Project" 180 n.5
Things Fall Apart Achebe, Chinua 76, 119, 134
Thoughts and Sentiments on the Evil and Wicked Traffic of the Slavery and Commerce of the Human Species, humbly submitted to the inhabitants of Great-Britain by Ottobah Cugoano, a native of Africa (Cugoano, Ottobah) 111
Tide of Fortune: A Family Tale (Madhvani, Manubhai) 69 n.3
Toivanen, Anna-Leena 151
Transwonderland, Nigeria 176
travel 171, 205–6, 209, 212 (*see also* migration)
travel writing 167–80
Tristão, Nuno 106
Tutuola, Amos
   Palwine Drinkard, The 119
Tveit, Marta 4–5
   "Afropolitan Must Go, The" 61–2

unhomely 180 n.3 (*see also* home)
United States. *See* America
universalism 49
unworlding/worlding 104, 107–9, 111, 112–20
Ur-Afropolitans 111, 114
urban/rural tensions 89, 92–4 (*see also* cities)

Vassanji, M. G. 57
   And Home Was Kariakoo 59, 63, 64, 65, 66–7, 68–9
   Place Within: Rediscovering India, A 69 n.2
Vermeulen, Peter 212–13
victimhood 133 (*see also* suffering)
violence 19, 21, 22, 24, 155, 159
   homosexuality 139
   slavery 111

Virgin of Flames, The (Abani, Chris) 142–3

wa Thiong'o, Ngugi 121, 185
   River Between, The 134
Wainaina, Binyavanga 4–5, 73–4, 112
   "Discovering Home" 117
   "I'm a Pan-Africanist, not an Afropolitan" 186
Wawrzinek, Jennifer and J.K.S. Makokha
   Negotiating Afropolitanism 110
"We, Afropolitans" (Eze, Chielozona) 206, 211
We Need New Names (Bulawayo, NoViolet) 99, 104, 117, 175
Weheliye, Alexander G.
   Habeas Viscus 188–9
wellbeing 144–5
West-Pavlov, Russ 25
Western focus 7, 17, 77
   Africa 117
   African literature 117
   cosmopolitanism 26
   Ede, Amatoritsero 51
   modernity 26–7
   temporality 25
   travel writing 168–9
"What is a world? On world literature as world-making activity" (Cheah, Pheng) 203–4

Wheatley, Phyllis 114, 115
   Poems on Various Subjects, Religious and Moral 114
"white man's magic" 79, 80, 82
white supremacy 77, 80, 82–3
whiteness 72, 74–7, 78, 80, 81, 123 n. 2
"Why I'm Not an Afropolitan" (Dabiri, Emma) 73
William Heinemann publishers 119–20
world literature 17–18, 104, 105–6, 112–16, 118–23
   Barrett, A. Igoni 83
   Cheah, Pheng 25, 52–3, 87, 187–8, 197
   comparative approaches 188–9
   New World Afropolitanism 110, 112–13
   postcolonialism 52–3
   systems 6–7
worlding/unworlding 104, 107–9, 111, 112–20, 186
   Cheah, Phengh 187–8, 197

Xhosa people 92, 100 n.5

Yoruba Girl Dancing (Bedford, Simi) 58–9

Zeleza, Paul 160

www.ingramcontent.com/pod-product-compliance
Lightning Source LLC
Chambersburg PA
CBHW052035300426
44117CB00012B/1835